FEVER

GOLD FEVER

A ROLLICKING HISTORY OF THE AUSTRALIAN GOLDRUSH

GEOFF HOCKING

The Five Mile Press

Note:
Currency values quoted in text cannot be equated using direct conversion.
To gain an approximation of present values [2010] any amount should be multiplied by a factor of 30:1.

Conversion Table

One penny [1d] = approx. 1 cent [30c]
One shilling [1s] = 10 cents [$3]
One pound [£1] = $2 [$60]
One ounce [1 oz] = 28.3 grams
One pound [1 lb] = 0.454 kg
One ton = 1.02 tonnes
One inch [1 in] = 2.54 cm
One foot [1 ft] = 30.5 cm
One yard [1 yd] = 0.914 metres
One mile = 1.61 km

The Five Mile Press Pty Ltd
1 Centre Road, Scoresby
Victoria 3179 Australia
www.fivemile.com.au

First published as *To the Diggings!* by Thomas C. Lothian 2000
Republished as *Gold* by The Five Mile Press 2006
First published in this revised, updated and reformatted edition 2012

Printed in China

Internal design and typesetting by Shaun Jury
Cover design by Phil Campbell

National Library of Australia Cataloguing-in-Publication entry

Hocking, Geoff
Gold Fever: a rollicking history of the Australian goldrush/Geoff Hocking.
Rev. ed.
ISBN: 9781743009918 (pbk.)
Gold mines and mining—Australia—History—Pictorial works.
Gold mines and mining—Victoria—History—Pictorial works.
Victoria—History.
Australia—History.

994.5

CONTENTS

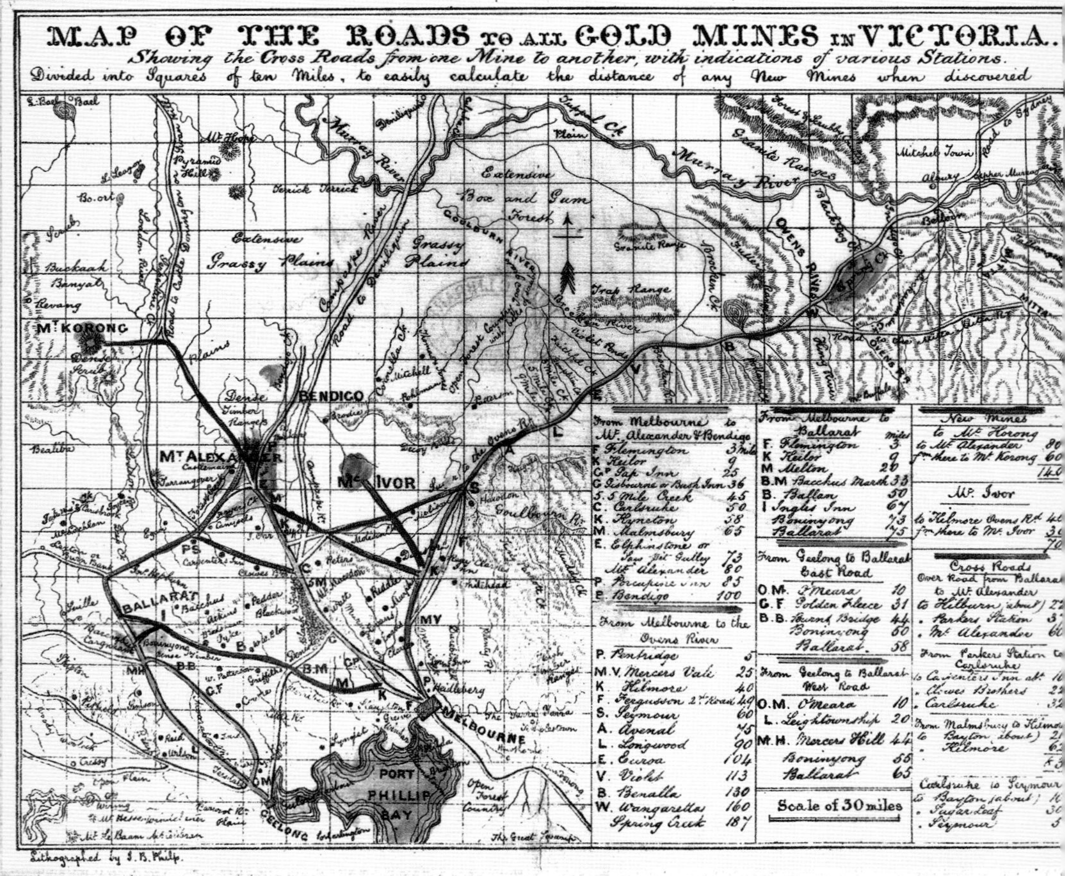

Map of the Roads to all the Gold Mines in Victoria
Lithograph by James B. Philp, c. 1853
(Picture Collection, State Library of Victoria)

This map indicates the major goldfields of central Victoria; from the left: Ballarat, Mountt Alexander, Mt Korong, Bendigo, and the Ovens in the upper right.

Although this map is clearly not to scale, the information contained would have served the diggers well on such a journey unaided by signage.

AUTHOR'S NOTE

I was born in Bendigo. I grew up in Chum Street, Golden Square, only a few hundred metres from 'Fortuna', the magnificent home of George Lansell, the Quartz King of the Victorian goldfields.

My first schooling was at Specimen Hill Primary, a small rural school perched on a rise of quartz-strewn, gravelled ground overlooking the valley through which the Bendigo Creek runs after heavy rains.

I can clearly remember we picked up specks of gold from the school playground on mornings after such a downpour.

Later, I was moved to Golden Square Primary, a larger school closer to the bed of the creek, right next door to the Golden Square Methodist Church, which was an imposing, spired building with a large mezzanine

High and Dry
Lithograph from *Mountains and Molehills* by Frank Marryat, 1853
(Courtesy of the Bancroft Library, University of California, Berkeley)

The buildings that lined the San Francisco streets were not at all like the bark huts and mudstone shacks that characterised the early Australian diggings.

Maybe the Californians thought they were going to stay in the West, whereas the adventurers on the Antipodean fields were only there for the easy gold—to get rich and get out as quickly as they could.

Here a number of ships left high and dry, after the bay had been reclaimed, have been converted to stores, factories, inns and accommodation for the diggers.

Junction of Pegleg & Sailor's Gully Bendigo
Hand-coloured lithograph
(Author's collection)

gallery that encircled the body of the interior, such was the size of the congregation of hearty-voiced Cornishmen who had rushed onto the Bendigo diggings after the discoveries there in 1851.

My great-grandfather was one of these stout and faithful Cornishmen who, as it seems, along with half the population of that coastal corner of Britain, had migrated to the colonies, eager to dig and tunnel their way to glory on the diggings.

I grew up among the landscape of the diggings, the names of the streets around recalling the 'roaring days'—Panton, Hargraves, Chum, Booth, Barnard, MacKenzie. We wandered along the gullies whose names honoured the diggers who had toiled there a century before—California Gully, Sailor's Gully, Long Gully, Job's Gully, Peg Leg, Adelaide, Tipperary, Golden Gully, and New Chum Gully, which ran opposite our home.

The diggers had recreated the idea of London in the dust and the mud of the goldfields—Pall Mall, Charing Cross and Park Lane were names given to meandering tracks that soon became the centre of this bustling town.

As children, we played on the great dumps of crushed quartz sand that stood as stark reminders of the extensive subterranean mining ventures that made Bendigo and the central Victorian goldfields among the richest places on earth. Up until the middle of the twentieth century tall steel poppet legs straddled the city; they dominated the skyline, strung out in

The Old England Hotel, Barker's Creek
(Private Collection)
Kentish-born John Hopkins Walter built his hotel in 1862, after the railway passed through Barker's Creek.

The author's maternal great-grandfather Charles Richard Ladd moved his family from the Avoca diggings, and took over the license of the Old England on 20 July 1889. The Ladds only stayed in Barker's Creek for another two years, when they moved up to Bendigo to try their luck there.

The Old England is on the western side of the railway line that runs from Melbourne to the Murray River at Echuca, opposite Specimen Gully, where in October 1851 Worley and Peters found the first gold of the Mount Alexander rush, just a few hundred metres into the bush.

This valley had been at the heart of Dr Barker's Ravenswood Run, a vast sheep-grazing property, typical of the holdings taken up by scores of squatters following the opening up of the district after Major Mitchell's expedition of 1836.

Just one month after Worley and Peters' find it was estimated that 67,000 ounces of gold had been taken in Victoria. 10,000 ounces had been carried by escort to Melbourne. By Christmas 1851 250,000 ounces of gold had been taken from the central Victorian region.

long lines from north to south, tracing the reefs that ran deep below the surface. The mines of central Victoria were rich indeed, and some of the owners and shareholders were the richest men of all.

My maternal grandfather, Fred Cronin, was born on the diggings, the son of a poor Irish lad who ran away to sea from a village to the north of Cork. When Fred was young he was mates with Leonard Lansell [the son of the mining magnate]; together they would muck about in the boats on the wide ornamental lake that nestled in front of Len's place, also in Chum Street. In later years Fred worked for Lansell at the Little 180, the great Hustler, and the Red, White and Blue mines, driving the steam engines that hauled the cages up and down the shafts. In later years several of his sons, my uncles, also worked in the mines until the closure of the last in the 1940s.

Fred married eighteen-year-old Alice Ladd, whose family was among the first at Carisbrook; she always claimed that her father was the first white child born on those diggings, and, given her advanced years

Diggers on Rout [sic] to Deposit Gold
Lithograph by S. T. Gill, 1852
(Rex Nan Kivell Collection, U1018. By Permission, National Library of Australia)

A pair of determined diggers stride purposefully through the bush on their way back to Melbourne to pay their gold into the Treasury.

With rifles at the ready and their mongrel between them, they look the type to brook no interruption to their purpose.

There were many, however, who had lost everything they carried as they made their way through the black and gloomy forests to and from the diggings. Some poor fellows were found stumbling, days later, back onto the diggings with little more than the shirts on their backs, the miscreants who had robbed them of their gold dust no doubt living it up in the nearest bush-inn or grog shop.

John Sherer recalls:

> Gangs of mounted bush-rangers, masked, and with pistols, are infesting all the roads, stopping the travellers, and even the gold transports . . . two men from Geelong were also attacked by three mounted diggers, who took all their gold-dust, money, and fire-arms, and bound them to trees. This happened in the broad light of day.
>
> — John Sherer, *The Gold Finder of Australia*, p. 16.

when she made these claims, we had no reason at all to doubt her. When her father decided to try his luck on the diggings they moved to Barker's Creek, just outside Castlemaine, and not far at all from Specimen Gully, where the first gold was found on the Mount Alexander diggings. My great-grandfather was, for a short while, the publican of the Old England Hotel, which still stands beside the Midland Highway.

As we grew up we were enmeshed in the culture of the diggings. The mines may have long gone, the 'roaring days' a faint echo, but our lives in the 1950s were little different from that enjoyed, and at times endured, by our grandparents. We attended the same schools, the same churches, sang the same hymns, and I am sure heard much the same sermons.

We entertained ourselves the same way, with Sunday School picnics, and church teas, in large groups of boisterous relatives who all seemed to live in the same area. We walked in and out of people's houses, knew everybody, and if we weren't related to them, someone we knew was.

The diggings ran a current through all of our lives. Every now and again, after inclement weather, the local paper would carry a report of someone's backyard disappearing, or half of the roadway collapsing, or a schoolyard opening up to reveal a shaft or tunnel long forgotten. As the towns developed, the Municipal Councils undertook to cap and seal the open shafts that littered the landscape; some were concreted over, but most were sealed with timbers and covered with earth, and every now and again one fell in, reminding us of our heritage.

Several Hocking brothers had emigrated, with their families, from Tucking Mill in Cornwall to the goldfields of America. My paternal great-grandfather was just an infant when he was first taken to America. Several of his uncles and their families stayed on at the mines in Montana, an aunt in California.

The great diaspora of the Cornish was never considered equal to that of the Irish, who fled their homeland after the potato famine, forced out by British 'plantationers' or carried away on convict ships. The Cornish migrated of their own accord, ready for great adventure, and eager to build a prosperous future through honest, hard work. At one stage Bendigo seemed an outpost of the Duchy of Cornwall. The predominance of the nuggety little 'cousin Jacks' and 'Jennys' on the Bendigo diggings was unparalleled anywhere in the country. Other migrant diggers in Bendigo, who showed no allegiance to the ancient Kings of Cornwall, would, when asked their religion, simply answer—'not Methodist'.

Bendigo has always had a large Irish population, and its Roman Catholic Cathedral was one of the last Gothic-styled churches built in the world. If any of our family were in hospital for one reason or another it was an act of proud defiance to refuse the attentions of any of the 'brides of Christ' on their hospital rounds. The family surname, Cronin, attracted the nuns like moths to a flame, but the Protestant Irish were pretty good at holding their own. Lessons learned in the enmity-ridden old country took generations to forget in the new.

Although Australia prides itself on the spirit of mateship born on the diggings, it was such division and lack of fraternity that also led to the battles fought there.

The rush to California in 1848 had attracted large numbers from around the world, including hundreds from Australia, to the west coast of America. When New South Wales announced the discovery of goldfields there, the early migration was largely internal, attracting diggers from the other Australian colonies of South Australia, Victoria and Van Diemen's Land, and back from California.

Alluvial gold washing, Mt Alexander gold-fields, c. 1852
Watercolour by John Skinner Prout
(National Library of Australia Collection)
This fanciful drawing of diggers panning in a wide stream with a majestic mountainous landscape in the distance has more of a European flavour than the hot and dusty reality of the Australian bush around Mount Alexander at the start of the rush in late 1852.

When the news of gold in Victoria was broadcast the unexpected news of gold in the 'south countrie' created almost unbelievable excitement worldwide. It seemed that the whole of the country was littered with nuggets, and the greatest rush of all was on. Gold mining suddenly became a serious business. This was worth leaving home for, leaving all behind and being born anew in the free spirit of the colonies. When professional miners arrived, the diggings took on a different hue. The spirit of the adventurers and the wild colonial boys was displaced by the earnest diligence of experienced mining men. The diggers at Bendigo were certainly among the best of these.

There was always a large and permanent Chinese population in Bendigo. When I was studying at the School of Mines I clearly remember the Chinese-born father of one of my teachers, as he took his daily stroll, up from the Chinese quarter in Bridge Street, past the school, and on into Bendigo.

We used to buy fireworks from him in his dark, timber and verandahed store. Long counters and high shelves lined the store, filled with all sorts

The Great Extended Hustlers Mine, Sandhurst, The Shafts and Surface Works
Engraving from *Illustrated Australian News*, 20 May 1873
(Picture Collection, State Library of Victoria)

Once these poppet-legs dominated the landscape across the Victorian goldfields. There was a romanticism about these timber and steel giants, each one bearing the name of the company that had come together to finance the deeper search for gold: Hustlers; Red, White and Blue; Deborah; Hercules; New Moon; Nell Gwynne; New Chum; Napoleon—and many more. These were the names that underwrote our lives.

Even though the mines have long gone, the same names appear on street signs, or new housing estates, or shopping malls, each a constant reminder of the heritage left by the energies of our forefathers.

of strangely, fascinating oriental goodies—bamboo kites with rice-paper wings, unusual vegetables, brightly–coloured clothing, and rows and rows of penny bungers, catherine wheels, tom-thumbs and rockets.

I stood and watched in Bridge Street the day a bulldozer ran through his shop and stripped the street bare of the Chinese houses. I rummaged through the rubble looking for anything of value that may have escaped the dozer's blade, but it was all gone. Today, descendants of the original Chinese families have built a museum to house the ceremonial dragons of which Bendigo is so proud; they have created a beautiful Chinese garden across the creek, and proudly honour the contribution their forefathers made to the spirit of the diggings.

In the 1960s I watched a workman hack into the great 30-foot-long oregon timbers of the Deborah Mine. He was claiming the metal pulley housings for scrap. The poppet legs of that mine are one of the few that

No. of Issue Folio

ABE LINCOLN

Tribute Company NO LIABILITY

Block of Scrip Certificate.

Date

Shares (how many)

Progressive Nos. of Shares

Name

Residence

Transferred from

No. of cancelled Issue

Received Scrip for

Date

Signed

No. of Issue Folio

Abe Lincoln Tribute Company

NO LIABILITY

NEW-CHUM.

SANDHURST.

Capital £2500 in 25000 Shares of £0.10.0 each

Registered under the Mining Companies Act 1871

This is to Certify that of is a Member of the above named Company and the Proprietor of Shares numbered therein upon which the sum of per Share has been paid up subject to the Rules and Regulations of the Company.

Dated this day of 187

Manager

N.B. THIS CERTIFICATE MUST BE GIVEN UP TO THE MANAGER ON TRANSFER OF THE ABOVE SHARES.

TRANSFER.

I, the undersigned do hereby sell and transfer to of of my within-mentioned Shares, for valuable consideration. And I authorise the Manager to Transfer the said Shares in the books of the Company.

Progressive Nos. transferred Dated this day of 187

Witness Signature of Transferror

Share Certificate, issued by the Abe Lincoln Tribute Company, New Chum Sandhurst (Bendigo)

(Author's Collection)

After three to four years the alluvial gold was played out, but it didn't herald the end of the diggings—the investors moved in instead.

The diggers went from a freewheeling itinerant band to investors, partners, shareholders, or as most likely, employees in the scores of mining companies that issued scrip from Queensland to Kalgoorlie.

The mining exchange became the new hive of frantic activity, where speculators who would never soil their hands again rushed to join in the second gold boom.

still stand today, the rest of it has long gone, the crushing battery, the winding shed, the engine house—even the sand dumps have almost disappeared beneath housing estates.

While we may be proud of the magnificent public buildings, the ornate Victorian iron lacework, and the stories of the wealth that came from the soil, the diggers of the first rush laid the foundation of both the cities of today and the lives we are now living. In the humble honesty of the miner's cottage we preserve the memories of our forefathers; in the remnants of their forgotten shafts, the mullock heaps, the rusting, broken machinery overgrown in the bush, the stone walls, the creekbeds, the silent poppet-legs, we honour their lives.

This new edition, now titled *Gold Fever*, continues to honour the memory of those who came in the early days, to understand the relationship between events on both sides of the Pacific, and the political and social changes that followed the opening up of Australia through the currency of gold.

CHAPTER 1

Gold! Gold! Gold!

Gold Hunting
The gold is found in a pure state in particles
from the size of a pea up to an ounce weight...
I have worked ten days, during which I got eight ounces...
— *Boston Transcript, 1843*

In 1842 some nuggets of gold were discovered by Francisco Lopez in the San Francisquito Canyon in California. Oddly enough, little attention was paid to this discovery.

The earth remained undisturbed until the the discovery of gold again in the valley in 1846. The gold rush that followed, was almost overshadowed by the constant warring over the territory by the two nations that contested it, the United States and Mexico.

The West had long been a prize unattainable to the Americans. The British held the key to Oregon, and the only other way into California was blocked by the Rockies. Mexico and the slave-owning southern states of America had little empathy with the northern states' attempts to spread liberal ideals across the whole continent. 'The fulfilment of our manifest destiny to overspread the continent' was the opinion of the *United States Magazine and Democratic Review* in July 1845. Resentment of the interference of foreign nations intent on preventing the annexation of Texas led to a resolution in the House of Representatives on 5 January 1846 to end Anglo-American occupation of Oregon. Belief in America's 'manifest destiny' was, in part, the justification for the invasion and eventual capture of California.

The 'Americans' in the Mexican province of California had long sought to take control of the domain they felt was rightly theirs. Although the first non-native landholder in California, John Sutter, had prospered following a grant from the Mexican government of 45,000 acres of the Sacramento Valley just west of the Sierra Nevada, he conspired with

Gold Mining at Sutter's Mill, Coloma (El Dorado County, California)
Oil by an unknown artist, c. 1855
(Courtesy of the Bancroft Library, University of California, Berkeley)
In this painting of Sutter's unfinished Mill at Coloma, in the valley where the first gold had been found, a pair of California '49ers take their rest in the shade of a timber-framed building. One leans against his bed-roll and cradle, the other strikes a pose characteristic of all working men, leaning on his pick.

renowned explorer, John Charles Frémont, and others who had an interest in California, to take the territory from the Mexicans.

Throughout the early months of 1846 the Americans and the Mexicans were involved in a stand-off, sizing each other up over the Rio Grande. After a large squad of Mexican soldiers surrounded a scouting party of American dragoons, killing eleven, wounding five and capturing the remaining 47, the United States declared war on Mexico.

Frémont, and fellow-travellers of the 'Bear Flag Revolution', immediately saw the opportunity to press home Anglo-European defiance of Mexican rule over California. They captured a large mob of horses belonging to the Mexican Army bound for Sutter's Fort, and took Governor Vallejo prisoner, holding him at the Fort. The Bear Flag of the newly proclaimed Republic of California flew for the first time on 14 June 1846. Frémont was chosen as leader of the new republic on 5 July.

The Republic of California was short-lived. On 7 July an American naval vessel steamed into Monterey, captured the capital, claimed all of the territory for the United States and raised the Stars and Stripes flag in Yerba Beuna on the 8th (Yerba Beuna was renamed San Francisco on 30 January 1847). The Bear Party recognised the inevitable and wisely joined the Union, and the Stars and Stripes flew over Sutter's Fort the following day.

Portrait of John A. Sutter
(Courtesy of the Bancroft Library, University of California, Berkeley)
It was on John Sutter's ranch at New Helvetia (Sutter's Fort), near today's Sacramento in California, that the first gold of the California rush was found.

It was sometime later that Sutter engaged carpenter James Marshall to construct a timber mill at Coloma on the American River (near what is now known as Sacramento City) to supply much-needed timber for a flourmill he was also building, and to supply the needs of the growing township of San Francisco. Here, on 24 January 1848 Marshall found some small nuggets of dull yellow metal glinting in the tail-race of the partly-built mill. Believing it to be gold Marshall took the nuggets to Sutter's Fort.

Sutter recounts the occasion when he was first shown Californian gold:

> It was a rainy afternoon when Mr Marshall arrived at my office in the Fort, very wet, and I was surprised to see him, as he was down a few days previous . . . I [had] sent up to Coloma a number of teams with provisions, mill irons, etc., etc. He told me then that he had some important and interesting news which he wished to communicate secretly to me.[1]

Alone, and with doors locked behind them, Marshall took a rag from his pocket and showed them to Sutter:

> [He] began to show me this metal, which consisted of small pieces and specimens, some of them worth a few dollars; he told me that he had expressed his opinion to the labourers at the mill, that this might be gold; but some of them were laughing and called him a crazy man . . . after having proved the metal with aqua fortis, which I found in my

Left: *James Wilson Marshall*
(Courtesy of the Bancroft Library, University of California, Berkeley)
James Marshall found the gold that would turn the attention of the world to California.

Right: *Sam Brannan*
(Courtesy of the Bancroft Library, University of California, Berkeley)
Mormon leader Brannan's exultant ride through the streets of San Francisco shouting 'Gold! Gold! Gold from the American River', ushered in the Californian goldrush.

> apothecary shop, likewise with other experiments, and read the long article 'gold' in the *Encyclopedia Americana*, I declared this to be gold of the finest quality, of at least 23 carats.[2]

At the time Marshall's discovery was kept quiet as a goldrush to California was the last thing Sutter wanted. After several years of upheaval and hostility, the war with Mexico was drawing to an end, and the Americans were poised to take control of all the territories of New Mexico, California and the Rio Grande border of Texas. 'The fulfilment of our manifest destiny' began in earnest as hundreds of American settlers from the East took the great wagon trails to the West in search of farming lands.

It was almost four months later, on 12 May 1848, that Sam Brannan, a storekeeper at Sutter's Fort, rode through the streets of San Francisco waving a gold-filled glass jar over his head, shouting 'Gold! Gold! Gold from the American River'. Gold fever infected all of the United States, and turned the attention of the world towards the American territory of

Sutter's Fort, California
(Courtesy of the Bancroft Library, University of California, Berkeley)
An American Flag can be seen flying over the main building of the fort.

The discovery of gold on the American River, which ran through Sutter's land, changed his fortunes forever, as most of his labourers soon deserted him for the gold diggings. His sawmill was never finished and, although he had invested over $25,000 in his flourmill, that also brought him no reward.

His hopes were dashed by the loss of 'his' California and were ultimately destroyed by the great influx of diggers in the autumn of 1848.

In fact, by the 1850s all that remained of Sutter's Fort was the central building. Its walls (two and a half feet thick, and fifteen to eighteen feet high) were all that withstood the onslaught of the rush to gold.

The fort, which had been a haven for immigrants, and had once offered hospitality to explorer John Frémont and mountainman Kit Carson, became just another relic of California before the rush.

Sutter had seen his vast empire taken from him bit by bit, first by miners, then by squatters, and finally his claim to his Mexican title was denied by the American government. Captain Sutter was declared bankrupt in 1852.

California. California was once again invaded, but this time the 'army' carried picks and shovels, and was intent on an entirely different prize.

California! Here we come.

The cry of 'Gold' reached right across the North American continent, it carried across the oceans, and was heard loudly along the eastern seaboard of Australia, across the mountains and into the bush. Gold enticed thousands to cross the hostile American heartland to the hills of Sacramento, and across the open seas to the frontier port of San Francisco, eager for their great adventure. California was the first to experience the mass migration to its shores that became the hallmark of subsequent gold discoveries.

Although the discovery of gold on the American River had been reported in the *Californian* as early as 15 March 1848, the news was not widely believed. The *California Star* also reported the discovery of gold on 25 March, but this item provoked little interest, as the new territory of California was more intent on its potential for investment and development than with the haphazard lottery of finding gold.

On 29 May the *California Star* reported that:

> the whole country from San Francisco to Los Angeles, and from the seashore to the base of the Sierra Nevadas, resounds to the sordid cry of GOLD, GOLD, GOLD! while the field is left half-planted, the house half-built, and everything neglected but the manufacture of shovels and pickaxes.

The streets of most Californian towns emptied of their men, the farms were deserted and the ports left idle as hundreds of men, shouldered their picks and shovels and headed for Sutter's Fort.

On 10 June the *California Star* added to the excitement:

> Spades, shovels, picks, wooden bowls, Indian baskets [for washing], etc., find ready purchase, and are frequently disposed of at extortionate prices . . . the probable amount taken from these mountains since the first of May last, we are informed, is $100,000, and which is principally in the hands of the mechanical, agricultural and labouring classes.

The newspaper also added that it was forced to cease publication as all its staff had taken off for the diggings.

The news continued to spread throughout California, but there it stopped. It was not until later in June that ships left anchored in San Francisco Bay could gather a working crew to sail back to the eastern seaboard. They carried the news of the find, and samples of the yellow metal, and with it the stories of ready wealth that soon became the stuff of legend.

The 1848 presidential election dominated the news in the eastern states up until 15 September, when the following small item from the Pacific coast appeared in one of the New York papers:

> Interesting from California –
> We have received some late and interesting intelligence from California. It is to the 1st of July . . . It relates to the important discovery of a very valuable gold mine. We have received a specimen of gold.

Coloma (El Dorado County, California) Hunter & Co.'s Express, c. 1848
(Courtesy of the Bancroft Library, University of California, Berkeley)

This engraving shows Coloma, where Sutter's Mill was sited, after the establishment of a sizable town in the valley where the first gold had been found.
Sutter's Mill is shown on the right.

Next page: *Miners Coat of Arms*
Britton & Rey, lithographer & publisher, 1856
(Courtesy of the Bancroft Library, University of California, Berkeley)

No matter where the miners went, the kit was much the same.

This American lithograph shows an extensive array of boots, hats, cooking equipment, a puddling cradle, pick and shovel, and the indispensable firearms.

The Colt revolver became the weapon of choice in California and was also popular on the Australian goldfields. Light, reliable and affordable, the Colt saved the life of many a miner, but also took the lives of countless others.

It is often recorded in the diaries and letters of diggers on the Australian goldfields that, upon return from work in the shafts all day, they would fire their pistols before retiring, and would do the same on awakening next morning.

The barrage of pistol shots was like the deafening roar of a great battle, but the diggers needed to ensure that their powder was dry and the pistols clean and ready for action, lest they were needed in defence of their owners in any emergency.

On 17 September the *Herald* correspondent 'Piasano' reported that the entire population had gone to the mines, many to return a few days later with hundreds of dollars in dust and nuggets. Spades and shovels sold for $10 apiece. Blacksmiths were making $240 a week. Why, even a child could pick up three dollars worth of gold in a day from the treasure streams.

Every seaport as far south as San Diego, and every interior town, and nearly every rancho from the base of the mountains in which the gold has been found . . . has become suddenly drained of human

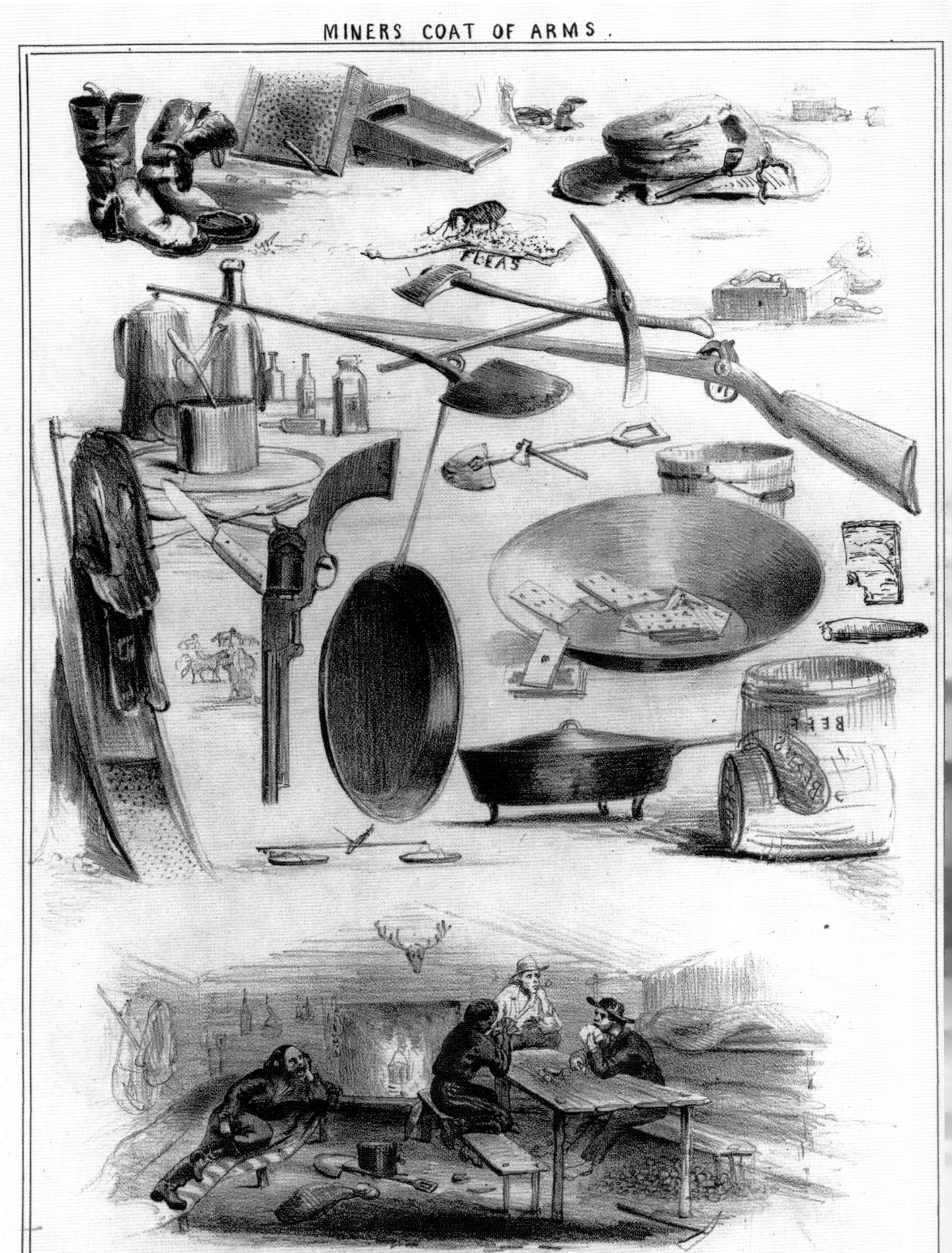
MINERS COAT OF ARMS.
FLEAS
Lith. & Pub. by Britton & Rey San Francisco

> beings. Americans, Californians, Indians and Sandwich Islanders, men, women and children, indiscriminately … there are at this time over one thousand souls busied in washing gold, and the yield per diem may be safely estimated at from fifteen to twenty dollars.

After the arrival of the Royal Mail Steamship *Europa* in London on 10 October, the editor of the *Times* scanned the papers on board for news from the United States. He discovered an item full of almost-unbelievable accounts of the success of the American goldfields, but concluded his report on page four of his paper with the following caution:

> the placer sand is said to be so rich, that if exported to England or the United States, it would be very valuable. Consequent upon this excitement, the price of provisions has increased enormously. We need hardly observe that it is necessary to view these statements with great caution.

The British, although defeated in the War of Independence a century earlier still maintained a strong and influential political presence and a feeling of propriety over its former colony. They openly distrusted 'the wily Yankee', and warned against rushing to the American diggings to 'swell the anti-British party in the United States'. Meanwhile, the British continued to expand their Empire. Although it stood alone in a world hostile to its monarchy, Britain believed in its right to influence the affairs of other nations.

At the same time all of Europe was in turmoil; the French people had risen and swept away the monarchy of King Louis Philippe; Austria and Hungary were at war; Italy was tearing itself apart in an attempt to become one nation, province was fighting against province, city-state against city-state, people across Europe were demanding the same rights for all citizens.

The Republic or the Economy?

Over half a million British had been transplanted to Canada, and thousands to other colonies all around the globe. With the end of transportation of convicts to Australia in 1840, the continued agitation of the Irish for freedom from British rule, the widespread devastation of cholera in almost all over-populated western Europe, Britain was determined to maintain security across its widespread domain.

The discovery and subsequent appeal of the California goldfields was seen by the British government as an opportunity to rid the British Isles of some of its unwanted population, yet it was also concerned about the large number of English who might leave the Empire entirely, through migration to America, an independent country over which Britain no longer had any constitutional influence.

Britain continued to hold an ambivalent attitude towards the Americans. In early November 1848 the *Times* scoffed at the reports of great finds in California, and went on to denounce the goldfields as a delusion:

> The discovery of gold in the Sacramento, like that of communism on the Seine, has produced a confusion of rank and a startling degree of equality . . . even politics have disappeared and republicanism ceased to be preached for the moment . . . we must hear more of this El Dorado before we bestow upon it . . . our serious consideration.

The *Times* expressed scepticism of the so-called El Dorado of California:

> There was need of many mines to gild the Mexican war, and to pay its expenses. These acquisitions have cost the Union twenty-five millions of our money. If in the course of twenty years, the principal and interest be repaid by the dust collected from the rivers of California, the Union may deem itself most fortunate.

Panoramic View of San Francisco, c. 1851
(Californian State Library Collection)

Wherever gold was discovered, the closest port saw hundreds of ships left untended. Crews absconded, heading for the diggings as quickly as they could step ashore.

It was the same two years later when diggers rushed to Australian ports. In Port Phillip Bay (Melbourne) ships' captains requested that passengers be carried ashore in light craft or on pilots' boats so they could lie at anchor a mile from shore. They feared that they would lose their crews and be unable to make the return journey to their home port.

At one stage captains and shipowners offered premium wages to encourage sailors, or anyone who was interested, to crew the ships back from Australia.

Few were interested, the lure of gold was too enticing, and ships lay at anchor for months on end.

Ship's captains had even requested that the gaols be opened to allow some prisoners to serve out their sentences as crew aboard a returning ship.

News items positive about the diggings were relegated to lesser pages of the paper. The *London News* made the cynical observation: 'that Brother Jonathon had taken California for its fine harbours and tallow trade, when, lo and behold. He found gold'.

The fear of republicanism was at the heart of most British attitudes towards the Californian diggings. If wealth could be readily accumulated by ordinary people, what impact would that have on the ruling classes? If those people gained economic power, how could the born-to-rule aristocracy manage to keep the population in its appointed place? If thousands of British subjects migrated to California, became wealthy and adopted American ways, what was the future for the rule of the monarch? What would be the influence, then, of the 'new Yankee' on the political aspirations of those at home and those already agitating in other colonies. This same fear was expressed some years later by Earl Grey, the British Secretary of State for the Colonies, when he advised Charles Joseph La Trobe, the Governor of the Australian Colony of Victoria:

> there is a spirit abroad which must be carefully watched and promptly brought under control if this colony (Victoria) is not to parallel California in crime and disorder . . . a sense of importance and independence arising from unexampled prosperity.[3]

Events soon got in the way of political point-scoring. By November 1848 the Californian diggings had proved so successful that the USS *Lexington* was able to leave San Francisco with $500,000 of gold bound for the east coast and the United States Mint. In December a Lt Lucian Loeser carried a tea-caddy holding 230 ounces (6.5 kg) of Californian gold into the Washington War Department, where it caused considerable excitement. President James K. Polk confirmed the reports of the Californian discoveries in a message to Congress on 5 December: 'the accounts of the abundance of gold are of such an extraordinary character as would scarcely command belief were they not corroborated by the authentic reports of officers in the public service'.

In Australia a Sydney newspaper of 31 August 1849 reported:

> there is now a shortage of farm labour in NSW, as many men, often recently arrived migrants, have gone to California to try their luck on the diggings. There were many doubters when reports of California gold reached Sydney late last year, but they were followed up by some samples, and the exodus began. Letters received in Australia tell of an up-river journey of 60 miles and a land journey of 70 miles until the diggings are reached. The work is hard and dangerous, and the living rough.

The diggings in California attracted all types of nefarious characters; hundreds left the eastern seaboard of Australia for California, where the pickings were thought to be easy and the rule of law not yet established, including old lags, the refuse of Britain's prison hulks, and more latterly those from the cells of Van Diemen's Land (Tasmania), known as Vandemonians. It is known that quite a few notorious bushrangers took themselves off, landing in San Francisco, as far away from the long arm of British Law as they could possibly be. The 'Sydney Ducks', as they were sometimes known, caused such a problem that vigilante groups were soon established to protect the citizens of San Francisco.

Those who kept to their old tricks suffered summary justice, without recourse to the niceties of trial by jury, gasping their last breath with their feet swinging just above Californian soil. In the early days the diggers took matters into their own hands, frontier life had given them that freedom, and they took the opportunity to govern themselves as they saw fit.

The success of the Californian goldfields saved the Western world from a devastating depression. The economies of Europe were struggling after months of war and revolution, while the end of the Mexican War had seen the cancellation of contracts, as the American Army shed its forces onto a struggling labour market, swelling the ranks of the already half-employed.

The excitement of the goldfields boosted demand for tools, for food and clothing, for transportation, for the planning of permanent townships, and the mobilisation of the hearts and minds of an otherwise dispirited people.

Merchants on the east coast of the United States also geared up to benefit from the demands of the diggers out west. Remarked one New Yorker in December 1848:

City of San Francisco (California)
Engraving by J. Clark, 29 May 1850
(Courtesy of the Bancroft Library, University of California, Berkeley)

This engraving shows sailing ships moored in San Francisco Bay.

By this time 'The Queen of the Pacific' (as San Francisco had become known) had grown into a bustling, substantial seaport. The port city boasted several hotels, churches, schools, hospitals and banks, as well as saloons, gambling halls and brothels.

It was close to the port, at 90 Sacramento Street, that the New York merchant Levi Strauss first established his dry-goods store. Here he was able to 'capture' the miners almost as they first stepped ashore, ready to be kitted out before they set off for the diggings.

It was in response to diggers' complaints that their trouser pockets were constantly tearing due to the weight of stone samples, and small nuggets, that Levi Strauss first thought to reinforce pockets at the corners with copper rivets.

He began to manufacture his own style of trouser using a broadly woven indigo-dyed cotton twill fabric, imported from the french town of Nimes, to make his copper-studded workman's trousers. He had an oversupply of the material on the shelves of his store at the time—kept on shelf No. 541.

It was in the Italian port city of Genoa, that denim had first been used to make trousers, giving the style of deep-blue trousers the name of 'genes', as a consequence Strauss's pants became known as '*gene de nime*'.

From a pair of reinforced workman's pants on the California goldfields to the most ubiquitous clothing product in the world, such an inauspicious beginning gave birth to the legendary 'Levis blue-jeans'.

> any person strolling along our docks cannot help being struck with the quantity of merchandise of all kinds, which is marked for shipping from this port alone, of which not less than $400,000 have been sent within the last thirty days.

Plans were laid for a railway to connect the east with the west, and goods were obtained from up and down the states. Philadelphia shipped hundreds of tons of flour, while the prices of clothing skyrocketed following the shipment of old stocks from Baltimore to the Pacific Coast. It was comparatively easy for merchants on the east coast of Australia to supply the Californian West, and merchants in Sydney made the most of every opportunity, the prices of picks, shovels and other mining equipment went through the roof as Sydneysiders shipped their stocks to California.

Go West Young Man!

The journey to the goldfields was not an easy one. New Yorker William Swain wrote to his family and friends back east from 'the Diggings' in California on 6 January 1850:

> tell all whom you know that are thinking of coming that they have to sacrifice everything and face danger in all its forms, . . . thousands have laid and will lay their bones along the routes to and in this country. Tell all that death is in the pot if they attempt to cross the plains and hellish mountains.[4]

Later, even after he had some success at the diggings he wrote again to his family still advising them to 'stay at home, for if my health is spared, I can get enough for both of us'.

The Way They Cross 'The Isthmus'
Tinted lithograph
Nathaniel Curry, c. 1849
(Courtesy of the Bancroft Library, University of California, Berkeley)

New Yorker, Eugene Ring, wrote of his experience crossing to California via Panama,

> that it was a fight for self from start to finish . . . the restraints of home were thrown off. No need of the mask of social life here, and men were reckless and natural . . .

Travelling from the paved streets of New York through the seemingly primitive lagoons of the Panama isthmus must have been quite a shock for the venturer unused to a 'natural' environment.

He assures his family he has no regrets about venturing to the goldfields. He remarks that, in fact, he had put on fifteen pounds in weight since leaving the East, and that he even seemed to grow in height, although he was suffering an attack of rheumatism, a complaint not uncommon among miners who spent half their days up to their knees in muddy water:

> I have not seen the hour yet when I regretted starting for California, nor have any one of our party ever regretted that we undertook the enterprise. I have seen hard times, faced the dangers of disease and exposure and perils of all kinds, but I count them as nothing if they enable me to place myself and my family in comfortable circumstances.[5]

Twenty-one-year-old Eugene Ring, another New Yorker, who had left his family behind and set off for the diggings in 1848 by way of Panama and South America, wrote of his first night on the trail:

> By sunset we had reached a country more rolling and more covered with trees and verdure . . . we made our first camping out. Seated on the ground around a crackling blaze, we passed the saucepan and boiled tea around, and felt ourselves borderers indeed. The tent was spread over the branches of a fallen tree for those to sleep under who wished; but John and I feeling above such effeminacy, of which a Boone or a Crockett would be ashamed, wrapping our blankets around us and lay down with our feet to the remains of the fire and watched the stars . . . until sleep closed our eyes.[6]

He also recorded his first view of the diggings around Coloma where the first gold had been found:

> In the centre of the valley through which runs the North Fork were clustered the various contrivances of buildings that made up the place, from a blanket hung across two poles, to a frame house. On the banks of the river and in the stream were the miners engaged in the different operations of gold washing. At the lower-end of the town on a bend of the river stood the 'Mill', celebrated as the spot where gold was first discovered, and beyond, the waters of the river hurried on.[7]

The exploits of the American West with its heroes, mountainmen, cowboys and Indians gripped the imagination of the mid-nineteenth-century

Placer Mining at Foster's Bar, California
Oil on millboard by Ernest Narjot, c. 1851
(Courtesy of the Bancroft Library, University of California, Berkeley)

The waterwheel was one of the constant features of all the goldfields.

This painting by French artist Narjot shows miners digging in the banks of the river, feeding the sluice-boxes that washed the earth in the hope that nuggets would be revealed.

A Native American can be seen in the foreground leaning against a boulder, arrows slung across his back, his hunting bow in his right hand.

The Native Americans were the losers in the rush to the diggings that overtook their homelands, destroying their hunting grounds and despoiling the river salmon runs that they had managed effectively for generations.

There were several tribes in the Sierra foothills when the rush began—the Maidu, Nisenan, Koukow, Miwok, Pomo and Yokuts—and a government report as early as 1848 recorded that half of the diggers were Native Americans. However, they were soon displaced by Europeans, and were exploited as cheap labour for these American settlers, who treated them just as the Hispanics had done before the rush.

Their population declined from 150,000 before 1845 to less than 30,000 in 1870. Syphilis, cholera, measles, smallpox and other epidemic diseases contributed heavily to this decline.

> I sat on the counter of a store in Jackson one evening, when a Digger Indian came in with several ounces of nuggets tied up in a rag.
>
> He put the package in one bowl of the scales and laconically spoke the word 'raisin'. The storekeeper leisurely walked around the counter, found a box of raisins and returning to the scales began dropping raisins, one at a time, as if they were too precious to part with, into the other bowl of the scale. When the raisins balance[d] the gold, he emptied them into a paper bag which he handed to the Indian who departed satisfied.
>
> —The Autobiography of Charles Peters: *Miners in the Sierra.*

Bar Room in the Mines
California Pictorial Lettersheets, No. 61, September 1861
(Courtesy of the Bancroft Library, University of California, Berkeley)
This view of a simple, single-roomed saloon on the Californian goldfields shows miners taking their recreation after hard labour at their claims.
They are seen here drinking [a common and extremely popular pastime] and playing cards.

desk-bound easterners who had looked on the goldfields as both a great Western adventure and a validation of their manhood. 'The West' entered the American psyche, just as the bushranger was to capture the imagination of Australian diggers several years later. For the native-born New Yorker, that first night around the campfire under starry skies was the stuff of penny novels, not of everyday experience.

Eugene Ring writes of an encounter with a Native American later on in his travels:

> as we neared each other I saw that he was a tall powerfully built man, the scantiness of his costume showing off his proportions to excellent advantage . . . an old red flannel shirt that would have reached the knees of a short man; carved reed passing through the lobe of each ear, and dangling against his neck, a bundle of arrows slung on his back, and a bow in his hand . . . I was remarkably attentive to his every point, movement and expression . . . particularly as I knew that in this section there had been much fighting between the miners and Indians; and many murders committed by the latter . . . he showed me

> the strength and force of his bow; which I offset by a sight of my Colts revolver for which he seemed to show a profound respect.[8]

A Great Business Opportunity

With the diggings not yet two years old, steamboats were plying the rivers, making four trips a day up the Sacramento River as far as Yuba City. The creek where William Swain was camped had 'no more than six houses built on it [when he had arrived]. Now, within a distance of ten miles, 150 dwellings are built'. In a letter of 16 January 1850 he added:

> The 'redskin' who four months ago roamed in his nakedness, the undisputed lord of these mountains and valleys, may be seen on the hilltops gazing with surprise upon the scenes below—the habitations, the deep-dug channels and the dams built. The sound of the labourer's axe, shovel, pick and pan are sounds new to his ear, and the sight one to which his eye has never been accustomed.[9]

The merchants on the diggings who supplied the miners made the most money of all. Swain finished his letter with the postscript: 'P.S. An onion in the mines is worth a dollar, and boots $40 per pair. I have paid $8 for a jar of pickles'.

Mary Jane Caples, was one enterprising lass who made her pile, but not by digging for gold:

> I concluded to make some pies and see if I could sell them to the miners for their lunches, as there were about one hundred men on the creek, doing their own cooking—there were plenty of dried apples and dried peeled peaches from Chile, pressed in the shape of a cheese . . . so I bought fat salt pork and made lard, and my venture was a success. I sold fruit pies for one dollar and a quarter a piece, and mince pies for one dollar and fifty cents. I sometimes made and sold a hundred in a day.[10]

Another sold some jewellery she didn't particularly value for $20:

> with this jewellery she purchased onions which she sold on arriving here for eighteen hundred dollars . . . she also brought some quinces & made quite a nice profit on them.[11]

Luzena Stanley Wilson used her time profitably while her husband was at his claim:

> I determined to set up a rival hotel. So I bought two boards from a precious pile belonging to a a man who was building the second wooden house in town. With my own hands I chopped stakes, drove them into the ground, and set up my table.
>
> I bought provisions at a neighbouring store, and when my husband came back at night he found, mid the weird light of the pine torches, twenty miners eating at my table.
>
> Each man as he rose put a dollar into my hand and said I might count him a permanent customer. I called my hotel El Dorado.[12]

California Forty-Niner
Quarter-plate daguerreotype
(Collection, Among Carter Museum, Fort Worth, Texas)

The art of photography was in its infancy in 1849, and it was such a novelty for the diggers that they rushed to have their images recorded to send back to their loved ones in the eastern cities.

This California Forty-Niner looks the epitome of the then popular idea of the western frontiersman: bushy-bearded and bold, with his bowie-knife thrust rakishly in his belt.

What would his family back east have made of this cavalier image? The rush to the diggings wrought great changes in such one-time office clerks, farm-hands and factory workers.

There were also plenty of women who plied the oldest trade in the book, and dancers and entertainers such as the notorious Lola Montez were in great demand, card players being most popular:

> In one corner a coarse-looking female might preside over a roulette-table, and perhaps in the central and crowded part of the room a Spanish or Mexican woman would be sitting at monte [a card game popular with Mexican gamblers] with a cigarita in her lips, which she replaced every few moments with a fresh one. In a very few fortunate houses, neat, delicate and sometimes beautiful French women were every evening to be seen in the orchestra. These houses, to the honour of the coarse crowd be it said, were always filled.[13]

Few women toiled at the diggings, although many had travelled from the East with their husbands; many had also sent their husbands ahead, looking to join them once they had become settled. One such women waited for three years for her husband, and then decided to pack up her children and set out to join him. When she finally arrived in the mining town of Jackson, she discovered that he had died just three months earlier. The journey out was rough enough, without turning straight around and heading back East, so she stayed, and took over the running of the store her husband had established, eventually becoming one of the success stories on those diggings.

Women who worked as cooks, or who took to washing the clothes of the miners, could make an easy $30 a day. One washerwoman claimed she had earned 'nine hundred dollars in nine weeks', and on hearing this one miner commented that if such women were common 'a man might marry and make money from the operation'.

The Chinese on The Diggings

There had been a Chinese population in California many years before the discovery of gold, and they had always been held in high regard—their services as labourers, carpenters, cooks and agricultural workers were always in demand. Before the goldrush the Governor of California had declared that he regarded the Chinaman as 'one of the most worthy of our newly adopted citizens'.

The discovery of gold in 1849 drew shiploads of Chinese away from their homeland, which had been through years of drought, floods and, often, violent political rebellion.

Compared to the migrant ships that carried diggers from Europe, the 60-day Pacific crossing for the Chinese was likened to the journey to the Southern states of slave ships from Africa. The conditions aboard the Chinese vessels were extremely unpleasant.

When the Chinese landed in California they faced both discrimination and open hostility from the European diggers, although at first they were still small in number. Extremely hard-working, the Chinese had been regarded by the authorities as valuable contributors to the frontier society; yet as their numbers grew and they spread across the goldfields, their European counterparts sought to force them back into the towns.

After the surface gold declined, and when the thousands of Europeans who had travelled across America from the eastern states arrived only to discover that the good times were over, they too fell back on the streets

The Bar of a Gambling Saloon
Lithograph by Frank Marryat, from *Mountains and Molehills*
(Courtesy of the Bancroft Library, University of California, Berkeley)

The Chinese took their place in frontier society alongside the Europeans. They worked hard, played at the same games and drank in the same bars, but were readily discriminated against as soon as things got tough for the Europeans.

While the Chinese were prepared to work long, hard and diligently for their gold, the Europeans expected to be able to pick it up easily from the ground, and for there to be a never-ending supply of easy money.

When the gold started to run out, they turned against the Chinese, who always followed them onto the diggings, reworking the old claims the Europeans had discarded, and the Chinese were forced off. When the Chinese looked for employment in the towns, the Europeans tried to force them from there as well.

Yet the Chinese persisted, claiming a lasting place in both Californian and Australian society.

of San Francisco and other frontier towns looking for the work that the Chinese had long regarded as their own.

At the end of the 1840s there had been about 4000 Chinese in California. By 1851 the Chinese population had risen to 25,000, and it was not long before the government that had once held them up as paragons of hard work and enterprise was to legislate to drive them away. In 1852, Governor John Bilger declared that 'the Chinese were a menace to the state'. Heavy license fees and taxes were levied on the 'Celestials' in an attempt to drive them from the diggings. Anti-Chinese activity was almost sanctioned by government and open resentment of the Chinese was the norm. The Europeans—the Americans—declared that California, and its gold, belonged to them and made repeated attempts to expel the Chinese from the diggings.

Chinese Gamblers, San Francisco
(Courtesy of the Bancroft Library, University of California, Berkeley)

The cry of 'California for the Americans' preceded the cry of 'No Chinese—Roll up! Roll up!' that was to ring out across the Australian diggings a decade later.

Just as on the Australian diggings, the Americans levied unreasonable taxes on the Chinese in a vain attempt to drive them from the diggings and from the country. In San Francisco the city attempted to enact what was known as the 'pig-tail ordinance', which required all convicted Chinese prisoners to have their hair shorn to within an inch of their heads, an almost unbearable insult to the proud Chinese.

In 1868 the Burlingame Treaty was agreed between the United States and China to grant 'reciprocal exemption from persecution on account of religious belief'[14] and to give Chinese citizens in the US the same privileges as citizens of America in China. The Americans saw this as a betrayal of the American workers, and resentment of the Chinese grew.

Across California the miners took the law into their own hands—just as they had joined together to rid San Francisco of the hooligan gangs who had terrorised the streets in the early days—they set themselves up as judge and jury, passing sentence this time on the Chinese. 'Committees of Vigilance' were established, challenging the government in the absence of real lawful authority. While their original intention was to rid the cities of criminals they soon turned their attention to other immigrant groups—and the Chinese, attacking them, destroying their business houses in the hope that they would leave the territory. Eventually it all got out of hand.

In Los Angeles on one night a group of Americans attacked and murdered nineteen Chinese by hanging and shooting, and stole more than $40,000 worth of their property.

The remaining population of more than 20,000 Chinese in California was not that easily dismissed. Even though they were harassed by officialdom, burdened by discriminatory taxation, and even attacked and murdered by vigilante groups, they persisted remaining to become an integral part of American society.

Edward Hammond Hargraves. Discoverer of Gold in New South Wales
Oil painting by Thomas Balcombe, 1851
(Mitchell Library Collection, State Library of New South Wales)

Hargraves had been in California in 1849 where he learned the art of gold-panning.

It is said that he recognised a similarity between the Californian gold-bearing landscape and the landscape around Bathurst where he had farmed before he joined the California rush.

He sailed back to Sydney in 1851 determined to find gold in the creek-beds and before long success was his.

Gold in the Antipodes

Only three years after the goldrush had invigorated the United States and captured the imagination of the world, attention shifted across the Pacific to the new discoveries in the Antipodes.

Edward Hargraves was one of hundreds who had left Australia for the diggings in California. While gaining invaluable experience in the California rush, he became convinced of the likelihood of deposits of gold in Australia—the hills of Sacramento, where he had first tried gold digging in 1849, bore a striking similarity to the country around Bathurst in central New South Wales.

Hargraves left California in 1851 and returned to Australia. As he boarded the ship an American digger called out to him, 'There's no gold in the country you're going to, and if there is, that darned Queen of yours won't let you dig it'.

Hargraves removed his hat and, striking a defiant pose, rejoined, 'There's as much gold in the country I am going to as there is in California; and Her Most Gracious Majesty the Queen, God bless her, will make me one of her gold commissioners'.

He was soon proved right when, in the first months of 1851, he washed out some gold beyond the Blue Mountains near Bathurst. Before long the ships that once had carried diggers away from Australia's shores now brought thousands of eager diggers and adventurers back to the great 'antipodean El Dorado'.

The Second American Rush

Gold had also been found in Montana as early as 1851, and again in 1858. The first really big discovery was at Bannack in 1862, and on 26 May 1863 the discovery at Alder Gulch once again fired the imagination of those in the south, but the gold rush to Montana was never to achieve the same legendary status as California's.

The finds were made at the same time as the news of Australian gold was first broadcast, and the biggest rush only a few months after the outbreak of the American Civil War.

While the discoveries of the late 1850s may have drawn miners back from the rush to Australia, the civil war that raged across the south had a devastating impact on every American state, almost overshadowing the excitement of the new goldfields.

The Montana gold rush saw gold worth over $100 million taken from a 14-mile-long valley near Virginia City. The rush had all the hallmarks of the good old days of 1849, but the war had robbed the west of its innocence—in the bad, bad west the gunfighter was abroad, and the diggings had become a hard, brutal place of outcasts, deserters, roughriders, those without future, without homes, without hope. As on the subsequent Australian diggings, the grog and the girls were close at hand, ready to take that gold and send the diggers, pockets emptied, back to their claims.

In January 1891 prospector Bob Womack struck the El Paso lode in the Cripple Creek field, south of Denver, Colorado. On 4 July Winfield Scott Stratton staked out the aptly named 'Independence' claim, one that eventually returned him millions, ensuring his title as one of the 'Bonanza Kings' of Cripple Creek.

Panorama of Virginia City
Photograph by Carleton E. Watkins, c. 1876
(Courtesy of the Bancroft Library, University of California, Berkeley)

Watkins, a San Francisco photographer, went to the Comstock Lode near Virginia City, Nevada, in 1876.

The view shows the frontier town surrounded by waste sand dumps, (a sight familiar to the citizens of the Australian towns of Bendigo and Ballarat towards the end of the nineteenth century), steam and smoke belching forth from the engine rooms of the stamping mills.

The goldfields did little to enhance the natural environment. In Australia the legacy was of fine 'Victorian' towns, but in many cases the American West seemed to lose its towns as quickly as the gold ran out, becoming ghost towns once mining had ceased.

Watkins's photographs were prepared as stereoscopes, a popular viewing method in the late nineteenth century. Double images, mounted side by side on card, were inserted in a viewing holder 15 cm in front of a pair of magnifying binoculars. The effect on the image was to create a three-dimensional impression of the object in the photographs. A double-mounted image is shown in full above.

North to Alaska

On 12 August 1896 gold was found on the Klondike Creek on the north-west Canadian border with Alaska. It was almost a year before the news of this discovery reached the United States which was, at that time, in the depths of serious financial recession.

When, in 1897 two steamers returning from the Yukon River landed on the west coast of the United States, one at San Francisco, the other at Seattle, both disembarking prospectors toting sacks filled with gold, some worth more than $100,000, the cry of 'North to Alaska' echoed across the continent. Over the next three years more than 100,000 prospectors rushed onto that freezing goldfield, the most inhospitable goldfield of all.

Towards the end of 1899 gold was discovered near Nome on the north-west coast, but this rush was worthless, leaving 30,000 desperate men starving and stranded there on the beaches only a few months after it began.

LOLA MONTEZ IN CALIFORNIA

Lola Montez—'The petted companion of Louis Napoleon; the idolised dancer of the swells and wits of the capitals of the Old World, with the near relatives of royalty and the beaux of Paris for her intimates.'

The most infamous seductress of her day, 'femme fatale' Lola Montez was born Maria Delores Eliza Gilbert in County Sligo, Ireland in 1818—or possibly 1821.

Her mother was the illegitimate daughter of an Irish member of Parliament and her father was a British Army officer. He died of cholera soon after the family had moved to India. Lola's mother re-married and although her step-father, Ensign Patrick Craigie, was fond of Lola, as a child she already displayed the unconventional and independent spirit that would characterise her adult years, she was shipped back to Scotland to be educated by the Calvinist Craigie family.

Lola Montez[s]
Sixth-plate ambrotype, photographer unknown
(Courtesy of the Bancroft Library, University of California, Berkeley).

In most American references Montez appears spelt with a 'z'.

In Australia her name was spelt Montes.

This was not a happy mix for the wilful Lola. Aged 11 years she was packed off again, this time to boarding school in Bath. At the age of 16 years she ran away from school, eloping with Lieutenant Thomas James. After five years she had had enough. Leaving her husband behind she took to the stage—and the rest is history. Lola became the most fashionable courtesan in all Europe. She was the lover of Kings, the muse for poets, writers and artists, even bedding the equally fashionable Franz Liszt. After an aborted betrothal to Ludwig, King of Bavaria, she abandoned Europe for the 'new world' arriving on the California diggings in 1853.

Her arrival in San Francisco caused great excitement: A newspaper editorial ran the line: 'What if Europe has exiled her? This is of no consequence . . . she is Lola Montez, acknowledged Mistress of Kings! She is beautiful above other women; she is gorgeous; she is irresistible; and we are genuinely proud to welcome her.'

The Californian diggers certainly appreciated her ample charms [which she had once thrust into Ludwig's face to prove they were all her own], and all the trappings of European elegance that she had brought with her to California.

On her arrival she established a saloon in the rough-and-ready mining town of Grass Valley, which she furnished with Louis XVI cabinets, ormolu mirrors, gold leaf, jewellery and a large deep-red-topped billiard table with dragon-carved legs. She had Kanaka houseboys, and a pet bear was kept for the entertainment of her guests—among them were senators and millionaires, and, of course, the diggers, who adored her.

While Lola may have been a great lover, her dancing skills were criticised by some in the media not captivated by her charms. Annoyed by constant, carping, opprobrium Lola left to seek a new audience on the Australian diggings, arriving in Port Phillip in August 1855. This woman, who had been referred to in the British press as 'La Belle Horizontale', probably had much to put behind her when she left for Australia.

Lola's House in Grass Valley
(Courtesy of the Bancroft Library, University of California, Berkeley)

CHAPTER 2

First Gold in Australia

Rumours of the discovery of specimens of gold had been circulating throughout the colonies for many years before the Australian rush began in 1851. In earlier times specimens of gold embedded in quartz had been displayed as curiosities in the shops of Sydney.

As early as 1823 a convict working on a road gang near Bathurst was flogged for having a lump of rough gold in his possession. He was charged with the theft of a gold watch that had disappeared about the same time as he was showing his nugget. As he wouldn't reveal where he had found his gold, it was concluded that he had stolen the watch and melted it down. The poor fellow received 150 lashes as the reward for his 'discovery'. Others who had also found nuggets were quick to learn from this salutary lesson. Another shepherd who brought several pieces

Sheep Station Point, River Turon [NSW]
Colour lithograph by C. Rudston Read.
Frontispiece to *What I heard, saw and did on the Australian goldfields*, C. Rudston Read, published by Hullmandel & Walton, London, 1853
(Rex Nan Kivell Collection NK11147. By permission, National Library of Australia)

of gold to Sydney converted them to cash 'with as little ceremony as possible'.

An old prisoner named MacGregor, who had been assigned to a squatter up-country, displayed a piece of pure, waterworn gold on one of his visits to Sydney. He was ordered to show the spot where it had been found on his master's run, but refused to do so, obviously hoping to keep the secret for himself. He was in prison for debt when the rush began in 1851, and a party eager to take off for the diggings paid his debts and secured his release in return for showing them where he had found his gold. However, once near his old haunts MacGregor disappeared.

Edward H. Hargraves, Australian Gold Discoverer, first found at Ophir, Feby. 12th 1851
Hand-coloured lithograph by George French Angas. Printed by C. Goddard, Sydney, c. 1851
(Rex Nan Kivell Collection, U4111. By Permission, National Library of Australia)

Hargraves is credited with the discovery of 'Australian gold' around Bathurst in New South Wales.

He had successfully tried his hand in Summerhill Creek, then left the district until John Lister and the brothers William and Charles Tom, whom Hargraves had previously instructed in panning methods, found the first payable gold at Ophir.

It was Hargraves, however, who made the announcement when he took Ophir gold in to show the Colonial Secretary, and it was Hargraves who received both recognition and eventual reward.

Lister and the Toms contested Hargraves's claims, but were defeated. They tried again forty years later, and finally received the recognition that had long been denied them.

1839—The Australian Alps

Explorer Count Paul de Strezlecki found gold in the Australian Alps in 1839. Although he believed that it existed there in large quantities, he was also advised to keep his discovery from public knowledge, as the authorities were fearful of the consequences if the large and often restless convict population became aware of the existence of gold in the colonies.

1840—Strathloddon, Victoria

A nephew of William Campbell, the licensee of the Strathloddon Run, found gold at Campbell's Creek in 1840. Campbell, when shown a pannikin filled with 'clean, pure, heavy gold', demanded that it be kept a secret 'lest people should come and turn up the soil and the shepherds abandon their flocks'. He feared undesirables would overtake his sheep run.

1844—Hartley, New South Wales

The Reverend W. B. Clarke showed the Governor, Sir George Gipps, some specimens of gold that he had found near Hartley. Upon seeing the yellow specks the Governor reacted in the same manner as had Campbell four years earlier in Victoria, exclaiming, 'Put it away, Mr Clarke or we shall all have our throats cut'.

1846—Montecute, South Australia

Although some gold had been mined at Montecute as early as 1846, at this time South Australia's mining destiny lay in its rich copper deposits. When the rush to New South Wales and Victoria almost depleted South Australia of its menfolk, there were attempts to find goldfields in the hills around Adelaide. However, gold in any quantity was not discovered until diggers returning from Victoria tried their luck in the creeks of South Australia late in 1852.

February, 1849—Glenmona Station, Victoria

A shepherd boy named Thomas Chapman started a small goldrush after he found gold at 'Glenmona', Messrs McNeil and Hall's station in the Pyrenees, 100 miles north-west of Melbourne. He claimed to have found 350 ounces of gold, which he sold to Brentani, the jeweller, in Melbourne. He agreed to lead a party back to the spot, but ran away as they neared the station, obviously fearing the consequences of his actions when discovered by his employer.

The news still got out, and was reported in the *Argus* on 6 February. Governor La Trobe sent troopers to the station to prevent any trespass on the land, but were surprised to find thirty or forty men already at work. Unfortunately, the diggers had dug only one small hole, and were quickly sent packing, their bags empty. They concluded that the nugget sold to Brentani must have been some melted plate, and that there was no gold in Victoria at all. Thomas Chapman was not seen again.

The government escort and mail containing the gold, arrival at the Treasury, Sydney, on 21 August 1851
Pen and wash drawing by Marshall Claxton, Engraved version published *Illustrated London News*, 24 January 1852
(Rex Nan Kivell Collection, T2241. By Permission, National Library of Australia)
The excitement caused by the arrival in Sydney of the Government Gold Escort and mail containing gold is recorded in this contemporary drawing by the English artist, Marshall Claxton.

12 February 1851—Summerhill Creek, NSW

When the veteran of the California diggings, Edward Hargraves, announced his find in the *Sydney Morning Herald* on 15 May 1851, there were already several hundred diggers working at Summerhill Creek, near Ophir.

Although Hargraves is credited with the discovery of gold in Australia, it took several years before he was granted the reward he believed was justly due to him. He was not shy, however, when he considered how important his find was for New South Wales. After he had washed out five panfulls of gravel from the creek-bed, finding gold in all but one, he had exclaimed to his companion:

> This is a memorable day in the history of New South Wales. For this day's work I shall be created a baronet, you will be knighted, and my old horse will be stuffed, put into a glass-case, and sent to the British Museum.[1]

His prophetic rebuff to the American digger several years earlier was fulfilled when he was made Gold Commissioner in Her Gracious Majesty's Colony of New South Wales. When the news broke that an Aboriginal shepherd boy working for Doctor Kerr, of Bathurst, had found a nugget in the Murroo Creek that weighed two hundredweight, the rush to these diggings took off in earnest. The *Bathurst Free Press* reported on 16 July 1851:

> Bathurst is mad again. The delirium of gold fever has returned with increased intensity. Men meet together, stare stupidly at each other, talk incoherent nonsense and wonder what will happen next. A hundredweight of gold is a phrase scarcely known in the English language. It is beyond the range of our ordinary ideas.

While nuggets of such size were certainly unknown on the Californian diggings, they were quite common in Australia.

The rush to the Colony of New South Wales that followed Hargraves's discovery echoed the rush to California, and again filled Australia with excitement. Just as in California, homesteads were left deserted, farms abandoned and towns emptied of men, the ships that had carried diggers from the east coast of Australia across the Pacific to California now headed south again, rushing the diggers home, while thousands poured across Australia's colonial boundaries, heading for the goldfields.

Victoria was separated from colonial rule by New South Wales on 11 November 1850. Six months later Hargraves announced his discovery. So many able-bodied men had left Victoria for New South Wales that La Trobe [now the Lieutenant Governor of the new Colony of Victoria] posted a reward for the discovery of Victorian gold, in the hope of reversing the depopulation of his newly proclaimed colony.

With their eyes fixed on a reward, one way or another, it seemed that from then on every itinerant shepherd, every farmboy, carrier or journal-bound office clerk spent their idle moments dreaming of discovering gold.

June 1851— Clunes, Victoria

Clunes claims to be the site of the first discovery of gold in Victoria, even though there is evidence of gold found elsewhere earlier. William Campbell (of Strathloddon Run) claimed to have found gold as early as 1840 at Campbell's Creek, near Castlemaine, eleven years before

Cradling and Panning
Engraving by W. Hatherall, from *Cassell's Picturesque Australasia*, 1889
(Private Collection)

Hargraves had made his discovery at Summerhill Creek in New South Wales.

The news of the Californian diggings had encouraged Campbell to do some further exploring of his own. He had examined geological reports from California and concluded, in much the same way as Hargraves, that gold should be found in similar country. On a visit to fellow-squatter Donald Cameron's station, 'The Clunes', he investigated a large quartz vein and concluded 'that it was the most likely place I knew to find gold in'. At this time Campbell did little to further his investigation until on a later visit he encouraged Cameron and others to accompany him on a 'search for gold'.

> In the course of a few minutes I had the satisfaction of having the correctness of my expressed opinions verified by the discovery of a gold mine in Australia, on the exact spot where I said I thought it would be found.[2]

It became known later that Campbell had found rich golden stone on Donald Cameron's station as far back as March 1850, but the find was

The Diggings at Spring Creek (Creswick)
Wood engraving from C. Cooke, *Illustrated Australian News*,
Ebenezer and David Syme, Melbourne, 1 March 1869
(Picture Collection, State Library of Victoria)

From the memoirs of Mary Ann Berry:

> On the way [there] we saw, near springs a great herd of kangaroos bounding along. We arrived on 15th August '53. I think it highly probable that I was the first white woman to set foot in that part . . . There was a terrible bushfire on the 9th January, 1854. We had to take the children and stores to a place of safety, and burn a patch round the tents, by which we managed to save them.
>
> Father's bad luck was persistent, as the holes he sank were duffers. Eventually he sold one claim for £1; the purchaser secured £500 of gold from it!

Mrs Berry was the daughter of John Mason, who was associated with the first discovery of gold at the head of Creswick Creek.[3]

From *Creswick Memoirs* (collected 1908–12), first published in the *Creswick Advertiser* in 1940.

concealed until Campbell announced his discovery in a letter to Mr James Graham, 'a prominent public man in Melbourne', where he stated that, on 10 June 1851, 'within a radius of 15 miles of Burbank [near Clunes], on another party's station, he had procured specimens of gold'.[4]

Just as so many other discoveries before them had been kept secret, they also kept this one to themselves for fear of the consequences for the squatter if his run were to be overtaken by diggers. Under pre-emptive rights Cameron had ownership of the land on which his homestead was built, so at least that was safe from digging, but the rest of Clunes was open for exploitation if the news got out.

When the rush to the goldfields in New South Wales caused a mass migration from Victoria, spreading panic across the colony, Cameron decided that his discovery should be made known, hoping to stem the rush to the north. The announcement was made to the Mining Committee in Melbourne on 8 July 1851, and within days 'a rush of diggers was soon upon the ground, where they remained working until a richer mine was discovered near Buninyong'.

Once the rush was on and the shepherds had become diggers, and the diggers were turning up the soil, the claimant to be the first to have discovered gold on any field where the government could levy a license fee was entitled to a good reward. Campbell's reticence, and later claim, led to confusion, as there were others who were sure that they had been the first.

James William Esmond, a veteran of the Californian diggings who had returned to Australia on the same ship as Hargraves, was erecting a building on another station nearby.

Dr George Bruhn, a German physician turned prospector, was looking for gold in the Pyrenees when he saw specimens at Cameron's station that he was informed had come from Clunes. In the course of his travels he told Esmond. Esmond put the experience gained in 1849 to work, and he, too, found gold at Cameron's station on or about 28 June 1851.

Although it seems that it was Campbell who made the first discovery at Clunes, Esmond was the first to work the claim.

All three—Campbell, Bruhn and Esmond—were rewarded.

July 1851—Anderson's Creek, Warrandyte, Victoria

At almost the same time, Louis John Michel and a small party of prospectors found gold at Anderson's Creek, north-east of Melbourne, near Warrandyte. Henry Frencham, who was to feature prominently in a later discovery at Bendigo, was also in this party.

20 July 1851—Mount Alexander, Victoria

From the *Argus*, 8 September 1851:

> Dear Sir,
> I wish to publish these few lines in your valuable paper that the public may know that there is gold found in these ranges about four miles

Gold-Fields on Mount Alexander
News Letter of Australasia, No. 75, November 1862
(Author's Collection)

Mount Alexander was named by Major Mitchell, who passed this way in September 1836. When Mitchell wrote in his journal on 30 June 1836, 'As I stood, the first European intruder on the sublime solitude of these verdant plains', he had no inkling of the great invasion that was to destroy this solitude for ever.

South Australian Police Commissioner Alexander Tolmer, travelling through in March 1852, described the hustle and bustle he had observed on these diggings:

> Let the reader imagine thousands of bearded, uncouth looking men, dressed in dirty short jumpers, with trousers the colour of yellow ochre, busily at work – some filling carts with gold-impregnated earth, and carting it to the bank of the creek, lined with cradles, where washers were in full operation.
>
> The cradles were placed lengthwise with the water which was at the time of the thickness of cream, and of a yellow colour. Those who worked the cradles, held the handles with one hand, and with the other broke the lumps of earth with a stick, and stirred up the contents, keeping the cradles constantly rocking, whilst others stood by with ladles of some kind, and kept baling water continuously into them.
>
> Others again were carefully washing into large tin dishes, the deposits that had fallen through the sieves of the cradles and onto the boards beneath.
>
> — Alexander Tolmer, *Reminiscences of an Adventurous and Chequered Career at Home and in the Antipodes*, 1882

Tolmer's South Australian Gold Escort had carried the first gold back to Adelaide in November 1851.

> from Dr Barker's home station, and about a mile from the Melbourne road, at the Southernmost point of Mount Alexander, where three men and myself are working. I do this to prevent parties getting us into trouble, as we have been threatened to have the constables fetched, for being on the ground. If you will have the kindness to insert this in your paper that we are prepared to pay anything that is just, when the Commissioner comes.
> In the name of the party,
> John Worley,
> Mount Alexander Ranges, 1 Sept, 1851.

In July 1851 three shepherds and a bullock driver had been working in the outer reaches of Dr Barker's Ravenswood No 1. Run in the foothills of Mount Alexander, in central Victoria, where they found some nuggets of dull yellow metal in a creek-bed at what was eventually to be named Specimen Gully. Although their find was later recognised as the first on the Mount Alexander goldfields, when two of them, Worley and Peters, returned to the homestead and showed the specimens to the overseer, no-one believed that what they had was gold.

Although gold had been discovered at nearby Clunes some months earlier, it was Worley's announcement of their find in the *Argus* newspaper on 8 September 1851, that sparked the biggest rush of all to the Australian diggings. Before long Mount Alexander and Forest Creek were the diggings that captured the imagination of 'new chums' the world over.

The alluvial Castlemaine field was to become the richest the world had ever seen.

Just three weeks later, on 27 September, 10,000 ounces of gold were sent by escort to Melbourne. By the middle of November it was estimated that 67,000 ounces had been taken from the district. By the end of the first year 250,000 ounces had been taken from this central Victorian region, only four months after the first nuggets were found in Specimen Gully.

Major Mitchell, who had crossed through this region in 1836 had described the richly pastured land as 'Australia Felix'; the thousands of diggers who followed the discoveries of 1851 plundered Mitchell's dream, laying the foundations of a society, based not on agriculture and sheep-herding but on quartz, iron and steam.

Ballarat in 1851, as viewed from Bath's Hotel
The Discovery of Gold – 1851, engraving from *Victoria and Its Metropolis*
(Private Collection)

> 'Hundreds on hundreds of tents were clapped down in the most dusty and miserable of places; and all the ground was perforated with holes, round or square, some deeper, some shallower, some dry, some full of water.
> All between the holes the hard, sand-coloured clay lay in ridges, and you had to thread your way carefully amongst them if you did not mean to fall in.
> Still horrider stenches from butchers' shops and garbage pits: the scene thickened, and tents after tents, stores and bark-huts crowded upon you like a great fair.'[5]

8 August 1851—Buninyong and Ballarat, Victoria

Before the goldrush, Ballaarat (later spelt Ballarat) was an almost forgotten outpost of the Yuille brothers' sheep-run.

Buninyong was at the centre of several runs taken up by squatters in 1838. The first settlement began there in 1841 when timber splitters and teamsters settled their families in the valley. There were over fifty families in the area, with shepherds and timber-cutters on the lonely outreaches of the runs.

A hut, built by pioneer George Gabb, served as a hotel, and Campbell and Woolley moved their store next to it. A blacksmith soon joined them, and in 1844 Dr Power set up his medical practice. In 1847 the Learmonths sponsored the building of a church and schoolroom, and the Presbyterian Minister, Rev. Thomas Hastie, became the first clergyman and teacher in the district. At this time Buninyong was the largest inland township in Victoria. It could have become an important trading centre but for Hiscock's discovery in August.

Thomas Hiscock is given the credit for the discovery of the Ballarat goldfields. In early August 1851, while he was searching for a lost cow, he picked up a piece of gold-studded quartz. Within a few days he had washed out two and a half ounces of gold from the gravels in the area around the Yarrowee Creek.

Unbeknown to Hiscock when he made his discovery in August, James Esmond had similar success in Clunes just weeks before.

Hiscock communicated his find to the editor of the *Geelong Advertiser* on 10 August 1851, and it was this newspaper that later urged the government to reward both men as the discoverers of Victorian gold. In 1853 the committee charged with the task of conferring the reward for gold discovery concluded:

> It is obvious that Mr Hiscock's discovery at Buninyong, by attracting great numbers of diggers to the neighbourhood, was the cause of the discovery of Ballarat. Ballarat is, in fact, upon the same range, and at no great distance...[6]

Hiscock was awarded his £1000.

When the first Commissioner came onto these diggings to collect the first license fees, the early Buninyong yield was very poor, and the disappointed diggers were either unable to pay or saw no reason to give what they had to the government. Most of the diggers simply vanished into the bush.

On 18 August 1851 the government proclaimed legislation granting the Crown rights to all gold found on Crown lands, while at the same time ruling that it was illegal to be found searching for gold without a license. A fee was set at 30 shillings a month, imposed on all male adults on the goldfields, whether engaged in mining activity or not. It was this fee, introduced on 1 September that was eventually to cause this and the subsequent Governor so much trouble.

As Commissioner Armstrong patrolled these disappointing diggings, a crowd of diggers took refuge in Mother Jamieson's Inn, maybe the first inkling that the Ballarat diggers were unlikely to bow to the demands of the government officials. Among them was John Dunlop, a seventy-year-old veteran of the battle of Waterloo, and a young Irishman, James Regan. They slipped quietly away from the inn, and made their way into the darkly wooded forest. They trekked along the White Horse Range on Yuille's Ballarat station, until they came upon a small hill on the northern edge of the run. Towards the end of August Dunlop and Regan panned the first gold of the Ballarat diggings in a creek running south from the foot of this hill, a tributary of the Yarrowee. The point, known later by the misnomer of Poverty Point, was one gully away from the more aptly-named Golden Point, where over 20,000,000 ounces of Ballarat gold were later found.

Within six weeks there were 2000 tents near Golden Point, with more than 10,000 men encamped there. The din from the rocking of the cradles could be heard more than three miles away. French adventurer, the photographer Antoine Fauchery, recorded the scene:

> No doubt the place I am passing through was not considered rich enough to be worth working; but a hundred paces further on still, the holes are closer together, and about ten minutes after finding these first traces of gold-seeking, at the top of a plateau at the extremity of which the road ends, the horizon widens and I am overlooking 'The Ballarat Gold Fields'.
>
> The sun is declining. At my feet I can just manage to see the diggers' tents scattered about. Workers, with pick and shovel on their shoulder, fan out in all directions. Fires are lit at different points, and my heart grows heavy at the thought that here I am, alone once more, about to enter a new sphere. The barking of dogs warns me that it would be imprudent to venture here at this hour, and, rolled up in my blanket, and stretched out at the foot of a tree, I put off until tomorrow my first appearance on this stage.[7]

Between 21 September and 31 December 1851, 30,323 ounces of gold from this field were carried by the gold escorts to Melbourne. When the news of the rush to Ballarat reached England early in 1852, hundreds of experienced coal and tin miners from Cornwall, Scotland and Wales set out on the six-month-long voyage. They landed in Port Phillip, only to be told that Ballarat was played out. When they arrived on the diggings, they found them almost deserted.

Rev. Hastie later described the peaceful valley before the rush where he 'often passed the spot on which Ballarat is built . . . and there could not be a prettier spot imagined'.[8]

Eagle-hawk Gully, Bendigo, Victoria
Hand-coloured lithograph by G. F. Angas, 1852
(Rex Nan Kivell Collection NK6288/A. by permission, National Library of Australia)

> Mr George Inness, a resident of Buninyong since 1845, informs me that he discovered gold in July of that year at the Black Hill, Ballarat, but he kept the circumstance a secret. His movements were watched however by Hiscock the blacksmith, who was in the habit of sharpening the miner's picks. Hiscock some time afterwards began prospecting on his own and found gold at Hiscock's. If Inness' statement is correct the existence of gold was known in Victoria much earlier than is generally supposed—C. W. Langtree (1888).[9]

October 1851—Sandhurst [Bendigo], Victoria

24-year-old William Johnson from Sydney picked up a bit of slate with a small spur of gold imbedded in it and showed it to old Ben Hall, a shepherd who had his hut by the Bendigo Creek. After examining the slate, Hall threw it back into the creek.

The area around a chain of waterholes where Golden Gully met the Bendigo Creek was frequented by sheep-herders. However, it was not until Margaret Kennedy and her companion, Mrs Farrell, had gone to the Bendigo Creek to try their hand at panning while their husbands were away looking for shearers—and found quite a bit of gold—that any serious investigation of the creek was attempted.

Left: *Mrs Margaret Kennedy*
Right: *Henry Frencham*
(Photographs courtesy of James Lerk, Bendigo)
Margaret Kennedy and Henry Frencham were is dispute over who was the first to discover gold in Bendigo. Mrs Kennedy and her companion Mrs Farrell were eventually granted the reward, and thus the honour, although Henry Frencham,who had been fossicking along the same creek at the same time maintained that he deserved the same recognition.

Specks of gold had been picked up at various times. The squatters were well aware of the impact a gold find would have on their prospects, so they tried to keep any news of gold from the shepherds and the shearers until the sheds had been cleared. It was impossible, though, to keep a lid on the rumours of gold discoveries in central Victoria, particularly as such news had so long been awaited.

The news of the find on Dr Barker's Ravenswood No.1 Run on the foothills of Mount Alexander rapidly made its way into every shepherd's hut across the rolling valleys. Mrs Kennedy and Mrs Farrell had been to Forest Creek, and observed for themselves the method of gold panning there.

Kennedy's husband was overseer of the Ravenswood Station and Patrick Farrell was a cooper employed by Gibson and Fenton to construct barrels for tallow. The flocks were scabby and Fenton had decided to boil them down after the shearing had finished.

Farrell had no work at the beginning of September, so after obtaining some rations he said he was going down to Forest Creek but, unknown to Fenton and Gibson, he turned back for the Bendigo Creek. Farrell, his wife and Margaret Kennedy were quite successful in their endeavours,

Kangaroo Flat
Watercolour by George Rowe, 1857
(Bendigo Art Gallery collection)

This painting by Rowe shows a scene familiar to all who ventured onto the diggings. Tents line the meandering creek, and the immediate landscape is denuded of trees as the diggers cleared almost all the land around for shaft timbers, firewood and building materials.

It took almost a century before the vegetation returned to these valleys, but the great stands of box and ironbark eucalypt were gone forever. Only scrub and stringybark grew in their place for many years.

The creek-beds became the site for villages, then the towns, and English trees soon lined the streets, irrevocably changing the nature of this ancient landscape.

stashing away quite sizable number of nuggets. Just as Worley and Peters had learned at Specimen Gully only months before, itinerant shepherds panning for gold on the squatter's run enjoyed little favour from the authorities.

The well-known chain of waterholes was not necessarily an isolated or lonely spot. By all records there seemed to have been people coming and going all the time. William Sandbach and his brother, who also worked on Gibson and Fenton's station, shearers' cook Johnson, John Ross, shepherd Ben Hall, hut-keeper Charles Asquith, someone named O'Donell, Fenton, Robinson and James Ross were all in and out of the district, with one eye on the sheep and another in the gullies.

Mrs Kennedy feared that 'they would be murdered some night, as it was known they had gold', so they armed themselves in their primitive shelter. One night, listening to the sounds of the bush outside, they heard footsteps trampling through the bush. Patrick Farrell had loaded his pistol with cooper's rivets, and Mrs Kennedy took up a rusty old bayonet, while Mrs Farrell armed herself with a tomahawk as her husband fired off a shot into the night. 'We will fight for it', he declared, but it appears

The Prospector
Oil on canvas by Julian Ashton, 1889
(Art Gallery of New South Wales Collection)

that the shot had frightened the intruder away. It was only after this event that Farrell went off to Forest Creek and obtained digging licenses for them all.

Returning to the sheep run some weeks later, the shearer's cook, Johnson, again saw Mrs Kennedy and Mrs Farrell with their skirts hitched up, knee-deep in clay, filling tin cans with gold. He also observed old Ben Hall scooping up a billycan of gold, letting the pieces trickle slowly through his fingers, and exclaiming, 'This is better than shepherding, boys!'.

It has long been debated who actually made the first discovery at Bendigo, but Mrs Kennedy and Mrs Farrell were probably at the right place at the right time. So, it appears, was the journalist and avid prospector, Henry Frencham, and his party of Robert Atkinson and fellow-reporter James Ogilvie Ross, who had followed the creek from the White Hills, picking up gold as they went, and were now prospecting very close by. By this time Frencham was quite an experienced prospector, and had been scouring the creeks around the White Hills north of Mount Alexander, making his way along the creek on the Ravenswood Run, picking up 'specs' as he went.

At the same time Fenton and Gibson were also prospecting in a nearby valley, convinced that they too had found the first gold in the Bendigo area.

After Frencham also saw Kennedy and Farrell hard at work, he dispatched one of his party, the one-armed Henry Byass, to Forest Creek to seek out Captain Harrison, to report that gold was discovered on the Bendigo Creek. The announcement was made as Byass posted bills across the diggings along Forest Creek, that 'women were getting quart-pots of gold on Bendigo Creek'.

The Woolshed Diggings
Oil by A. W. Eustace, 1856
(Burke Museum Beechworth Collection)

The Woolshed diggings were on David Reid's 'Wooragee' station. As often happened, the activities of the miners forced the squatters to look elsewhere for land suitable for their investment.

Reid left 'Wooragee' and took up grazing at Barnawatha station.

February 1852—Beechworth, Victoria

Gold had been discovered as early as 1846 in circumstances almost exactly the same as the find at Sutter's Mill in California in the same year. It was not until the rest of Victoria was overwhelmed by gold fever that any serious discovery was made.

The first recorded discovery of gold in Beechworth was near one of the outlying shepherd's huts on David Reid's 'Wooragee' station, a large sheep run that soon became the centre in the north-east of the same frantic activity that was happening further south.

> I was at my station at Wooragee [afterwards known as Gemmel's station]. In the evening, two young men came and asked to stay for the night. I got into a conversation with them, and they mentioned that they had been with Mr Smyth surveying the mountains on geodetic

> work, and that they had been discharged. They said to me, 'This looks like gold country'.
>
> I asked them if they knew anything about gold, and they said they had been to the California diggings, and that if they had the tools they would try that part of the country . . . My shepherd, a man called Howell, . . . asked to be allowed to go with the two men . . . On the third day after they started, they discovered gold on the creek in front of the outstation hut, that stood where Beechworth now stands.
>
> The three men sunk some shallow holes two to three feet deep on the edge of the creek, and washed the stuff on the rock in a dish. Howell returned and mentioned the matter to me. Then the news got about that gold was found in the creek, and men came from Albury and from Wangaratta . . . They sank alongside the first claims, and got good gold. Then a great rush set in, and men came from all parts.[10]

Reedy Creek, four miles from Beechworth, soon became the richest gold-producing area on the field. John Johnson, from Sydney, first worked the creek in 1853. He was soon joined by Duncan (Dan) Cameron, James Lonnie and others. It was Dan Cameron who, in 1856, when campaigning for his election as the first Member of Parliament for Beechworth, created a world-wide news phenomenon, when he rode into Beechworth on a circus-pony that was shod with 'golden' horseshoes.

May 1852 —Yackandandah, NE Victoria

The diggings at Yackandandah were opened by a digger named Carrol.

Fifty-three years later, in an article written to the Mines Department in Melbourne squatter David Reid explained how he had found gold in Yackandandah in early 1846, four years before Carrol, in exactly the same way as gold had been found in California:

> In 1845, or the beginning of 1846, I commenced the flour-mill, long known as Reid's Mill. We were cutting a race to bring water to the wheel. One day we were examining the stuff being dug out, and I took up a bit, and said, 'This looks like gold'. Afterwards gold was discovered in California in a similar way, later on, the ground around Reid's Mill was worked for gold, so that I actually found gold before its discovery in California, by Sutter in his mill race.[11]

Autumn 1852—Eaglehawk, Victoria

The rush to Eaglehawk began in the autumn of 1852. It was followed by further rushes to the Whipstick and the low scrubland of Myer's Flat later in winter. When the news reached the Beechworth diggings on the Ovens River, so many picked up their picks and shovels and struck out for Eaglehawk that Beechworth was almost deserted.

The dense scrubland known as the Whipstick was crisscrossed with the 'circuitous, detached and disconnected' tracks of the diggers. This was uninviting country, flat, hot, gravelly, and in places almost impenetrable, men easily became lost, and several died, unable to find their way out, but it held the nuggets that were the goal of every digger. 'Old Harry' Moorehead and 'Old Dan' Stewart were just two of those who were rewarded with a 22 ounce nugget; others found nuggets weighing 63 and 372 ounces.

The scrub was so thick that, at a place called 'Drunken Scotchmen's', two 'tall, bushy-whiskered mates' were able to work away undetected, coming out every couple of weeks to sell their pockets full of gold. It was only when their pack-horses were followed back into the scrub that they had to share their discovery. The rush to their remote gully was then on.

1852—Tilba Tilba, New South Wales

Traces of gold were first discovered in the streams flowing from Mt Dromedary in 1852 by cleric and amateur geologist, the Rev. William B. Clarke.

There was also a short rush to the mountain in 1860, but, even though this had died almost as quickly as it had started, the Dromedary was not forgotten.

October 1852—Onkaparinga, South Australia

W. Chapman, a digger returned from Bendigo, washed out some gold in the Onkaparinga valley near the old Wheatsheaf Inn on the Echunga Road. The next day he was asked to do the same again, only this time he was watched by a crowd of over sixty, including the Colonial Secretary and several mounted police troopers. To guard against fraud, Chapman was ordered to take off his coat and roll up his shirtsleeves (any claim on the reward for such a discovery was closely investigated). He scooped up a dish full of dirt, washed it through, poured the dirt off—and showed nothing.

Miners on Mt Dromedary, (Tilba Tilba)
(Rex Nan Kivell Collection, TT138. By Permission, National Library of Australia)
Mt Dromedary is a large granite boulder-strewn outcrop near Narooma, on the central New South Wales coast.
The difficult terrain meant that miners employed some creative architectural style to keep their tents anchored to the hillside.
Winches, pulleys and flying foxes were used to bring gear up and down, as well as buckets of ore for crushing.

The crowd was easily disappointed, and soon became angry at the 'swindler' Chapman. At that point there were many who would have liked to hang him from the nearest tree. Just as well for Chapman, he performed 'a quick twist of the dish, the rest of the dirt was shot out, and gold was seen gleaming in the bottom of the pan'.[12]

The rush to the Onkaparinga was on. There was so much excitement that day that everybody rushed to get something to use for washing out gold, even hats were used to pan out the stream, and there was so much noise that 'the horses broke their fastenings and galloped away into the bush'.[13]

Some mines were soon worked in the Barossa, at Gawler and Mt Pleasant, and there were some that were very rich indeed. However, the most gold South Australia ever saw was that carried back to the South Australian Treasury by Alexander Tolmer's escorts or brought back in returning diggers' swags. When describing the rush to Echunga in his report of 2 October 1852, the Assistant Gold Commissioner remarked that it was unlike any of the three eastern colonial fields:

Miners' Camp on the South Australian Diggings
(Photograph Courtesy of the State Library of South Australia)
Wherever the diggers went they had to make do with the materials at hand to create some rudimentary shelter for themselves.

It was only in later years, after the first rushes had died away, that attempts at 'permanent' dwellings were made.

This crude hut made of packing cases, bush poles, bark and scrub is home and hearth to quite a large party of diggers.

While there was a sustained rush to the diggings on the Barossa, and in the north-east of the colony on the desert fringes in the late 1880s, the *South Australian Register* reported the early demise of the diggings around the city of Adelaide on 7 February 1853:

> *The Gold Fields.*– Although there is at the diggings everything to indicate gold in large quantities, none have succeeded in realising their hopes. The majority content themselves with what they can get on Chapman's Hill and Gully, knowing that, if a fresh place is discovered, they will stand as good a chance as those who have spent months in trying to find better ground. The quantity of gold taken to the Assay-office, during four consecutive weeks, amounting to less than four thousand ounces, the Governor has proclaimed that after the 17th of February the office is closed.[14]

> since my last report sixty licenses have been issued, making it a total of three hundred and fifty-six . . . many families of respectability have arrived, and are now living in commodious tents. The presence of well dressed women and children gives to the goldfields, apparently distinguished for decorum, security and respectability. From the feeling of greater security and comfort, combined with cheapness of living, all classes of diggers are unanimous in their preference of this place to Victoria.
> [Signed] A. J. Murray.[15]

South Australia had never been a transportation colony, so its citizens were assumed to be a bit above the rougher society of Victoria and New South Wales, and most certainly above those of Van Diemen's land.

February 1853—Stringer's Creek [Walhalla]

Ex-convict Edward Stringer, and mates, William Griffiths and McGregor, found the first gold that opened the Walhalla diggings.

June 1853—Mt Tarrangower, central Victoria

Tarrangower had been a pastoral run since 1839 when squatter Lachlan McKinnon settled in the area now known as Maldon. Like many others McKinnon had followed in the footsteps of Major Mitchell who had first passed through the region in 1836, and he had taken up a large tract of land on which to settle and fatten his flocks.

At Tarrengower, unlike most other goldfields, the discovery is not credited to a shepherd occupying his daylight hours washing a bit of stuff out in the creek.

Polish sea-captain Captain John Mechosk found the first gold in June 1853. This discovery saw the end of the pastoral era, as over 20,000 diggers rushed to the boulder-strewn granite hills in search of alluvial gold.

July 1853—Buckland River, eastern Victoria

An American, Pardoe (or Pardew), had been secreted on the lonely Buckland River 60 miles from the Spring Creek diggings for four months before the news of his discovery there finally reached the outside world in July 1853. Within ten days a rush of over 500 diggers a day invaded his profitable peace and quiet.

3 August 1853—Waranga, central-eastern Victoria

The first discovery on the Waranga diggings was reported in the *Argus* of 3 August 1853. A sawyer searching for timber saw the similarity of the terrain to that of Bendigo, and was lucky enough to pan out some gold in the St Louis Creek.

October 1854—'Canton Lead' [Ararat], Victoria

Joseph Pollard discovered the first gold in Ararat in north-western Victoria in 1854. This sheep-herding country had been opened up by H. S. Wills in 1839, and, as on almost all other goldfields, the squatter saw his run taken over by diggers.

More than 700 Chinese, travelling across country from Robe in South Australia scratched out some gold on 29 June 1857.

I Have Got It
Oil by Eugène von Guérard, 1854
(Picture Collection, State Library of Victoria)
This digger celebrates his good fortune as he washes out a pan with a good show of nuggets. Von Guérard's painting records the bustling activity on the early alluvial goldfields, with pan, puddling tub, windlass and shaft in evidence.

This large group of Chinese didn't make it as far as the Bendigo diggings where they had been heading. The 'Canton Lead' was one of the richest alluvial leads in the colony and the rush that followed laid the foundations for the town of Ararat.

The Chinese suffered indignities wherever they went but it was at Ararat where they suffered the meanest treatment of all. Chinese miners

Gold diggings, Ararat, 1858
Oil painting by Edward Roper
(Mitchell Library Collection, State library of New South Wales)
The district around Ararat was settled soon after Major Mitchell's tour of discovery in 1836.

had toiled diligently in their shafts for over six months; digging, timbering and driving further and further into the ground.

Once the news of this goldfield was abroad thousands of Europeans rushed to Ararat. Seeing the advanced state of the mines on arrival, the diggers decided to take over. As a ploy, some suggested that the Chinese might not have had the required residence tickets.

On 4 February 1858, a small party of European diggers demanded that the Chinese show their tickets. When the Chinese were unable to do so, the Europeans invaded their shafts and evicted them. Sixty to seventy claims, worth over £1000 each, were jumped. The Chinese had almost all reached the bedrock where the gold was to be found, and their prize was denied them.

CHAPTER 3

A World Turned Topsy-turvey

Although there had been several reports of the discovery of gold in Victoria throughout 1850 and early 1851 it was the announcement of the find in the foothills around Mount Alexander that captured the imagination of the newly separated Colony of Victoria and then the rest of the world. The reward offered by Governor La Trobe for the discovery of payable gold in the Colony had borne fruit.

Topsy Turvey—Our Antipodes
Engraving by John Leech
Follies of the Year, London, c. 1860
(Rex Nan Kivell Collection, S2826. By Permission, National Library of Australia)

The established class distinctions which regulated British social intercourse had little relevance to the reality of life on the goldfields, for on the goldfields even the lowliest could become wealthy overnight, and those used to giving orders could have no luck at all.

Here the recognised world has certainly been turned upside down, the scruffy diggers are being waited upon by 'learned' gentlemen and elegant ladies.

Newly-found riches changed everything.

> We can scarcely tell who are below the middle classes. The diggers appear in labourer's garb, but many of them have a great deal of money. I have known clergymen, gentlemen's sons, men of education, in the County Court cells; many of them in rags.
>
> — Dr John Milton addressing the Legislative Council [Victoria] in 1854.

A City of Melbourne Solicitor
Lithograph by S. T. Gill
De Gruchy & Leigh, Melbourne, 1866
(Picture Collection, State Library of Victoria)
This down-at-heel character was well known on the streets of Melbourne at the time. He is seen here serenading a 'lady of the streets', who also looks a bit the worse for wear.

A fear of the law, and indignation at injustice, are implied in John Worley's announcement in the *Argus* on 8 September 1851 [pp. 44–5]. It indicated the prevailing sentiment among the working class in Australia that, while they feared the law and recognised they were subject to the Crown and to the established order, they were also gaining confidence in their desire for universal suffrage.

Workers' rights were not yet recognised as a movement, or even acknowledged as such, although a group of English farm labourers, known as the Tolpuddle Martyrs, had already spent some years in Australia after they had been banished to the Antipodes for daring to request some form of civil justice for working people. Workers across the Western world were beginning to demand 'a fair go'.

The discovery of gold bought instant wealth to the new colony, through migration, investment, trade and royalties paid by the Crown. At the same time it freed the workers from servitude, creating an independent workforce that needed no master.

The government acted swiftly to curtail the independence of the labouring class. The imposition of a license fee on all diggers seemed the disincentive needed to keep the shepherds with their flocks, the sailors on their ships and the troopers at their posts. However, it was to no avail. All that it achieved was to set the diggers against the government and its license, and fostered a system of corruption, discrimination and bureaucratic chicanery that was eventually to bring the goldfields to insurrection. From the beginning, the government, quite reasonably, demanded compliance with its fees, but by the actions of its goldfields administrators was simply seen to punish its subjects as it lined its own pockets.

'An English Gold Field' and 'A Gold Field in the "Diggins"'
Punch Magazine, London

The popular papers in England were fascinated by the great exodus to the colonies. They profited by it, promoted it, and, in the style of most newspapers even today, took their turn at cynicism and outright condemnation.

The illustrations shown express a cynical yet comedic view of the goldfields. The one at left shows a group of happy little English children safe in their bountiful homeland; the other depicts the debauchery of a 'living hell' that could be life in the colonies.

For many, Australia did become a living hell. For those without luck, on whom Mother Fortune showed no favours, Australia was the farthest from the delights of a remembered home that they could possibly imagine.

Britain Awaits the News

Almost six months had passed between the time of the news of the first discovery at Bathurst in New South Wales and the news of the discovery at Mount Alexander in Victoria. While the London press was desperate for further revelations of the great finds west of the Blue Mountains, they had not expected similar news from the newly established colony of Victoria.

When ships arrived back in British ports carrying news of gold in the gullies at Buninyong, gold in the creeks of Creswick, gold beneath the surface of the gravel pits at Ballarat, and gold in the foothills of Mount Alexander, London was ablaze with excitement. The Californian fields no longer held the same fascination, yet the gold finds in the central highlands of Victoria—so recently described by the acclaimed explorer, Major Mitchell, as 'Australia Felix', where so many sons of Caledonia had recently taken up vast and profitable cattle and sheep-grazing runs—captured the imagination of the entire population.

Victoria had never been a penal colony, and the cessation of transportation in 1846 had placed heavy demand on labour for the building and development of colonial infrastructure in the southern colonies. Following the rushes to California, and then to Bathurst, there was also a severe shortage of rural workers, labourers and maidservants—hearty lads and wholesome lasses whose labour was needed to keep squatters, and merchants, profitable.

The popular press in Britain offered all kinds of encouragement to aspiring emigrants who wished to go to the diggings. Scores of books and pamphlets rolled off the English printing presses. One such work, published in 1852, was John Dunmore Lang's *The Australian Emigrant's Manual*, in which Lang counselled both for and against throwing caution to the wind in the rush for easy riches. Lang exhorted the migrants to do their best, reminding them

> that they are going to that distant land to assist in laying the broad and deep foundations of what will ere long be one of the mightiest empires upon earth, I would simply say to all who possess the mental and moral qualities: 'Go where comfort and a moderate independence await the honest and persevering exertions of every prudent and industrious man'. Such persons are sure to rise in the social scale in the Australian colonies, as compared with their position and means of influence at home. For although we have had enough people in times past, under our wretched system of government in these colonies, who would gladly have raised themselves into the position of colonial aristocracy, with rank and titles to authorise them to keep down all classes around them, the prospects of these aspirants have been sadly blighted of late by the levelling and equalising tendencies of the gold discovery; and there is now no part of the world in which it is more true than it is at this moment in Australia, that . . . 'A man's a man for a' that' . . .[1]

Another comprehensive work was the *Emigrant's Guide to Australia* written by the enterprising John Capper, whose advice ranged far and wide. One chapter, entitled 'Who Should Emigrate and How, with a Few Words to Those Who Had Better Remain at Home', offered advice that seems based more on the need to encourage rural workers and domestic servants to choose Australia to replace those who had rushed to the diggings than to encourage the inexperienced to chance their arm on the 'glittering lottery':

> Young unmarried women unacquainted with any form of farm or agricultural occupation would be of little use in the new colony.

View of the North Shore, Port of Melbourne, 1852
Engraving from a drawing by William Frederick Evelyn Liardet
(Picture Collection, State Library of Victoria)

The Melbourne ports were crammed with hundreds of tall ships unable to make their return journey after their crews had taken off for the goldfields.
Edwin Canton Booth wrote in 1873:

> It was of course impossible to keep the news [of the gold discoveries] away from the sailors, and to restrain men who had 'signed articles' for forty shillings per month from rushing off to a spot less than a hundred miles away, where they could gain as many pounds a day as they could earn on board ship in a year, was simply impossible.
>
> The law was powerless, for the guardians of the peace had joined in the general s tampede, and gone away in their hundreds to the diggings. Masters of vessels, finding their utter powerlessness in the matter, adopted a very sensible plan of making the most of things. They entered into a alliance with their officers and men, moored their ships as safely as possible, left one man in charge, and started for the gold regions in a body.. .the bargain made by the masters was faithfully carried out so far as seeking for and dividing the gold went.
>
> The return to the ship was a different matter. The Captain was bound to go back, but in the great majority of instances the men remained behind, having parted from their old commanders in perfect friendliness, both the richer and more contented than when they started.
>
> — Edwin Canton Booth, *Australia in the 1870's*, Virtue & Co., London, 1873–6, pp. 21–3.

> The drawing-room accomplishments of singing, dancing, painting, crochet would stand no shadow of a chance against the highly prized virtues of churning, baking, preserving, cheese-making and similar matters.[2]

The goldfields were the great leveller, where the notion of equality and liberty were tested. Jack did become as good as his master, no matter how hard the master worked at keeping him in his place. Just as the British tried to dismiss the Californian discoveries in case Queen Victoria's subjects rushed off to enjoy the fruits of true freedom, so did the British government attempt, for pecuniary purposes, to keep a lid on migration.

The great need was in the fields, not the goldfields, in the milking sheds not milking the earth, in the kitchens not out under the stars.

Lang discussed the mood among the elite in Britain who regarded the diggings with suspicion; they believed that the lure of quick riches promised by 'tall tales' from the colonies had caused the working class to eschew service in their rush to emigrate:

> There are certain mawkish sentimentalists in this country—certain people who pretend to be a great deal better than everybody else—who strongly encourage emigration to Australia, but who endeavour to persuade the emigrant to in a sort of whining tone by no means go to the diggings, as if there is something wrong in going there![3]

Yet, fuelled by reports in the press and fervour for adventure, excited emigrants soon filled scores of sailing ships. Entire villages packed up their tools—farm boys, working girls, clerks, lawyers, doctors, seamstresses; they came from all walks of life, from all classes, creeds and political persuasions—and headed for the diggings.

GREAT BOURKE STREET, MELBOURNE

Great Bourke Street, Melbourne
Hand-coloured engraving by W. Ralston from *News Letter of Australasia*, c.1880
(Author's collection)

A pair of lounging diggers stand out among respectable townsfolk as they promenade the streets of Melbourne.

With a nonchalant air, and no doubt pockets filled with the profits of gold-digging, these lads appear confident they are equal to all around them—gold has made it so.

John Capper, in his *Emigrant's Guide to Australia* [pub. 1852], offered this advice to gentlefolk considering a trip to the colonies:

> Let men, for instance, avoid all sorts of fancy waistcoats, dandy boots, or costly cravats and ties; let women shun the idle vanities of silks and satins, of lace and ribbons, of many flounces and fashionable bonnets; and let both men and women forget that there are such things in the world as kid gloves, lavender water and toilet tables.[4]

Capper was fully aware of the rough-and-ready frontier life that awaited new chums when they stepped ashore at Hobson's Bay. The streets of Melbourne did not resemble the elegance of Regent Street or the charm and bustle of Piccadilly in any way; the immigrant was set down in a dirty, dusty, or muddy, settlement of only a few hundred houses, and with virtually no amenities.

A New Chum and a Dirty Man Having a Discussion
Pen drawing by Edward Charles Moore, c. 1854
(Rex Nan Kivell Collection, T1762. By Permission, National Library of Australia)

The diggings were a great leveller. This comic drawing by E. C. Moore has the caption:

> '*New Chum*'. (to dirty looking man)
> I say my man, I'll give you have a crown to carry my box to an Hotel for me.–
>
> *Dirty Man* – You see my boot don't you? – It's unlaced – Well I'll give you a five pound note to lace it – You look hard up.

Such warnings, and there were many, seemed to have gone unheeded. Journalists, social commentators who wrote 'home' constantly, reported auctions of goods carried all the way from England, which were of no use to those setting off for the diggings. John Dunmore Lang offered advice against investing in goods in the hope of a quick profit in the colonies:

> I once advised an intending emigrant, who was going out to Australia with a capital of £1000 . . . not to expend one farthing of it in merchandise. But he preferred taking the advice of the captain . . . and he

> accordingly invested the whole of his fortune in goods. The result was, he lost upon everything, and was ruined.[5]

One writer who had a good business of his own at home advised: 'Go if you will; but you will probably be a great fool if you do'.[6] Few heeded the advice of the diarists, who, by the way, had already seen 'El Dorado' and were making their fortune by talking, at home, about their experience in the new world. In contrast to the nay-sayers one wrote in his diaries, that the diggings were:

> a truly wonderful place . . . the Chinese is jostled by the Russian. The polite Frenchman is abused by the African negro. The people of our own country are called to order by its more precocious offspring the American . . . Men from all nations sit down at the same table and drink from the same bowl, they each talk and sing in their own tongue, get drunk according to their own fashion, quarrel, jangle, fight and embrace and [then] . . . reel off to their own beds.[7]

The diggings became a great melting pot in the south that was to turn the whole world topsy turvey.

CHAPTER 4

The Last of England

The popular press in England was caught up in the rush 'to the diggings'. The great colonial adventure captured the imagination of the entire population and spurred thousands to throw caution to the winds and sail for the other side of the world.

The press was filled with tales of life on board ship, the hardships encountered on arrival at Port Phillip, disease, shipwreck, the excitement of relationships developed over the long voyage. The diggings were celebrated in hundreds of popular songs, plays, books, editions of lithographs, watercolours and mementoes collected as souvenirs.

As Henry Kingsley wrote:

> the discovery of Australia . . . opened a career for young gentlemen possessed of every virtue, save those of continence, sobriety, and industry, who didn't choose to walk and couldn't afford to drive; and, viewed from this point its discovery ranks next in importance after the invention of soda-water—a sort of way of escaping cheaply from the consequences of debauchery for a time.[1]

While it may be imagined that the majority of immigrants to Australia were from the ranks of the 'respectable poor' who would have saved long and hard to put together the fare, it is surprising to realise the large number of the educated, well-connected, middle and upper classes who were also set for the diggings.

When dramatic changes to several laws to do with property, debt and estates brought about a reduction in legal business, a reduction in plaintiffs and court cases, a large number of practitioners of the legal profession, particularly graduates of Trinity College, Dublin, made the journey to Australia. They carved out distinguished careers for themselves far from the green fields of old Ireland, and often far away from the dusty goldfields. One Irish lawyer wrote in his application for a job at the Colonial Office in Melbourne in 1854 that 'the disgraceful

DEPARTURE OF MRS. CHISHOLM, IN "THE BALLARAT," FOR AUSTRALIA.

Departure of Mrs Chisholm in 'The Ballarat' for Australia
Wood engraving, published *Illustrated London News*, 15 April 1854
(Rex Nan Kivell Collection NK4182/99. By permission, National Library of Australia)

Emigration to the colonies at the time of the goldrush did not abate, even after the feverish excitement of the first rushes had died away.

Caroline Chisholm had earned a reputation for her earlier work with homeless and wayward girls around The Rocks area in Sydney, establishing workhouses and dormitory accommodation. A staunch Roman Catholic she aimed to steer young girls on Sydney shores away from moral danger, finding appropriate work for them in service, which would hopefully lead to a good Christian marriage.

With the large numbers of single men on the diggings, who, without female company were prone to questionable social behaviour, alcohol and moral abuse, Mrs Chisholm saw female emigration as one way to arrest the inevitable moral decline of men living 'roughly' in the mining camps.

In concert with novelist Charles Dickens, they lobbied the British parliament, eventually finding the means by which they could encourage girls to migrate.

At the time Britain saw the rise of a class of well-meaning, and influential, middle-class social reformers and Chisholm was regarded as one the most effective of them. Although she suffered some criticism of her emigration schemes her reputation as a notable Victorian philanthropist is confirmed in this engraving published in the *London Illustrated News.*

state of the bar . . . induced me to look to the colonies as a better field for my exertions.'[2]

As Kingsley wrote in the opening pages of his memoirs of life on the diggings:

> Yes, that's the land for me! A continent in itself, inhabited by only a few civilised beings and wild aborigines, while millions of acres of good land are waiting settlement by people of the right stamp, . . . a

The Last of England
Oil by Ford Maddox Brown, 1852–55
(Birmingham City Museum & Art Gallery)

This poignant image was painted soon after Brown and the pre-Raphaelite artists Rossetti and Holman Hunt, farewelled fellow artists who had responded to the call of 'the diggings'. Among them were Thomas Woolner, who was to become the pre-eminent sculptor of the Victorian age in Australia.

Brown spent months on this detailed painting, which depicts a melancholic couple with their child, hidden beneath her cloak, as they sail out from England leaving the white cliffs of Dover behind them.

country possessing a genial climate and unlimited resources; while, more attractive than all, rumours are afloat that rich goldfields have been discovered in several parts of it. Who knows but that it may turn out to be a second California? Irrespective of gold, there is elbow room there . . . Under the Southern Cross there is room for all.[3]

The spirit of adventure struck deeply into the hearts of one group of distinguished English artists and writers. The poet Alfred Tennyson wished to go himself and try his hand at digging, but he restrained himself at the request of his wife. The Pre-Raphaelite Brotherhood, a group of bohemian artists in London, had hit a low patch in their fortunes and were considering migration as a body, in the hope of reversing that fortune, returning to England and being able to work unencumbered by the need of patronage. Their fortunes changed at home, and only three artists set out on the journey: sculptor Thomas Woolner, and artists Bernhard Smith and E. La Trobe Bateman, sailed from Gravesend in July 1852. They were farewelled at the dock by Danté Gabriel Rossetti, Holman Hunt and Ford Maddox Brown, who was so moved by the emotional departure that he painted *The Last of England* soon after.

The poignant narrative within this simple image was echoed time and again as thousands of others left their home in search of adventure and a new and better life.

Charles Dickens was another commentator who stood at the quayside watching a strange collection of his countrymen and women climb aboard one ship bound for Port Phillip. He shares his observation in *Household Words*, 17 July 1852:

> Old men with grey hairs and faltering steps; young girls, pale from the factory or the garret; countrymen in smock-frocks; lean-faced artisans; mothers with infants in arms; stout servant girls . . .; two or three newly wedded couples . . .; a knot of oily-headed, sleek-visaged shopmen, and city clerks; a few hale-looking country lads and lasses . . . I should have thought they were sailing to Botany Bay, by the dismal misery written on the faces of those on deck!

Leaving home may have filled Dickens's Micawber with a 'bold buccaneering air', but it filled most others with mixed emotions of expectation and fear. Embarking on a journey of four months or so halfway round the globe in cramped and spartan conditions, through calm and storm, disease and dismay, to step ashore at last—into what?

Ford Maddox Brown's melancholy image is an accurate one, contrasted with the buccaneering air affected by his friends who sailed out 'armed to the teeth . . . stocked with corduroys, sou'westers, jerseys, fire-arms and belts of little bags to hold the expected nuggets'.[4]

Emigrants Embarking from England
(La Trobe Picture Collection, State Library of Victoria)

The rush to emigrate to the colonies became a social phenomenon where thousands of men women and children, old and young, able, and at times not so able, took up the challenge of making a new life in a new land.

Through the marketing skills of the Emigration Societies and the promotional tours conducted by the likes of Mrs Chisholm, ships set sail from the English ports loaded to the gunwales with expectant emigrants taking their last look at the shores of 'home'.

Some would not survive the rigours of the long sea voyage, others would s uccumb to the dangers of the Australian bush, while many never became rich enough to ever consider returning home.

Almost all left with the expectation that they would soon make their pile, and change their lives forever. One thing was certain, however: no matter what lay before them, their lives would all be changed by the experience of life at 'the diggings'.

On arrival at Port Phillip most were shocked at the state of the fledgling settlement. Few emigrants had expected a frontier town of unmade streets, crude inhabitants, mean and inadequate accommodation, and exorbitant prices. So many ships arrived in such a short time that a tent city was established on the south bank of the Yarra River, affording reasonable accommodation for the new arrivals before they rediscovered their 'land-legs' and began the march to the diggings.

Records show that, at times, there was an almost unbroken line of hopeful new chums making their way across the Keilor Plains out towards Diggers' Rest (the first day's resting place for most) on the Mount Alexander Road. There was also a similar line of the successful and the not-so-successful on their way back again, either to spend up big in Melbourne or to look for employment in the town.

Portrait of Caroline Chisholm
Lithograph by Thomas Fairland, M. I. Laidler, *Advance Australia*, London, 1 September 1852
(Rex Nan Kivell Collection, U6413. By Permission, National Library of Australia)

Mrs Chisholm was at heart a philanthropic gentlewoman.

The desire to do her Christian duty and rescue fallen women, while at the same time transforming the male-dominated society in the early colonies into a community stabilised by the influence of 'home and hearth', led her to pack hundreds of destitute girls into sailing ships bound for Australia.

Although she assisted the girls to find a worthwhile place in the colonies, once ashore they either found employment, found a husband or 'fell' again.

She suffered criticism from many quarters, and was accused of transporting prostitutes to the colonies without regard to the type of society she was creating.

Good Business for Mrs Chisholm

Emigration was big business. The cessation of transportation in 1848 had put an end to cheap labour, and the discovery of gold in America in 1849 saw thousands of able-bodied Australians leave for the diggings there. The landed gentry in the colonies saw their livelihoods at a standstill, crops left unharvested, flocks untended, shops and factories without labour.

The rush to populate was pushed along by several forces at once: the need to provide labour for the colonial enterprises—this generally meant rural, pastoral and domestic workers for the squatting classes; the need to provide for the dispossessed at home, the large number of homeless and unemployed from the outer reaches of the British Isles, the Irish, the Scottish and the English poor; the need to counter the depopulation following the American discoveries; and the need to create a stable colonial community through the migration of women suitable for marriage to the large number of men who had come alone to the diggings.

The British Colonial Land & Emigration Commissioners had not always been able to meet the demands of the colonists before the gold discoveries, but in 1852 they were deluged by over 700 letters a day from hopefuls desperate to be granted permission to sail. By the middle of 1852, 18,000 had applied for assisted passage to Australia.

The following advertisement was typical of the enticements to encourage emigrants to Australia, not to dig for gold, but to join in the hard work necessary in the building of the new nation:

> WANTED: An opportunity now offers itself to all married persons of useful occupations particularly to agricultural labourers, carpenters, builders, stone masons, shepherds and blacksmiths of obtaining a free passage to Port Adelaide in South Australia (SA).
>
> A free colony where there are no convicts sent and where every person who immigrates is as free as he is in this country. Besides the classes of persons enumerated above, bakers, blacksmiths, braziers and tin men, smiths, shipwrights, boat builders, wheel-wrights, sawyers, cabinet makers, coopers, couriers, farriers, mill-wrights, harness makers, boot and shoe makers, tailors, tanners, brick makers, lime burners and all persons engaged in the erection of buildings are always in great request. The applicants must be able to obtain a good character reference as honest, sober, industrious men. They must be real labourers going out to work in the colony, of sound body, not less than 15 and nor more than 30 years of age, and married. The rule as to age is occasionally departed from in favour of the parents of large families. As a general rule each child is considered as extended the age plus one year. Sisters of married applicants are allowed to go free if of good character.
>
> The province of SA is a delightfully fertile and salubrious country, in every respect well adapted to the constitution of Englishmen and is one of the most flourishing in all our colonies. It is well watered and there have never been any complaints from the colonists of a want of this valuable element. On the contrary, the letters from Cornishmen who have written home are very satisfactory on this point. It should be borne in mind that complaints of a scarcity of water do not apply to Adelaide but to other settlements not connected to SA.
>
> Immigrants wishing to obtain a free passage this year must now have that opportunity if they apply immediately to Mr. I. Latimer, Truro, who is employed by Her Majesty's colonization commissioners to engage for that fine first class teak built ship, the 'Java' of 1200 tonnes.
>
> The ship's accommodations are unusually spacious and lofty and are so arranged as to ensure the comfort of all passengers. She will

Emigrant Ship, Between Decks
Wood engraving from *Illustrated News*, London, 17 August 1850
(Rex Nan Kivell Collection, U5948. By Permission, National Library of Australia)

Adelaide. Hindley Street from the corner of King William Street; looking west
Hand-coloured lithograph from a drawing by George French Angas, 1846. Published by Thomas McLean, London, 1847
(Rex Nan Kivell Collection NK4742. by permission, National Library of Australia)

This inscription [in part] accompanied this picture of this already well-developed Adelaide thoroughfare:

> Hindley Street, which is about a mile in length, is the principal part for shops and public business, and presents an animated and bustling appearance. The ground in this street, and in King William Street, which intersects it, is very valuable; and is being rapidly built upon by the merchants and tradesmen . . .

Emigrants Landing at the Queen's Wharf
Wood engraving by Fredrick Grosse, Melbourne, c. 1861
(Rex Nan Kivell Collection, S2853. By Permission, National Library of Australia)
Although those who arrived in the early days of the rush were landed on the muddy shore of Liardet's beach, over a mile or so from the town, it was not long before the docks of Port Phillip were made ready for the hundreds of ships to follow.

> carry 2 surgeons and 2 school masters, the latter of whom will be regularly employed in teaching the immigrants and their children. The vessel will call at Plymouth to take in Cornish passengers and on or about the 16th of October but in order to ensure a passage application should be made forthwith.[5]

The Highland and Island Emigration Society was established to assist the inhabitants of the Isle of Skye and other islands on the west coast of Scotland to look for passage to Australia. Potato disease and a subsequent famine had all but destroyed the islands, and it was remarked that, even after migration, the 'docility' of these folk made them of little use to their employers. It appears that after so many years eking out a pitiful existence on their windswept islands that it took many years under the southern sun to rehabilitate them.

The English philanthropist, Caroline Chisholm, and the Family Colonization Loan Society set out to attract a better, stronger, more suitable class of prospective migrant. Caroline had accompanied her husband, Captain H. Chisholm, from Madras to Australia in 1848. It was in Sydney that she saw the poverty of the lives of destitute, unemployed women,

Hobson's Bay from the Signal Staff, Williamstown
Hand-coloured lithograph by Edmund Thomas, R. Quarill & Co, Melbourne, 1853
(Rex Nan Kivell Collection, U2621. By Permission, National Library of Australia)

The first land fall for emigrants to the Colony of Victoria was Hobson's Bay (Williamstown) which was some distance from the new port of Melbourne.

Smaller craft, steamers and ferries were able to take the expectant new chums further up the river to land on the shores of Melbourne on the Yarra Yarra River.

and was made aware of the bawdy, boozing lives of unaccompanied men on the diggings. Caroline believed that the introduction of family life to the diggers would do much to redress the awfulness of their frontier lives. She believed that the influence of her women, 'God's police' as she referred to them, on the lives of the frontier men would do much more than would any moralising priest or didactic schoolmaster.

She organised convoys of women, going from farm to farm seeking employment for them as she went. Her expeditions were outstandingly successful. Before long Chisholm had established the Family Colonization Loan Society, which sponsored females to travel to the colonies, where they contracted to repay their debt to the Society after they had secured a position or a marriage partner.

Mrs Ellen Clacy, who sailed for the diggings with her fiancee in 1852, writes:

> No one in England can fully appreciate the benefits her [Mrs Chisholm's] unwearied exertions have conferred upon the colonies. I have met many of the matrons of her ships, and not only do they

> themselves seem to have made their way in the world, but the young females who were under their care during the voyage appear to have done equally well. Perhaps one way of accounting for this, is the fact that many of those going out by the Chisholm Society are from Scotland, the inhabitants of which country are particularly fortunate in the colonies, their industry, frugality, and 'canniness' being the very qualities to make a fortune there.[6]

But there were also those in the colonies who, at the same time, disagreed with Caroline Chisholm's almost evangelical promotion of the positive benefits of colonial life.

Polish gold-digger Severyn Korzelinski who had been at the Forest Creek and Bendigo diggings, writes in his memoirs: 'Mrs. Chisholm, painting only the bright side of Australia, omitted its defects'. He felt that Mrs Chisholm, in effect, was carrying on 'what amounted to trafficking in women'.[7]

Caroline Chisholm's agent in Melbourne took females straight off the migrant ships as they docked. They were sorted and most sent straight up to the bush. Of course this suited most of the arrivals as they did not really know where to go or what to do, and it suited employers very well. Those who were not taken up could look forward to an extended period in one of Mrs Chisholm's 'emigrant houses', where food rationing was so carefully worked out that the girls were given just enough to keep them alive. They took any offer from any comer, simply to escape.

Korzelinski commented:

> they were prepared to grasp at every opportunity and agreed to go with a sailor, ex-convict, anyone . . . nor was there any difficulty in obtaining a woman from the emigrant house. Whoever wished arrived, picked one out to his liking and carried her away with him after reimbursing the institution a few pounds which the government had spent on clothing, because usually the women had arrived in Australia in tatters.[8]

There are records of hundreds of women at a time being sent to the diggings to save the diggers the time and effort of travelling to Melbourne in search of a wife. At one time any man on the Castlemaine diggings who desired a wife simply had to prove that he had £10, and he could take a woman, a dowry of a similar amount, a tent and a pair of blankets.

Primrose from England
Oil on canvas by Edward Hopley, c. 1855
(Bendigo Art Gallery collection)

This charming and nostalgic painting was donated to the Bendigo Art Gallery in 1940 by George Lansell Jr, son of George Lansell Sr, the Quartz King of Bendigo.

The painting depicts the arrival of a potted primrose on the docks at Port Phillip. This lovely fantasy is based upon an actual event, and depicts the longing that migrants can feel for 'home', and the ease with which a simple reminder can transport them back to that long-since-departed place.

What a great collection of colonial characters there are in this painting—the beaming Dickensian gentleman in his topper, the merchant, the farmer and his child, a bold digger stands back in the shadows, a rustic Scot beams towards the artist in the foreground. Others crowd at the door, the housemaid, the trooper, in the distance the tall masts of a sailing ship at the dock, while a group of young women gaze longingly at the potted blooms.

An Aboriginal is seen partially hidden in the shadows on the right. This may well be an allusion by the artist to the condition that Aboriginals had found themselves in following the colonisation of their homeland by Europeans.

It may also be the softness of that flower that contrasts so greatly with the comparative harshness of Australian flora that has them longing so wistfully for home.

But what sort of future was that for a young girl who would be likely to be left in an empty tent after the money ran out, and seeing her digger 'husband' take his leave to repeat the 'marriage' somewhere else?

'Let them reflect well on the unpaved streets, and the dust blowing every few days in Melbourne until you cannot see your own hand; on the heat, the flies, the mud, and slush, the moment there is rain, before they quit the smooth pavements and the comforts that abound in England. Let them reflect too, on the rude, chaotic, and blackguard state of the lower society in this suddenly-thrown-together colony',[9] wrote William Howitt in his book *Land, Labour & Gold* in 1853, in warning to young maid-servants whom a correspondent of his was seeking to send to the colony. It was a warning to all young girls who may have looked towards the goldfields as a place for excitement, and more probably, emancipation from household service in England:

> As to girls marrying here—the great temptation—that is soon accomplished; for I fear that lots of diggers get married almost every time they go down to Melbourne to spend their gold. A lot of the vilest scoundrels are assembled from all the four winds of heaven. Nobody knows them; much less whether they have left wives behind them in their own countries; and they marry, and go off, and are never heard of again . . . the experiment, however, is so awfully hazardous, that I should carefully avoid in all cases promoting it.[10]

Marvellous Smellbourne!

One hundred days away from Britain's shores, the migrants who had travelled so eagerly to the other side of the world were rarely prepared for the frontier society they were to find at the end of their journey. Most formed into digging parties of half-a-dozen or so on board ship, and upon landing spent the first few weeks in the colony putting together supplies necessary for the journey north. This gave them some time to explore the township of Melbourne, whose streets at that time were a far cry from the leafy avenues and promenades of London, Liverpool or Dublin.

Most writers describe the disgusting scene on arriving at Port Phillip. Slaughterhouses lined the river—wooden buildings with fenced yards to one side, holding the wretched beasts standing among the decapitated heads of their kind. Pigs snuffled about in the filth, tearing the flesh from discarded bones. On the riverside entrails, blood, gore and the stripped carcasses of rotting animals trailed into the river, creating a filthy and malodorous welcome to the newly arrived immigrant. Crossing to the other side of the river offered little respite from this gory scene.

New Chums, Refreshing Sleep. 10/- a Night – Hard up! Compulsory sales – Melbourne, Dec. 1852
Watercolour by William Strutt, 1852
(State Parliamentary Library Collection, Victoria)
This painting depicts the common experience shared by new arrivals at Port Phillip. Highly-priced accommodation, and expensive goods and provisions meant that many who were financially ill-prepared sold what they could to help finance the next leg of their expedition.

Rendering plants, tanneries, fellmongers and wool-washers spewed their filthy aroma into the fetid air while the river was both source and sewer of the malodorous brew being created on the river's edge, enshrining the title on the port of—'Marvellous Smellbourne'.

Although Melbourne had tried to keep the river clean for domestic use up until the 1850s, and bathing in the stream above the fresh-water mark at Queen's Bridge had been banned for a long time, the sheer crush of humanity that flowed into Melbourne during the goldrush placed incredible demands on the town's services. Things may have been worse: floods in 1842, '44, '48 and '49 swept most of the foulness down the river, including more than 2500 sheep penned by the riverside at Philpott's boiling-down plant.

The dusty, at times boggy, streets were littered with garbage, dead and decaying animals; for miles around the outskirts of town the bush glittered with the broken shards of discarded champagne bottles:

> I have scarcely seen a tree under which do not lie the remains of bottles which had been dashed against it, as they have been emptied. Nay, I see whole bottles lying thrown out all about the outskirts of the town, which not a soul thinks it worth his while to pick up . . .[11]

Gold Diggers Receiving a Letter From Home
Oil attributed to William Strutt, c. 1860
(Art Gallery of New South Wales)

News of home was eagerly awaited by the immigrants who no longer classed themselves as new chums but as 'diggers'.

Strutt's painting shows a pair of diggers reading their way through a pile of mail that has just arrived on one of the migrant ships.

Mail was regularly carried to the diggings, as the postal services were always one of the first agencies to be established on any of the goldfields.

Camping on the Road
Hand-coloured lithograph by Cyrus Mason, c. 1855
(Rex Nan Kivell Collection, U2490. By Permission, National Library of Australia)

William Howitt reflects that the bottles are a passable blight, but only showing 'a recklessness of expense; but the dead horses and bullocks are disgusting'.[12]

It seemed that the citizens regarded their worn-out animals as criminals, and preferred to execute them where they fell, which was often at crossroads. Howitt continues:

> the other evening we saw a bullock's head, with a large pair of horns, lying on the road, as if the animal, according to Milton's description, were just created and rising out of the earth, having as yet only got its head free.[13]

Life under canvas may have seemed exciting and adventurous at first, but the flies, mosquitoes, heat and dust soon took their toll. So many had arrived that the young town could not accommodate them in the few hundred houses that had been constructed by the first settlers and merchants. A tent city was established south of the Yarra below Princes Bridge, which had been opened in 1851, to accommodate the thousands of new arrivals who could find no other place to stay. The town charged

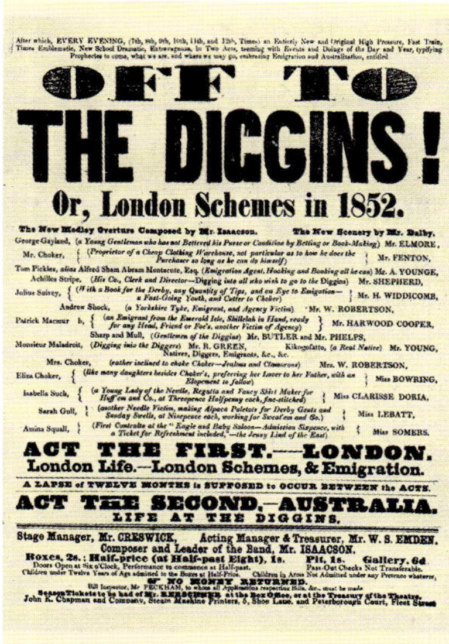

Left: *Advertisement for Castlemaine tent-maker H. Winks*
All kinds of products were created to assist in a successful voyage to the colonies and then in a successful venture on the diggings.

The fact that most merchants in London had little idea what the diggers would really find upon landing in the Antipodes did not deter them from making their pile at home.

Although there was a roaring trade in tents and other diggers' paraphernalia in England, there was still plenty of opportunity for entrepreneurs in the colonies like Mr Winks to make their own bit 'of hay while the sun shone'.

Winks operated his business from the Market Square, Castlemaine.

Right: *Off To The Diggings! Theatre poster, c. 1852*
Off To The Diggings was a rollicking comedy of errors, in the French-farce style popular in British theatres at the time. Filled with British archetypes: the upper-class nob and the working man, and woman, get well and truly mixed up on the diggings.

immigrants and others who had made their way into Melbourne before striking out for the diggings 5 shillings a week on each tent. Among these tents a little city had been established, known as Little Adelaide, where a number of families from South Australia, who had been seduced by the prospect of the Victorian diggings, were camped out, as they could not afford the prices of accommodation in the town.

For many the tent city gave them the opportunity to set up their gear and test their ability as 'campers' before they really put themselves to the test. Mrs Ellen Clacy took a stroll along the river one Sunday, in the company of her brother and a friend, along the river towards the Botanical Gardens. They came across two tents pitched on a slight rise beside the river:

Canvas Town, South Melbourne
Hand coloured engraving from *Victoria and Its Metropolis: Past and Present* published 1888
(Author's Collection)
A tent city was established on the south side of the Yarra river in Port Phillip [Melbourne]. Mt Macedon, from the summit of which Major Mitchell first spied the bay only 15 years before, looms on the horizon, reminding the tent dwellers of their goal, which lay a further 40 or 50 miles on from that brooding landmark.

> not far enough away from Melbourne to be inconvenient, but yet sufficiently removed from its mud and noise, were pitched two tents, evidently new, with crimson paint still gay upon the round nobs of the centre posts, and looking altogether more in trim for a gala day in Merry England than a trip to the diggings.[14]

What a jolly sight these tents must have made when they were eventually set up among the cacophony that was the diggings. The peacefully pleasant scene of canvas set among the gardens on the gently flowing river contrasts sharply with Clacy's description of her last night on the diggings some weeks later at the end of her colonial adventure:

> Imagine some hundreds of revolvers almost simultaneously fired—the sound reverberating through the mighty forests, and echoed far and near—again and again till the last faint echo died away in

> the distance. Then a hundred blazing fires burst upon the sight—around them gathered the rough miners themselves—their sun-burnt, hair-covered faces illumined by the ruddy glare. Wild songs, and still wilder burst of laughter are heard; gradually the flames sink and disappear, and an oppressive stillness follows . . . broken only by some midnight carouser, as he vainly endeavours to find his tent.[15]

There were those who were never to experience the camaraderie that took over all life on the diggings. Life in Melbourne proved too distasteful, and they simply returned on the ships that had brought them out, having never even landed their sea-trunks. There were those who simply did not have the stamina to withstand the ravages of the new colony and succumbed to its excesses—excesses of heat, dust, flies, disease, alcohol, robbery or murder. It was the harsh new land that took away from many the pale-rose flush of England.

Howitt writes:

> Hundreds have already gone back again, cursing those who sent such one-sided statements of the goldfields and of the climate. Thousands have been struck down, and many are still lying on their backs, from the effects of the change in climate . . . dysenteries, fevers, and rheumatism, which will cripple many for life, and have already carried many out of it. New as are these diggings, there is a tolerably populous cemetery on a hill here; and some who crossed the sea with us are already sleeping there.[16]

Yet the discomforts endured in Melbourne did not deter most diggers from their quest: 'But for ourselves, we are no whit daunted. We shall dig, and we shall buy gold; and whether we shall get more or less, we shall be picking up information for an ultimate object'.[17]

That ultimate object was adventure, and the adventure was for gold!

HARD TIMES AND MIGRATION SCHEMES

Charles Dickens & Mrs Chisholm

In 1847 The 3rd Earl Grey, British Secretary of State for War and The Colonies, devised an emigration scheme to satisfy both the demand for domestic servants, and for marriageable young women, in the largely male-dominated Australian colonies, while also reducing overcrowding in Irish workhouses, the result of the years of famine. He proposed to send out more than 4000 Irish orphans to relieve the chronic shortage of female labour in the colonies. Several ships disembarked the Irish orphans: the *William Stewart*, *Mahomed Shah* and the *Pemberton* brought several hundred orphan girls, but before long Grey changed his mind. He decided not to send out immigrants but exiles, convicts who had served part of their sentences in British gaols.

Philanthropist Caroline Chisholm, who had championed the cause of immigrant women since her arrival in the colony in 1841, publicly attacked Grey's change of mind. She opposed the resumption of any form of transportation of convicts, a system that had ceased seven years earlier following repeated protests by the prominent citizens of the new society.

Instead she advocated a systematic form of assisted emigration, which helped hundreds of women make the journey to Australia to fulfil the secondary aim of the 'civilisation' of men on the diggings.

However, Mrs Chisholm was not without her critics. What seemed to have begun as an altruistic effort to help the homeless, vagrant and unemployed women on the streets of Sydney to redemption through hard work became a profitable business for Chisholm. The Emigration Society that she eventually helped establish is reported to have returned her £3 per girl.

She did meet considerable criticism of her efforts to stabilise goldfields society through the benefits of 'hearth and home'. Many critics in the colonies accused her of 'trafficking in women', yet she continued to perform what she saw as her Christian duty, and was considered by others to have been worthy of the title of 'Australia's first saint'.

Chisholm and the Family Colonization Loan Society sought to send out a better class of future colonist than simply emptying Imperial gaols. She toured England extensively, promoting the colonies in the hope of filling 'her' ships—and, as some were wont to complain, her pockets as well.

English author, philanthropist and social reformer Charles Dickens shared a common interest in female emigration with Mrs Chisholm. He wandered the foggy alleys and cobbled streets of London at night, where he encountered many young women who had taken to life 'on the game'. Through his 'Appeal for Fallen Women' Dickens was convinced that a new start was the only hope for the 'permanent reformation' of the fallen. His novels refer constantly to the promise offered by emigration and the redeeming possibilities of life renewed in the colonies.

Caroline Chisholm
Lithograph by Thomas Fairland
M. I. Laidler, 1 February 1851, London
(Rex Nan Kivell Collection, U6422. By Permission, National Library of Australia)

In 1847 Dickens opened a home for former prostitutes known as Urania House, in London's Shepherd's Bush. He believed that 'the prospect of marriage in a context free of past associations could be sufficient incentive for former prostitutes to give up their long-learned and enduring vices . . . these unfortunate creatures are to be tempted to virtue. They cannot be dragged, driven or frightened [into it]'. Dickens was also interested in similar work by Mrs Chisholm and her Family Colonization Loan Society, as he had also supervised the sending of proposed residents to both Cape Town and Australia.

After Dickens had visited Mrs Chisholm at her London home—apart from commenting on her bad housekeeping and her children's dirty faces, which 'haunted him' for some considerable time—he created the character Mrs Jellyby [based on Caroline] and 'telescopic philanthropy' for use in his novel *Bleak House.*

His characters, Little Em'ly and Martha Endell, were inspired by women he had met on the streets, and represented his belief that prostitution flourished in a male-dominated society, where class distinctions and sexual exploitation would ensure that a certain class of women was seduced into a state where the prospect of a respectable marriage was more than likely rendered impossible.

Both Dickens and Chisholm were actively promoting the same view. While they were genuinely concerned for the well-being of the women they encountered, this coupled with the demand for working-class emigration and the excitement of the gold discoveries in the colonies, ensured that the work of 'tempting' such girls to seek redemption through emigration was relatively easy and a very profitable outcome for all involved.

Dickens was satisfied that the outcome provided for 'the perfect penitence for these women—a kind of active repentance in their being faithful wives and the mothers of virtuous children', no matter that on arrival at Port Phillip they were most likely to be 'hitched up' to any old lag, hoary Vandemonian or lusty digger down on a spree, who was just as likely to leave them on the streets where they had found them when they took off back to the diggings. Often, the lives of these migrant girls did not change much at all.

The Earl Grey scheme ceased in May 1850, at the beginning of the Australian gold rush, when migrants of both sexes eagerly sailed away to the colony at their own expense.

CHAPTER 5

The Road to the Diggings

Almost every one of us brought too much on our back and at every stage we lightened ourselves. At one camping place three pairs of trousers were thrown away, one of which were mine, and at our last camp in the valley, innumerable articles were left. Our company left our table cloths or oil cloths, two axes, 1 counterpane, prospecting pan, camp kettles, pannikin etc. Some left everything they had, determining never to camp out again: flannel drawers, shirts, blankets, kettles, rugs etc., were all scattered about.[1]

—Thomas Arnot, 7 August 1852

The road to the diggings took the newcomer across a landscape that had known no plough, and no roadmaking gang had ever toiled to ease their journey. The diggers trekked across windswept plains, forded rushing streams, climbed granite-strewn slopes and tramped into darkened forests of gnarled, black-trunked eucalypts.

With their gear strapped to their shoulders or pushed before them in hand-carts the diggers cursed the heat, flailed at flies and swatted at mosquitoes; when the season turned to winter they shivered in the cold, soaked by the rain, but few were beaten by the sheer effort that was their start in their 'rush to the diggings'.

> It was a melancholy sight. Four hundred miles they had dragged along their carts, over gully, swamp, and mountain, leaving the richer diggings of the Turon and of Bathurst behind them to gather at the Ovens [Beechworth], as they had been assured, hundredweights of gold![2]
> —William Howitt, 1853

One young fellow, who had spent a long time at Bendigo, had his horse stolen by a group of escaped convicts just out of Albury. It had pulled his cart from Bendigo to Sydney onto the Turon and back, to be taken

The rush to the Ballarat goldfields in 1854
Watercolour by S.T. Gill, Melbourne, Victoria, 1872
(National Library of Australia collection)

This is one of a series of paintings of goldfields life commissioned by the Victorian government in 1872. Here Gill recalls the almost ceaseless rush of humanity heading for the diggings.

The going was tough: hills to climb, valleys to traverse and boggy creeks to cross. All the while the diggers carried all they owned on their backs or trudged beside a cart as they made the slow journey to the latest rush.

Every possible variety of digger is shown here: from the Chinese with their baskets across their shoulders; the fortunate digger with a pack-horse; the unfortunate lugging his heavy wooden cradle strapped to his back; the family with a cart, father and son walk by the horse's head while mother sits perched upon all their worldly goods.

Diggers and their wives, one cradling an infant in her arms, have stopped for a rest and watch the passing parade. For them there appears to be no urgency, their gold will still be there for them whenever they arrive, and wherever that may be.

Gill shows us what equipment they have carried with them as they begin their great adventure: a pot, a pan, a washing dish, a shovel and pick, rifle, bed-roll and tent. These basic goods the foundation of a new life on the goldfields.

by thieves halfway back again. He had kept one nugget of seven or eight ounces as a remembrance of old times and feared that he would have to sell it to finance his way back to Bendigo.

The road through the forests was fraught with danger, and bushrangers and thieves seemed to wait at every turn.

Attack on the road was such a common occurrence that all who recorded their own stories of life on the diggings make reference to what they themselves had the mispleasure to experience:

The New Rush
Colour lithograph by S. T. Gill, c. 1854
(Bendigo Art Gallery collection)
A ragtag army of diggers makes its way to Bendigo.

Most diggers carried everything they owned on their backs. Only a lucky few had horses, and only those newly arrived from the old country with funds ready for adventure could afford the hire of a carter's dray.

Although there were many new chums who attempted to carry everything they thought they would need, the roads were soon littered with the trappings of polite society that were of no use at all in the bush, or were simply a burden best discarded.

In the towns and on every field the digger's auction was a common sight, as men sought to grab back a few shillings spent on non-essential goods they no longer wished to carry to the next rush.

Towards evening, a party of four, returning from the diggings, encamped a little distance from us. Some of our loiterers made their acquaintance. They had passed the previous night in the Black Forest, having wandered out of their way. To add to their misfortunes, they had been attacked by three well-armed bushrangers . . . two of the poor men had been wounded, one rather seriously. Hardly had they recovered from this shock, than they were horrified by the sudden discovery in a sequestered spot of some human bones, strewn upon the ground beside a broken-down cart. Whether accident or design had brought these unfortunates to an untimely end, none know; but this ominous appearance seemed to have terrified them even more than the bushrangers themselves.[3]

Melbourne 1855, as seen from the north, near the road to Mt Alexander
Lithograph on tinted paper by Henry Burn
(Picture Collection, State Library of Victoria)

Crossing the open grassy plains to the north of Melbourne took all of the first day of any journey to the Mount Alexander and Bendigo diggings.

After a single day of toil with a swag over the shoulder, pick and shovel in hand, the small settlement at 'Digger's Rest' was a welcome sight.

This drawing shows a pair of diggers resting by the side of the road as the heavily guarded gold escort makes its way back to the Treasury.

Melbourne's growing skyline can be seen, not too far away, stretching across the horizon. The first Exhibition buildings dominate the scene, an indication of the wealth of a city being built on gold, while the old flagstaff still sits out in open country.

To this report Ellen Clacy adds that her party doubled their watch on that night.

One young adventurer wrote to his mother back home in England with this request for a 'life-preserver':

> I wish you had sent out one of Colt's revolvers, or a pair of good duelling pistols as I am more in want of them than anything I can mention. For Baker's revolvers they are asking £16 or £18 each, and for pistols that are 4/6 at home, 45/-. The town is in a dreadful state . . . This week ten bushrangers were taken. Their beat is on the road to the diggings, travelling in parties of 4 or 6. They stopped everyone they met, took them into the bush, stripped them naked, tied them to trees, and there left them until someone came by and released them.[4]

The roads were crowded with travellers all intent on one purpose:

> In one week upwards of 2000 people were counted on the road to the Bathurst diggings, and only eleven coming down. Hundreds of men, of all classes, threw up their situations, and leaving their wives and families behind them, started for the diggings. Whole crews ran

Road to Bendigo from Forest Creek, 1852.
Hand-coloured lithograph by S.T. Gill
(Author's Collection)

It was a tough haul up to the Bendigo diggings for both man and beast alike. The last hill to climb before the long descent into the wide dish-shaped valley of the Bendigo diggings took its toll.

Here carts have been abandoned, bullocks strain beneath the bullocky's invective and diggers stop for a breather before they crest the 'Big Hill' and then down across Kangaroo Flat to the Bendigo Creek.

> away from their ships, which were left to rot in our harbours . . . the roads were crowded with travellers, carriages, gigs, drays, carts and wheelbarrows: mixed up in one confused assemblage might be seen magistrates, lawyers, physicians, clerks, tradesmen, and labourers.[5]

As they tramped towards their El Dorado the new chums were passed by others heading back to town, pockets filled ready for a spree, and there were others who had had no such luck and were already keen to give digging away; troopers crashed through the bush, mounting guard over flatbed drays carrying boxes of gold ready for the Treasury, and there was the ever-watchful villain lurking, waiting for the unwary or the careless.

Apart from the bleached bones of a few unfortunate diggers, the roads were also littered with the wrecks of expeditions gone wrong, animals that would pull no more simply left to die by the side of the road, goods piled high as merchants waited for relief, or discarded as yet one more traveller sought to lighten his load. Bullock drays made their painfully slow progress towards the diggings. It took a journey of three, four or more weeks to get supplies up by wagon, the goods carried this way arrived with a highly inflated retail value, but the diggers on the fields had little choice but to pay the going rate or do without.

Many an entrepreneur made a start in commerce by judiciously investing in a drayload of goods that would bring a handsome profit on the diggings. Diggers who had banded together often invested in a pair of horses and a dray to carry the goods they thought essential on the diggings, but soon sold the beasts on arrival, as the cost of feeding and watering, combined with the difficulty keeping them corralled or safe from thieves, was prohibitive for most.

The end of the journey was near when a party became aware of a dull roar in the distance, a roar like slow-rolling thunder. The rocking of hundreds of cradles, the loading and discharging of hundreds of buckets set up a cacophony that grew louder as they approached, eager for their first sight of the diggings:

> Our longing eyes at length obtained a view of El Dorado—Forest Creek. It was a sight! Mounds of earth lying beside holes presented the dismal appearance of a graveyard . . . the whole scene to a new chum was one of unspeakable squalor, surpassing all that his eye had seen or his fancy woven . . .[6]

Another remarked as he topped the rise that led down to the Forest Creek diggings: 'its appearance was novel to us all, and the tents gave the impression that an immense army was in camp there'.

After several days on the road in an environment so unfamiliar and in many ways so hostile, the first sight of the diggings must have set many a stout heart a-flutter.

FAST TRACK TO THE DIGGINGS

By the Lights of Cobb & Co.

Travelling across the seas to the colonies was the easy part. All a hopeful digger had to do was load his goods onto the boat, sit back for 100 days and there he was, landing all his gear on Australia's shore.

In the early days getting up to the diggings took a bit more effort. Unlike the American goldfields, which saw steamboats in service on the Sacramento River soon after the first rush, the trip to the colonial diggings was usually over uncharted territory—boggy plains in winter, a dust bowl in summer, through dark bushranger ridden forest—and then tramp for days on foot.

In July 1853 four enterprising young Americans who had gained some experience out West and on the Californian goldfields with Wells Fargo and the Adams Express Co., established their own coaching firm in Melbourne.

Up until this time passenger coaches in use were British imports, which had solid metal suspensions and steel-rimmed wheels totally unsuited to Australian conditions.

Freeman Cobb and his partners, James Swanton, John Peck and John Lamber, established the firm Cobb & Co., using light, leather-sprung American coaches built in Concord, Massachusetts. The first coaches ran between Melbourne and Castlemaine, the closest diggings to Port Phillip. They employed hundreds, kept countless horses, which were changed every ten miles on the run, scores of stablehands and drivers, hotel-keepers and changing-station attendants.

Cobb & Co. was famous for the quality of its service and for the skill and popularity of the drivers. One of the most famous of them all was Edward Devine, a great 'character', also known as Cabbage-tree Ned, who drove the Ballarat to Geelong run. Ned had even convinced his passengers that he had trained a kangaroo to meet the coach, take delivery of the mail, and carry it away in its pouch for delivery. Just after he had told this improbable story, his coach rounded a corner, and there stood a kangaroo by the side of the road. 'Nothing for you today, Jack', shouted Ned as the coach rolled by. To the astonishment of Ned's passengers the kangaroo simply turned and hopped away.

Ned was the driver of the 'Great Coach'; pulled by twelve grey horses, it could carry 90 passengers. At one stage Ned carried the first English cricket team to tour Australia.

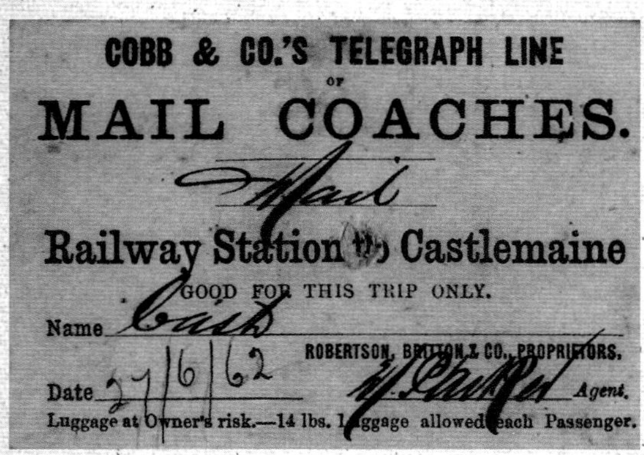

COBB & CO.'S TELEGRAPH LINE
OF
MAIL COACHES.
Mail
Railway Station to Castlemaine
GOOD FOR THIS TRIP ONLY.
Name Cash
Date 27/6/62
ROBERTSON, BRITTON & CO., PROPRIETORS.
Agent.
Luggage at Owner's risk.—14 lbs. Luggage allowed each Passenger.

(Ticket courtesy of the Castlemaine Old Residents and Pioneers Association)

The largest of Cobb's Australian-built coaches was a double-story 'Leviathan', a massive coach which ran between Castlemaine and Kyneton. The lead horses were so far out of reach of the driver's whip that he carried a bag of stones to throw at them to get their attention.

Cobb & Co. established a reputation for safety, comfort and reliability; as a result the firm managed to continue operation long after competition from the ever-extending railways which had begun reaching out to all corners of the country by the 1860s.

As the railways pushed further and further across Victoria, linking most of the major gold-producing centres with Melbourne, and with the discovery of vast new deposits in northern outback Queensland, Cobb & Co. moved their headquarters to the New South Wales goldfields town of Bathurst in 1862.

Coach-Driver Ned Devine
(Picture Collection, State Library of Victoria)
Legendary coach-driver, 'Cabbage-tree' Ned Devine, showing the grip on the reins that made him famous.

Freeman Cobb had sold his interest the previous year to James Rutherford and his partner, NSW coaching agent Walter Hall. [The Hall brothers, Walter and Thomas, had gained a lot of experience on the Victorian goldfields, both had been involved in the uprising at the Eureka Stockade, although it appears that neither took part in the battle].

Even though Freeman Cobb no longer had any interest in the company, the name Cobb & Co. was retained and remained synonymous with the excitement and romance of coach travel in the 'roaring days'. Walter Hall and James Rutherford continued to provide the service that Cobb had made famous for a further sixty years until, no longer able to compete with motorised transport, the last horse-drawn coach made its final journey in 1924.

CHAPTER 6

Under Southern Skies

Life under Southern skies! While the English press was filled with both the excitement of the adventure and news of great nuggets, it also offered many cautionary tales, generally to no avail. The movement away from tired old Europe and out into the new world was too enticing, too seductive, too liberating, to deny. The notion of a new start to life where one could be free and make one's own way, with prospects not denied by social position or accident of birth, seemed too attractive to ignore.

The diggings paid no heed to class or creed; there all men were equal. As J. W. Bull wrote of the men drawn together on the Forest Creek diggings in March 1852:

> Take a picture perfectly true. Here are four men working in a claim; next claim on one side four Californians; on another side, four Tasmanians [coarse fellows] and not far off a party of Melbourne men. All these men are on an equality as to their pursuit.
>
> Did the well-bred men descend to the general manners of their surroundings? As a rule no. Civil and sociable remarks pass. The roughest of the men see and adopt, as far as they can, the manners of the gentlemen, and begin to see themselves to be respectable.

Frank McKillop, editor of the *Mount Alexander Mail*, wrote of the population on the diggings in 1855:

> The population of the field! What a heterogeneous collection! Nearly every race on earth was represented, with British greatly dominating—all on an equality in the eager scramble for gold. There were French, German, Italian, American and Chinese settlements.
>
> The bulk of the diggers were a manly, hardy and intelligent class of men—Britain's best to open up a new country and to carry forward British institutions and British ideals. They were for the most

Night Scene on the Diggings
Watercolour by John Skinner Prout
(National Library of Australia Collection)

The camaraderie of the diggers is evident in this painting of camp life: the diggers have gathered to entertain themselves at the end of the day:

> the evenings are a delight at the end of the day's work, being both novel and picturesque. From every direction weary diggers are to be seen returning to t heir canvas homesteads, hundreds of fires are kindled and illuminate the scene, and at each tea is made and mutton roasted. The evening meal finished, the air is filled with the sound of firearms being fired, in order to be reloaded anew before the night.[1]

> part strangers to each other these blue-shirted, horny-handed, stout-hearted diggers, many having been delicately nurtured, but social distinctions were unknown on the goldfields in this new land.[2]

The diggings offered all the opportunity to begin afresh, to be at the beginning of the birth of a new kind of society, a community where all 'men' were truly equal, where prejudices of class and creed were superseded by cash. The gracious boulevards of London were left far behind, the verdant sward of the Emerald Isle a distant memory, the purple heath and misty-shrouded crags of the Highlands a fading echo. On the diggings all was as new, here was land never tilled by plough nor trod by the hard hooves of grazing cattle. No crowded streets, or darkened alleyways, no tenement or chilling croft, the diggers could stake their claim where they pleased, and set themselves to toil, or not, as the fancy took them.

The Gold Diggings
Oil on canvas, artist unknown, c.1855
(Rex Nan Kivell Collection, NK24. By permission, National Library of Australia)
The diggers' camps were free-wheeling, multi-cultural, and democratic where all men, no matter their status or title were equal under the spell of gold. Like sprawling military encampments, although with considerable less discipline, the camps offered freedom—equality, liberty and fraternity—those ideals so often bitterly sought by so many down-trodden abroad, and taken for granted on the Australian goldfields.

However, it was not long before the gentle valleys looked as if they had been the scene of a great battle.

> Nature had been rudely disturbed and peace and purity had fled for ever; Mount Alexander looked frowningly down on the desecration and desolation of Nature's bower, the crystal stream had vanished and a muddy, repulsive flow had appeared, the green carpet of Mother Earth had been cruelly rent and soiled and unsightly heaps, etc. were offending the eye along the streams and slopes, trees had been felled, the birds had hurried shrieking away, bearded, begrimed men were feverishly burrowing like moles into the earth scarring the face of nature, the air was filled with the discordant shouts of men, the noise of the cradle and the reports of firearms.
>
> At night as far as the eye can see the camp fires of the invading Goths and Vandals were burning—two long, irregular strings of luminously, iridescent beads. The beautiful had given way to the

General View of the Diggings, Ballarat
Watercolour by Henry Winkles, c. 1853
(Rex Nan Kivell Collection, R4749. By Permission, National Library of Australia)
Once the diggers descended on a rush it didn't take long before the earth was turned upside down.

Wherever the miners went the landscape was left in ruins, open shafts pitted the ground, gullies lay clogged with silt and gravel, streams muddied, diverted, dammed and often destroyed.

The diggers often left as quickly as they had come, rushing from place to place. The Australian bush seemed endless with open space to spare; once one gully lay ruined there was another over the hill, fresh, lying in wait for the attentions of the rapacious, greedy diggers.

> materialistic, peace has departed, and pandemonium reigned—all in less than a month.[3]

The arrival of the Commissioners brought some kind of focus to the encampments. They generally positioned their 'Camps' on vantage points overlooking the main diggings. In Bendigo they set up on a hill overlooking what is now known as Rosalind Park, on a rise still known as Camp Hill; on Forest Creek they first established themselves at Red Hill, Chewton, but later removed to the junction of Forest and Barker's Creeks, also on a slight rise that is still known today as 'Camp Oval'. The well-ordered Commissioners' Camp on the Ballarat diggings was set up once again looking across the diggings, while the diggers' tents followed the line of the creek or were set with their backs to the trees.

It was not long before the vastness of the diggings and the jumble of canvas and bark dwellings made it extremely difficult for the diggers to locate one another, or even to find their own way back to their own tents. Traversing the diggings at night was extremely hazardous, especially if one had been 'out on a spree'. Apart from the tents and ropes and fallen trees, the terrain was littered with open shafts and deep and abandoned holes. Many an unwary digger was located in the morning, slumped at the bottom of an abandoned shaft, after putting a wrong foot forward in the dark.

Flags were flown to indicate whose tent was whose. A Union Jack here, a Scotch Thistle there, the Fleur-de-lys, the Texas Star, all indicated the nationality of the occupants, and often served to inform of the languages spoken within. At Campbell's Creek one hotel was named The Five Flags, as five languages were spoken behind the bar. Stores were identified by their flags or letters emblazoned on their roofs. Bryce Ross, the correspondent for the *Melbourne Morning Herald*, compiled a directory of important or established dwellings in which he listed each tent in the order it stood in the gullies or along the flats, this directory enabled newcomers or those seeking stores or old friends to locate one another among the sea of canvas. Ross compiled his directories for almost all of the diggings, including Ballarat, Bendigo, Forest Creek and the Ovens, and turned his knowledge into a successful enterprise.

There were also numerous large trees left around the diggings that were used as noticeboards; the trees served for a long time to display messages from one party to another, to advertise goods or to carry government notices: 'the Digger's Intelligencer,—a fine old gum on whose weatherbeaten trunk was to be seen numerous postcards, some pasted on, some wafered on, some nailed on' was an important meeting point, and served to establish communication among the hordes of itinerant diggers who passed back and forth from rush to rush.

There were literally dozens of drays and heavily-laden carts arriving each week, followed by hundreds more on foot, who were intent on the diggings:

> The drays were laden with flour, corn, potatoes, sugar, tea, spirits, bottled beer, and the like, as well, as spades, buckets, &c. On the roadsides were stores displaying plentiful assortments of tin ware of all sizes, hanging in front—tea-kettles, bales of flannel, shoes, boots, ready-

Golden Point, Ballarat
Watercolour by David Tulloch, 1851
(Rex Nan Kivell Collection, T2253. By Permission, National Library of Australia)

> made clothes, &c.; in fact, all such things as diggers are in constant want of.[4]

It was possible to buy goods on the diggings that were no longer available on the streets of Melbourne, shipowners would unload their cargo straight onto bullock drays that headed out immediately for the goldfields, such was the profit to be made from the newly-enriched diggers.

Although it was illegal to sell any alcoholic liquor on the diggings, grog was in great demand, and the carriers took great pains to keep up the supply. Kegs of grog were carried to the diggings hidden among other goods loaded on the drays:

> We loaded in Elizabeth Street, at a merchant's named Smithson. Our loading was general stores and grog. The grog was in 5-gallon kegs, and addressed to different people, for there was no spirits allowed to be sold on the diggings. It was placed in the middle of the dray, and the sugar, tea, etc., packed all round it and over the top, so the troopers could not see that we had any grog on board.[5]

Mining camp
Watercolour by David Tulloch, c. 1855
(State Library of New South Wales)

Rudimentary stores sprang up everywhere on the diggings as merchants prepared to capitalise on the demand for supplies.

Stores were identified by flags flown, usually, on a freshly-cut bush pole.

Few stores could afford to specialise in the early days, as most attempted to make the most of every opportunity, trading in whatever was available and whatever they could bring up from the nearest port.

At times almost anything at all could be had on the diggings.

John Chandler, who had carted goods to and from all the early diggings, continues:

> all spirits found in any tent or store, were seized, and carried to the Commissioner's camp and destroyed. But there never was a law so much evaded, for in nearly every instance, one tent in five was a sly grog shanty . . . had we been caught, we should have our horses, drays, and loads seized.

He concludes that, although the government tried to keep grog off the diggings, he had never seen so much drunkenness. In 1853, when the government gave up its prohibition, and granted licenses to sell liquor, Chandler noted: 'they gave every little shanty with two or more rooms, a license. They always go to extremes'.[7]

The Diggers Take a Mid-day Meal
Illustrated Melbourne Post, 9 August 1862
(State Library of New South Wales)

As the canvas communities grew around the creeks, life there entered a familiar pattern. Digging parties divided themselves into working teams, which took shifts or turns in the pits and at the windlass, some even worked around the clock in an effort to make as much as possible in the shortest time and take the next steam packet home.

The day's work was hard for men who were largely unused to physical labour.

Artist, digger, adventurer—the Frenchman Antoine Fauchery complained of the arduous labour, an aching back and blistered hands, but recorded in his diaries the pleasure of the campfire and a well-deserved rest at the end of the working day.

As a goldfields-wide practice every evening, and again in the dawn, the diggers fired their pistols into the air, ensuring that they had kept their powder dry and were prepared for any emergency. The noise was deafening as hundreds of firearms exploded simultaneously, shattering the peaceful twilight.

The cradles may have stopped and the digging ceased, but the evenings were still alive with the sounds of all creation as the songs of all nationalities were taken up on the cooling night air. Italians caroused at their operas, Germans had their 'oompah' bands trumpeting away, playing waltzes first heard by the Danube; and always the haunting strains of the lone Scottish piper stirred a thousand hearts far from the 'shores of Loch Lomond'.

Mount Alexander, Gold Diggings, Australia
Robert Shortreid Anderson, *Glasgow Examiner*, 30 October 1852
(Picture Collection, State Library of Victoria)

This lively lithograph indicates the bustling activity that characterised the diggings.

Diggers seem like ants in their exertions, running from here to there and back again, seduced by the prospect of instant wealth.

Coffee tents and sly-grog shops were everywhere, the Chinese opened restaurants that catered for all tastes, little flocks of sheep were driven into butchers' pens ready for slaughter, as the demand for fresh meat was readily satisfied by the squatters upon whose runs the diggers had camped. Large tents were converted to theatres, where the leading performers of the day trod 'the boards', often rewarded with a shower of gold if they were any good, or hastened off stage in a shower of stones if no good at all. Circuses toured the diggings, and on Sundays, when by decree all digging ceased, tree stumps or drays were mounted by itinerant preachers who spread the word to the faithful.

The diggings quickly became a rough-and-ready parody of European society:

A Good Day's Work
Hand-coloured lithograph, Cyrus Mason, Melbourne, 1855
(Rex Nan Kivell Collection, U2493.By Permission, National Library of Australia)

A party of digger-mates examine their reward for a good day's work as they retire to their tent.

James Bonwick described the diggers' domestic arrangements in a survey of Bendigo in the early 1850s:

> [The diggers] live in canvas homes, or huts of bark and logs . . . Our furniture is of a simple character. A box, a block of wood, or a bit of paling across a pail, serves as a table. Some luxurious ones positively have rough stools as seats: the majority recline upon their beds, or make use of a log, the ground, or a pail turned upside down . . .
>
> After a hard day's work one is not disposed to be too particular about the evening meal, and the mode in which it is prepared . . . [some] will content themselves with dry or flat Johnny cakes, which are simply flour and water, with the addition of greasy accumulation of cookery, hastily prepared in the frying pan. Many lose health by inattention to meals . . .

He remarks on the danger to health:

> The sitting on the damp ground induces piles. Most attacks of sickness resolve themselves into fevers of the low typhoid type, as the powers of life are soon exhausted here . . .[8]

However, most diggers believed that the rewards far outweighed the risks.

Went to the consecration of the large tent which has been erected as a R.C. place of worship. There was such a crowd that it was almost impossible to get inside. Dr Goold, R.C. Bishop of Melbourne, preached. Afterwards I walked to Canadian Gully, now pretty well the centre of the principal diggings. Found a great number of stores, eating houses, smithies, etc. had sprung up. Also to my surprise came upon Henri d'Orleans, who is now running a much decorated 'Lemonade tent'. He is doing a grand business during this hot season by selling all

Old Ballarat, as it was in the Summer of 1853–54
Oil painting by Eugene von Guérard, 1884
(Ballarat Fine Art Gallery Collection)

> sorts of cooling drinks, and excellent havana cigars at 2/- a piece.[9]
> —Eugene von Guérard, 1852.

Although there were those whose main aim was to get in, get rich and get out, there was also a large body of colonists who had no intention of returning to the country that had spurned them, and thousands more who were keen to make a new life far away from the gloomy streets of London, or from wherever else they hailed—no matter how rough and tumble that life was in the beginning.

The diggings provided adventure that many had never dreamed possible, offering freedom, opportunity, camaraderie, excitement and cherished memories. As Ellen Clacy climbed aboard a slow-moving dray, ready for her return journey home, she gave the diggings a parting look, later recording in her diary somewhat wistfully, 'a slight turn in the road, and the last tent vanished from my sight. "Never," thought I, "shall I look on such a scene again".'[10]

Like so many thousands of others Ellen Clacy had greatly enjoyed her colonial adventure. She had seen the diggings, and tucked away her memories of the excitement and experience of an unusual life lived under southern skies.

CHAPTER 7

A Glittering Lottery

'The diggings are a mere lottery. There is not above one out of a hundred that do well here; and no one need go without £200 in his pocket . . . several of the Great Britain's first-cabin passengers are wheeling water for sale throughout the streets of Melbourne . . .'—so wrote the son of an Ayrshire gentleman who emigrated to the colonies in May of 1852.[1]

One newspaper of 17 November 1852 reported that the rush to Port Phillip was so great that, in just a few days seven ships had arrived, adding a further 3600 souls to the fledgling township. After a long voyage, cramped and crowded below decks, most stepped ashore to find a crowded township, without adequate lodgings or services, and with overpriced goods and outrageously priced foods.

In the early days when the towns had emptied of their menfolk, wages for any kind of position had skyrocketed; but by 1852 oversupply of labour had cut these wages right back. There were also hundreds of disappointed diggers returning from the goldfields looking for just enough work to make the fare home, so that any chance of finding a position to tide the unwary traveller over until he got his land-legs was now almost impossible.

For the hundreds who had expected easy pickings, the diggings failed to live up to expectation. Only one year after the first discoveries the alluvial gold was all but gone, and then the real digging commenced. The days of the adventurer were rapidly coming to an end, yet the merchants' ships were still bringing hundreds at a time into an environment that was not about to satisfy them all. John Sherer wrote in 1853:

> Of the 200 who came out in the *Blackfriar*, and went to the Diggings, nearly all have returned, and those remaining are earning only enough money to subsist on . . . crime is very prevalent—in fact, the colony is getting bad altogether; and should the Diggings fail, I do

Prospecting for Gold, or Rewarded at Last
Hand-coloured lithograph, c. 1860
From *Sketches of Australian Life and Scenery*, Paul Jerrard & Son, for Messrs Newbold & Co., London
(Rex Nan Kivell Collection, U2822. By Permission, National Library of Australia)
In this lithograph, diggers who had been on the field for some time are seen sharing their experience and good fortune with a new chum.

Their next move was to sell their claim, 'rich with nuggets', to the inexperienced gentleman and move on, to let him find out for himself how little they had left behind and ponder on how much it had cost him.

> not know what will be the consequence. The convicts shoot you in a moment . . . in fact, it will be a complete California in a few months, if the Diggings keep failing as they have for the last two months.[2]

Yet still they came. The ships poured their eager human cargo onto the docks, and the roads to the diggings were filled with an almost endless stream of hopefuls who still believed that after a few weeks at the diggings they would fill their pockets, return to Melbourne, and then home again on the next steam packet available—rich, experienced, and set for life.

No matter where the diggers went they were confronted with the same bustling scene:

> The first sight of the . . . diggings, after passing through tents scattered here and there for nearly five miles, is that which you would imagine to be a citadel thrown to the ground, and some thousands

> of men running about like rabbits in burrows, all having an appearance of deep yellow earth—yellow clothes—yellow hands—yellow faces—yellow everything, and working in closely-compacted pieces of ground as thick as possible over the whole surface of the hill or mountain.[3]

Antoine Fauchery, the photographer who left behind a marvellous pictorial record of the diggings, wrote in his letters published in Paris in 1857, that 'the only resolve to take on the diggings is to make a fortune at one stroke and then get away, without even looking back'.[4]

Many believed they too would return to their mother country, but they simply 'spent, wasted, swallowed!' what they had won in the greatest lottery of them all, condemning themselves to exile forever in this very foreign landscape.

The diggings were regarded by many as a lottery, where some win, and win handsomely, and many others lose—and when the winnings did come, and the gains were spent at the bar in some grog shop or splashed around with largesse in the streets of Melbourne, all it would take is another trip to the diggings to start all over again. Many diggers could not resist the 'easy come, easy go' attitude of this magnificent lottery, and were trapped by its attractions.

> There is a great restlessness among the miners, a constant shifting of their position, and exchange of holes by purchase . . . a man may gain but a small return, though he goes deeper than a neighbour almost adjoining him, who is literally gathering gold. The inequality of the distribution is remarkable, and gold-finding is a perfect lottery— at least with the present imperfect knowledge of the nature and cause of this inequality . . . the whole work is one of hazard.[5]

Fauchery may have been right—work hard, take the reward, and leave quickly. Only a few took that advice. He remembers a sailor named Antoine, a fellow-countryman, who had taken 126 lbs of gold from a claim on the Eureka line. Antoine had already 'dissipated the 50,000 francs' worth found at Bendigo' and was on his way to drink the remainder in whatever bar he could find. Fauchery met Antoine on his way to Ballarat a few months later, with nothing left but a pair of nugget earrings. He came across him again in Ballarat, where Antoine was found dead-drunk in the bottom of a 140-foot shaft. He had squandered over

Gold Washing, Ballarat Diggings, Victoria
Watercolour by William Strutt, 1851
(Victorian State Parliamentary Library Collection)

156,000 francs in that short time, 'easy come, easy go'. In fact, it seems that Antoine had been a very lucky digger, believing that it was as simple as digging a hole to get his gold, then he would 'buy a brig and take to the sea again'. But in the meantime the adventure of it all was totally captivating.

Fauchery relates the story of some other sailors who had also made a fortune in a few days and then left again on the same ship that brought them to Port Phillip:

> On the first voyage of the *Great Britain*, an immense steamship built in the Liverpool yards and sent out to Melbourne, the whole crew deserted within sight of the town, in Hobson's Bay. At that period no crew ever acted otherwise. Two of the steamer's passengers and three of the sailors formed a party and made for the mines.
>
> The day after their arrival, armed with tools whose use they did not yet properly know, one of the partners, no doubt anxious to familiarise himself with the emotion that seizes every individual sent below the surface on a rope, wanted to be lowered into a shaft, an

Diggers at Forest Creek, 1858
Photograph by Richard Daintree
(Picture Collection, State Library of Victoria)

The Forest Creek diggings were the richest alluvial gold field of them all, but it was not long before the earth was torn apart as eager diggers became miners and sought the gold that lay below the surface.

When the alluvial fields played out, the deep-lead mining regions took over. It was then that the Ballarat and Bendigo diggings came into their own. Whereas Castlemaine, Forest Creek, and the nearby diggings had limited success with deep-lead mining, Bendigo and Ballarat soon became the richest deep mining centres of them all.

This photograph by Richard Daintree shows a totally devastated landscape: walkways, trestling and tram-tracks criss-cross the deeply scarred earth, the shafts and tunnels almost undermining the hastily erected township of Chewton lining the road from Melbourne.

abandoned one—the first encountered . . . his companions laughed as they let him scramble down to a depth of about fifty feet, and the neighbours laughed at his companions.

Our man, at the bottom of the hole where no one had even taken the trouble to pierce any galleries, was seized by a new fancy: while he was there, why not push his investigations further? . . . taking one bit of digging with another, it was as good here as anywhere . . . so he asked for a pick and declared that he would not come out of the hole without adding another foot to its depth.

Pick and shovel were sent down, and he started striking out in all directions; his companions hoisted up the excavated earth, grumbling a little about a joke whose prolongation would only be a waste of time; officious neighbours asked if the 'old hand was trying to get home by the shortest way,'... suddenly the sound of two metals meeting rang out from the point of the pick; he stooped down: a shining yellow spot had been laid bare!

He dug around the patch, which grew larger, he scraped and dug out more earth, looking for a break in the continuity of the patch, which still grew larger! . . . after unheard of efforts, for you can't imagine how patches like this are encrusted and cling to the soil, it was at last brought to light; then it proved not to be a patch, it was a mass the size of a paving stone, a piece of gold set right in the middle of the hole—a piece of gold weighing 132 pounds!

I was not on the spot at the moment the man who made this wonderful discovery came up from the hole; I saw him only an hour later. He was a negro . . . he had hardly recovered from an excitement that was quite justifiable in such a case, his face still bore traces of that livid pallor peculiar to coloured people that makes the white lips stand out strangely from a grey mask. He was speaking very softly, like a man who has just committed a crime. His white partners were in little better case than he was; they were stunned by their success . . . one of them, however, came out of his torpor, shook the others, and the monster nugget, placed in the bottom of a bag slung on a long stick, was hoisted on to the shoulders of two of the fortunate proprietors and carried to the commissioner's . . . [see box below]

—Notable Nuggets—

The Sarah Sands

The monster nugget referred to here was later named the 'Sarah Sands' after the ship in which it was carried back to England.

The sailors who had discovered the nugget returned to England on the same ship that had brought them out—and after only two days at the diggings.

Both Eugène von Guérard and Fauchery described seeing this nugget just after it was brought to the surface. In fact, it was around this time (January 1853) that Fauchery had joined up with von Guérard's company as mates on the Ballarat diggings.

Von Guérard's group was an unusual one, consisting of an eclectic group of European middle-class artists and intellectuals.

Both von Guérard and Fauchery had female companions, young women of good breeding and similar background, who had accompanied them from Europe.

They were sometimes referred to as wives, at other times simply as good friends. In all accounts the young ladies were regarded as equals in the company, and took part in the business of gold digging as much as the men.

The Disputed Claim
Hand-coloured lithograph, Cyrus Mason, Melbourne, 1855
(Rex Nan Kivell Collection, U2491.By Permission, National Library of Australia)

Altercations between the diggers were not at all uncommon, sometimes a fight would break out or, as in this case, a trooper intervenes to settle the dispute.

The diggings were riddled with holes, shafts and underground tunnels. If the ground was thought to be good and nuggets ready to find, disputes over the legitimacy of the size and position of claims regularly flared up.

The prize was great, and every foot dug could make the difference between wealth or poverty.

> The day after this memorable event the five partners, who had worked all night and collected another 150 ounces of gold in a very small piece of ground, handed over to some enthusiasts, for a sum of £500 [12,500 francs], the chance of making a fortune after them in a hole whose exploitation had hardly begun. Satisfied with the result of a few hours' work, they announced their intention of making it back for Europe immediately.
>
> And actually, having gone back to town, they embarked on the same steamer that had bought them out, taking with them on one hand two hundred thousand francs' worth of gold, and on the other hand the memory of having been miners for two days.[6]

News of this discovery spread across the Ballarat diggings, and abandoned shafts in Canadian Gully became busy again near the site of the monster nugget. That week other discoveries were made, including one nugget weighing 94 lbs and another of 78 lbs.

Gold At Last!
Wood engraving, Ebenezer and David Syme, *The Illustrated Australian News*, 28 January 1874
(Private Collection, State Library of Victoria)

Diggers who had worked these claims bottomed out at around 50 feet, but big nuggets were found below this false rocky bottom, as lines of ancient creek-beds ran at various depths further below.

At one elbow on the Regent's Gully lead, a party of four Americans had taken 1,300 lbs of gold from a claim measuring only 24 square feet. Another on the Gravel Pit line had taken 900 lbs from an area 3 ft wide, 24 ft long and 8 ft deep.

Fauchery recalls: 'I once saw coming out of a hole at New Eureka a hatful of earth: this earth contained 17 pounds of fine gold'.[7]

The Ballarat leads took commitment and staying power, the shafts were deep, the work hard, and months would pass before any show of colour would repay tired diggers for their investment. Some never saw their reward. The week before Fauchery left the field seven diggers were killed in their shafts; some drowned, while others were crushed by a falling plank or bucket. In Fauchery's own claim one of his mates had his head 'horribly chipped' and his shoulder dislocated in an accident below ground.

There were some spectacular discoveries that left the world reeling at the sheer size of the nugget. John Deason and Richard Oates, two diggers from the island of Tresco, 31 miles from Land's End off the south-west coast of Cornwall, had followed the rush to Bendigo in 1854. They stayed for eight years before taking up a farm on the plains near Moliagul, about 37 miles to the west. They pegged out a claim, stripping the surface layer of the land and washing it in a puddling machine not far from where they made their historic discovery on the morning of 5 February 1869.

Deason was digging around a tree when he struck something solid at the base. 'Confound it! I've broken my pick', he cursed when his pick rebounded from beneath the roots. 'I wish I had broken it, if it had only been over some nugget.'

Unearthing the Welcome Stranger
Albumen silver carte-de-visite by W. Parker
(Picture Collection, State Library of Victoria)

Miners and their wives pose with the finders of the Welcome Stranger, Richard Oates and John Deason. Deason's wife is kneeling on the ground behind a large rock which is standing in for the nugget.

Still the largest nugget ever found anywhere in the world, the Welcome Stranger was discovered in the bush near Moliagul on 5 February 1869.

A minute later Deason called out to his partner Oates, who was ploughing in a nearby paddock, and told him to 'come and see what this was'.[8] There, sticking several inches out of the ground, 'like a boulder on a hill', was a mass of gold. They retrieved the nugget, which was almost 12 inches across and nearly the same in length. It was almost too heavy for them both to lift. They then covered it again, continuing to work as if nothing had happened. Later in the day they took it by dray to Deason's house, where they placed the nugget in the fireplace. The effect of heat on the gold forced it to expand, and quartz attached to it became brittle and broke loose. Even the quartz that broke away, after crushing and washing in Deason's puddling machine, yielded 10 lbs gold.

It was the weekend so the nugget was kept on the kitchen table, hidden under a cloth. Deason held a party for his friends, and later that night dramatically revealed the solid gold nugget. Once they had recovered from their shock at being the first to see the largest nugget ever found in all the world, he invited them to stay the night and help

John Deason, finder of the Welcome Stranger
(Private Collection)

Deason poses for a commemorative photograph with his pick and shovel, which we may assume were his authentic digging tools; however, just like the photograph taken at the site in Moliagul the day after the discovery the 'nugget' here is certainly not authentic either.

Small bits of quartz had broken loose when it had been placed in Deason's fireplace, and gold encrusted crystals had already been given to favoured onlookers and friends as keepsakes before it was broken up by the local blacksmith in Dunolly the first working day after it had been found on the weekend.

escort it to the bank the next day. The following day the nugget was taken into Dunolly to the London Chartered Bank where it was cut down for smelting.

It took Archie Walls, the local blacksmith, five hours to reduce the massive nugget of pure gold, 'as clean as well-cut Cheshire Cheese', into manageable pieces. Several of the gold-encrusted crystals were given to favoured onlookers and friends as keepsakes. The *Welcome Stranger* weighed 210 lbs. In 1869 it was worth £9210; Today, its value would be several million.

'As to the success or unsuccess of the Diggers, it cannot be denied that, if a man work hard and persevere, notwithstanding first disappointments, he is sure, ultimately, to produce for himself, at least a renumerative amount of wages . . . if a man, however, only but obtain his ordinary wages, or if he should not do this, he still has the chance of getting a prize in the great lottery of the auriferous field . . . the whole is a lottery, and essentially the lottery of the working man; where, for the price of his license – thirty shillings a month – and strong exercise of his muscular powers, he may draw a prize . . .'[9]

CHAPTER 8

No Place for a Lady?

A surprising number of women travelled to the early goldfields, and, contrary to contemporary opinion, not all were ladies of ill repute. While there were many who specialised in this trade rather than gold seeking, a large number had travelled to the diggings in the company of their husbands, and a number of well-educated ladies had simply come, captured by the spirit of adventure, just like their male counterparts.

One young lady from Dublin, possessing a good education, good birth and a handy sum left from her parents' estate, described her desire to join in the great adventure when she accompanied her brother and his mates on board ship headed for 'the diggings'. After committing £300 to outfit their expedition they set out for the experience of a lifetime:

> I was resolved to accompany my brother and his friends to the diggings and I felt that to do so in my own proper costume and character, would be to run unnecessary hazard. Hence my change. I cut my hair into a very masculine fashion; I purchased a broad felt hat, a sort of tunic or smock of coarse blue cloth, trousers to conform, boots of a miner and thus parting with my sex for a season . . . behold me an accomplished candidate for mining operations and all the perils and inconveniences they might be supposed to bring.[1]

She seemed to enjoy herself immensely on the goldfields. She arranged a sort of 'supplementary canvas chamber' within the tent occupied by her brother and travelling party, in which she slept, cooked and washed her clothes, and took to keeping watch over the 'heaps of gold dust and nuggets' they had found:

> Of course, my sex is generally known. I am called 'Mr Harry' (an abbreviation of Harriet); but no one intrudes the more on that account. I have become a sort of necessity, as I am always ready to do a good

Alarming Prospect, the Single Ladies Take Off for the Diggings
Watercolour by John Leech, c. 1852
(Rex Nan Kivell Collection, S2877. By Permission, National Library of Australia)
Distraught suitors offer marriage settlements that would once have had any single young girl swooning with delight. The lure of the diggings and the promise of an exciting match made in 'El Dorado' quickly abolished the image of a rose-covered cottage from the mind of the maid who had her heart set on gold.

> turn—the great secret, after all, of social success . . . I never refuse to oblige a 'neighbour'.[2]

For being 'neighbourly', for the cooking of an occasional pudding or the darning of a shirt, she was often repaid in small nuggets. After a short time she had accumulated about 10 lbs of gold:

> Wild the life is, certainly, but full of excitement and hope; and strange it is, I almost fear to tell you, that I do not wish it to end![3]

She writes of the enjoyable evenings spent with the diggers at the end of a day's labour in their shafts:

> You can hardly conceive what merry company gather in our tent every evening, or how pleasantly the hours pass . . . as to suitors, I have them in plenty, and not despicable ones either, I assure you.[4]

This letter contrasts with the picture generally painted of the women on the diggings, but this independent, educated and forthright young lady may well contrast with most others who had made the journey, not for the adventure but out of necessity.

Ellen Clacy told a similar story. She also travelled to the diggings with a party of men, one her fiancé whom she married just before their

—The Digger's Song—

by Mary Helena Fortune

Hurrah for the free new land!
  And hurrah for the diggers bold!
And hurrah for the strong unfettered right
To search in the hills for gold!
Dig! 'till each pore its tribute gives
  Which the burning forehead craves
But never a lingering look cast back
  To the land where we were slaves!

Breathe for a moment, one glad breath
  Throw up the shadeless brow;
Where is the paid taste–master's eye?
  We were never men 'till now!

Poem published *Mount Alexander Mail*, 14 December 1855

Belfast-born Mary Helena Fortuna followed her father, Scottish engineer George Wilson, first to Montreal, where she married Joseph Fortune, and then again to the diggings in Victoria, arriving in Melbourne with her son on 3 October 1855.

She gave birth to a second son in Buninyong and married again in Dunolly, this time to Percy Rollo Brett, a mounted policeman and son of an Irish clergyman. The marriage soon failed and he left for New South Wales, where he married again, apparently without first divorcing Mary.

She began writing in 1855, contributing articles and radical poetry to goldfields newspapers under appropriately male pseudonyms. She was once offered a position as sub-editor on the *Mount Alexander Mail* but the offer was withdrawn as soon as it was discovered that she was a woman.

One of the first female authors of detective stories in the world, her book *The Detective's Album* [1871] was the first detective fiction published in Australia.

In her declining years, with failing eyesight, and diminished by alcohol, she was still supported by *The Australian Journal* for whom she had once written under the name of 'Waif Wanderer'.

She lived past the turn of the century, although the date of her death is unknown.

Digger's Wife in Full Dress
Watercolour by George Lacy, 1852
(Rex Nan Kivell Collection, R4111.By Permission, National Library of Australia)

The women who promenaded as 'diggers' wives' had no benefit of bridal party, but assumed the role of wife to any digger who provided the wherewithal to play husband:

> She dressed sumptuously, and arrayed herself in the hues of the rainbow.
> Her satin dress, which always looked as if it had been made for somebody else, was overlaid with a massive gold chain, a brooch as big as a warming pan, and a lace collar more costly than clean.
> Her hands, which were as red as raw beef, and big enough to fell a bullock, were garnished gorgeously with rings, her movements were more energetic than graceful; her language more emphatic than precise, and she was surrounded by an atmosphere redolent of Eau de Cologne, onions and bran.

The wealth that gold had brought to these once-poor working-class folks may have bought their freedom but could not buy them class.

return to London. Clacy published a record of her travels in 1853. Her party travelled far and wide; she described the journey out, the arrival in Melbourne, then the long trek to Mount Alexander; from there they went on to Bendigo, the Ovens, and then back to the port.

On the road Ellen Clacy encountered bushrangers, murderers and thieves, but it was the topic of 'sly grog' that captured much of her attention, and disapproval.

A large number of 'crones' made their fortune in 'coffee tents' which were fronts for sly-grog establishments. Clacy wrote of one such establishment:

The Girls the Diggers Left Behind and What They had to Do!
Watercolour by William Strutt, 1852
(State Parliamentary Library Collection, Victoria)

This watercolour shows the grass widows of Melbourne, the women left behind to do men's work, while the only male on the street that creates any interest is an old gent in his top hat as the young ladies crane their necks for a glimpse of 'a man—a man!'

> To wander through Melbourne and its environs, no one would imagine that females were as one to four of the male population; for bonnets and parasols everywhere outnumber the wide-awakes [a diggers' broad hat].
> This is occasioned by the absence of so many 'lords of creation' in pursuit of what they value—many of them at least—more than all the women in the world—nuggets. The wives thus left in town to deplore their husband's infatuation are termed 'grass-widows'—a mining expression'.[5]

> [The coffee tent] was situated at right angles with ours and our shipmates, so the annoyance was equally felt . . . whilst her husband was at work farther down the gully, she kept a sort of sly-grog shop, and passed the day in selling and drinking spirits, swearing, and smoking a short tobacco-pipe at the door of her tent. She was a most repulsive looking object. A dirty gaudy-coloured dress hung about her shoulders, coarse black hair unbrushed, uncombed, dangled about her face, over which her evil habits had spread a genuine bacchanalian glow, whilst in a loud masculine voice she uttered the most awful words that ever disgraced the mouth of a man—ten thousand times more awful when proceeding from a woman's lips.[6]

Clacy is probably describing a pair of Vandemonian ex-convicts whose background and aspirations would be dramatically different to that of an educated Englishwoman on a 'colonial adventure'. For them, survival, in the colonies that had spurned them and separated them from the mainstream that was always wary of their type, was a desperate struggle. The Vandemonians were despised, feared and outcast, set apart from and against polite society.

Clacy described the influence that the fairer sex generally had on the lives of the diggers. Just as Caroline Chisholm was convinced of the civilising effect of female companionship, Clacy also makes the same observation:

> the interior of the canvas habitation of the digger is desolate enough; a box of wood forms a table, and this is the only furniture; many dispense with that. The bedding, which is laid upon the ground, serves to sit upon.
>
> In some tents the soft influence of our sex is pleasingly apparent; the tins are as bright as silver, there are sheets as well as blankets on the beds, and perhaps a clean counterpane, with the addition of a dry sack or perhaps a piece of carpet.[7]

The first woman to arrive on the Forest Creek diggings had pushed her barrow from Melbourne, taking four days to make the journey. She had brought a washing tub, but she intended to do no laundry:

> She was soon surrounded by diggers who quickly ran her a tent up, and she started in the grog line. She was a lady of colour, and the scenes witnessed about her place at night were something to be remembered. Twice in one week was her tent burned down by the police, but as quickly went up another, in about a couple of hours.
>
> But night at the diggings is a characteristic time: murder here murder there—revolvers cracking—blunderbusses bombing—rifles going off—balls whistling—one man groaning with a broken leg—another shouting because he could not find his hole, and a third because he had tumbled into one—this man swearing, another praying—a party of bacchanals chanting various ditties, to different time and tune, or rather minus both. Here is one man grumbling because he has brought his wife with him, another ditto because he has left his behind, or sold her for an ounce of gold or a bottle of rum.
>
> Sometimes a wife is at first rather a nuisance; women get scared and frightened, then cross, and commence a 'blow up' with their husbands; but all their railing generally ends in their quietly settling down to this rough and primitive style of living, if not without a murmur, at least to all appearance with the determination to laugh and bear it.
>
> And although rough in their manners, and not over select in their address, the digger seldom wilfully injures a woman; in fact, a regular Vandemonian will in his way, play the gallant with as great a zest as a fashionable about town—at any rate, with more sincerity of heart.[8]

Digger's Wedding in Melbourne
Lithograph by S. T. Gill, Macartney & Galbraith, Melbourne, 1852
(Rex Nan Kivell Collection, U999.By Permission, National Library of Australia)

Such weddings were popular with diggers who had come down to Melbourne eager and very willing to spend their gold. Champagne flowed freely, and the young ladies provided much sought-after female companionship—for the time being. The 'marriage' lasted as long as the gold; when that ran out so did they, and the diggers headed back to their claims.

> The manner in which the successful diggers' weddings are conducted exhibits the reckless extravagance of these men and their doxies; the former we have no hesitation in stating to be 'old hands' in the colony, who do such things out of bravado to eclipse one another in vain show; as they formerly drank champagne out of buckets and latterly devoured five pound notes between slices of bread-and-butter.
>
> — Samuel Mossman, *The Gold Regions of Australia: A descriptive account of New South Wales, Victoria, and South Australia. With particulars of the recent gold discoveries*, Orr, London,1852.

Any woman set among this society had to be either strong, accompanied and protected, or just plain tough, and it appears that there were plenty of tough 'sheilas' about, and there were boatloads of young women disembarking who were willing to take a chance in the marriage stakes in the colonies.

Ladies of Easy Virtue

Although prostitution operated on the diggings, the almost total lack of its description in most written records may indicate that it was either not all that remarkable, or that it was an activity best not recorded, after all what young man or long-departed husband would record in his diary a visit to a house of ill fame?

The *Hill End and Tambaroora Times* reported a visit to the Chinese camp on the Turon in 26 May 1875 that:

> ... every hotel and place of entertainment was entered. Large numbers of Chinese were found in most of them, but, contrary to expectation, comparatively few women ... a girl of about 18 years of age was seen in bed sipping tea preparatory to indulging in the pleasures of the pipe*. .. Occasionally in the street, a white object, seen indistinctly in the darkness that prevailed, was descried. A few paces would bring the visitor close enough to distinguish it was a woman 'out on her rounds'.

While the Chinese had no women of their own race with them on the diggings, they did use prostitutes for their own pleasure and for their own gain. It was quite common for European working girls to be engaged by the entrepreneurial Chinese, who saw no barrier to making a little out of every opportunity that presented itself.

John Chandler, whose carrier's dray was a familiar sight on the early diggings, recorded in his diaries that women would offer to travel with him. He remarked that they would go up with one man, stay on the diggings for a while, and then come back down with another:

> I have heard carriers boast of how many women they had taken up. As I was coming into Melbourne once I was met by a young woman, and she was good looking. She asked me for a ride, so I told her to get up. She invited me to go home with her. She soon let me know to what class she belonged.[9]

Chandler and the young woman pulled into the stables where he was to put up for the night; however, the thought of what he was about to do so filled him with dread that he panicked while taking the harness off his horses. When he returned to the dray she was gone. He thanked 'the dear Lord for delivering [him] from joining his body to a harlot'.[10]

While the intention of most who migrated was not to work on the

---

* The pipe referred to here is opium. Opium was readily available in the Chinese quarters. It was not illegal to partake of the pipe but most Europeans passed up the opportunity—grog, no matter how impure, was the diggers' mind-altering substance of choice.

The same article in the *Hill End and Tambaroora Times* described a scene common in Chinese encampments:

> In some cribs the dim lamps were enveloped in dense haloes of opium, the atmosphere was almost suffocating.

—The Great Social Evil—

Prostitution was common on the streets of London in Victorian times. Many 'enlightened' upper-class men held the view that 'Victorian morality' was a corruption of nature and repressive of natural, and no doubt some 'un-natural', proclivities. They saw working-girls as sexual innocents uncorrupted by Victorian repression: 'the fact that the girls had to open their legs to a succession of strange men was a matter of minor importance'. Brothel patrons were convinced that these women would enjoy the benefits of prostitution—clean accommodation, plentiful food and good clothing.

The moral reformers of the time were convinced that all were heading straight 'for hell in a handcart', and that redemption was only possible through marriage, family hearth and home.

For almost all working girls this was an unattainable prospect unless they were prepared to migrate. Thousands took the opportunity offered by the Family Colonization Loan Society, only to find themselves in much the same situation in the colonies.

The Great Social Evil
Cartoon by John Leech,
[London] *Punch*, 1857

streets but to find a good husband and make a respectable life, a lot of young ladies took the easy way out, making the most of their assets soon after they hit the streets of Melbourne. After all, they were a long way from home, and the intention was to find a partner who could keep them in the manner to which they had never before been accustomed. It was common for these women to 'marry' successful diggers. After they had had their fun, and emptied pockets of nuggets and dust, they left their 'husbands' and 'married' another, just down from the diggings.

Young working-class girls, domestic servants or rural labourers had little chance of improving their station in class-ridden English society, but were free to make their own place in the anonymity of the new world. Prostitution was endemic to the streets of London in Victorian times, as the upper classes took their pleasure at leisure among the working girls. Many of those who had been transported to the penal colonies were

Oh! My goodness gracious I'll be off—Hold on, Poll my girl, all right
Watercolour by George Lacy, c. 1860
(Rex Nan Kivell Collection, R3803. By Permission, National Library of Australia)

There were plenty of young women who weren't prepared to stay away from the diggings while their men had all the fun.

Many travelled with friends or male companions, with a brother and his mates; acting as cook and housekeeper, bringing some degree of civilisation to their calico encampment.

There were also plenty of convict girls who seized upon the opportunity to escape the drudgery of skivvying for a squatter, taking their chances along with everybody else.

categorised as prostitutes, yet they may more likely have been convicted of theft than of living a life of easy virtue. However, many probably used their feminine wiles to break away from servitude on arriving in Sydney or Port Phillip.

One such lass, Alice Armstrong, transported to Sydney from Ireland in 1845, absconded soon after landing, and was found carousing with a sailor in Bathurst Street, Sydney. The 20-year-old had been listed as a vagrant sixteen times, her crime of the theft of a watch was at the time of the great potato famine, which caused so much misery in her native Enniskillen. Her transportation did little to ease her misery. She married after she had pretended to be a 'ticket-of-leave' convict, and had arranged to be stationed to a position in the country. Her husband of only three weeks took off for the diggings in Port Phillip, leaving her once again to look out for herself. What hope did such a girl have for redemption? What future lay in store for her? What could she do that would enable her to make her own way?

The diggings provided just the right opportunity for prostitution to flourish and prosper, yet there is little written evidence, apart from the descriptions of the many girls whose charms were noted by a journalist or artist. William Kelly described the audience in the dress-circle boxes of the Queen's Theatre, Melbourne, in 1853 attending a performance of *Hamlet*:

> the dress circle was crammed beyond sitting posture with florid-looking women in too low satin dresses, some in their smeared hair, with their pinned bonnets dangling in front of the boxes; others crowned with tiaras like rose bushes in full bearing, and all hung around with chains, watches, collars, and bracelets of most ponderous manufacture.

He describes the diggers who accompanied them:

> their lords-in-waiting were habited in tartan jumpers or red worsted shirts, smoking short pipes, and indulging in indelicate attentions, which frequently 'brought down the house'.[11]

The third act of this particular play developed into an exchange of views between 'Hamlet' and several diggers from Eaglehawk, who wondered aloud about the depth of the grave and the return to the tub. 'Hamlet' gave up his soliloquy, and joined in the jolly repartee. At the fall of the curtain the cast was showered with nuggets instead of bouquets. The diggers and their companions were out for fun, and had enough capital to ensure their place on the social scene.

Almost all records tell tales of diggers' 'weddings'. The gold and jewellery, fine gowns and large rings that were bestowed upon young 'brides' were astonishing to all well-bred folk. The streets of Melbourne were treated to parade after parade as diggers celebrated their good fortune by the taking of a bride—of sorts.

> Hackney carriages were to be continually seen driving through the streets, filled with men and women of the most doubtful respectability—men with coarse blackguard-looking features, half finely and shabbily dressed, and some in their coarse working-clothes, and seated beside women tricked out in the most gaudy and expensive goods the shops of Melbourne could furnish.[12]

The Castlemaine Police Court
Drawing by George Rowe
(Castlemaine Art Gallery & Historical Museum Collection)

The prisoner, Catherine Crane, was brought before the Castlemaine Court charged with assault, against whom is not indicated in this drawing. What hope would this weary-looking crone have against the gentlemen arrayed against her?

Here stand the noblest legal minds, police magistrates, JPs and military personnel available for the dispensation of the best of British justice on the Mount Alexander goldfields.

She was fined almost £20, which was a huge sum at the time. Her offence must have been grave or else her trade highly illegal, and therefore profitable, for her to be able to sustain such a heavy impost.

It appears that on the diggings the courtroom was no place 'fit for this lady'.

In fact, the diggers and their 'wives' had so commandeered the hackney cab that respectable, sober gentlefolk would not be seen in one—the diggers by their crude extravagance and boisterous behaviour debased the elegance of the carriage trade:

> Gold-diggers think nothing of giving £50 or £60 for a couple of two-horse flies to drive a wedding party about the town for two or three hours. There are one or two of these weddings every day; the party driving up one street and down another half the day, showing themselves off, gradually getting drunk as the day advances. You would stare in London to see such a wedding; the whole party, excepting perhaps the bride and bridesmaids, smoking; and generally one, the drunkest of the lot, leaning half over the back of the fly, black bottle in hand, inviting the public to have a 'nobbler'.[13]

Plucking Mrs Chisholm's Chickens

Ellen Clacy suggests that the better class of eligible young men, the squatters and the provident diggers, who generally returned to Britain to marry, would not be satisfied with the immigrant lass, no matter how pretty, unless she was cultivated and of the right class, 'unless her manners are cultivated and her principles correct':[14]

> Much is said and written in England about the scarcity of females in Australia, and the many good offers awaiting the acceptance of those who have the courage to travel so far. But the colonial bachelors, who are so ready to get married, and so very easy in their choice of a wife, are generally those the least calculated, in spite of their wealth, to make a respectable girl happy.[15]

The class system that so many were seeking to escape was still accepted and understood by those who sat at the top.

When Bill Armstrong, a digger from Ironbark Gully near Bendigo, took a fancy to having a wife, he sold his half-claim, hopped aboard the Cobb & Co. coach, and arrived in Melbourne determined to get for himself one of 'Mrs Chisholm's Chickens'. He took a bath, visited the barber and fitted himself with a new set of clothes, then at midnight presented himself at the Women's Hostel. He had convinced the matron of the hostel that he had been so busy in preparation for his intended that he was unable to appear any earlier.

After some time a young girl appeared at the door, to his great relief she was 'a winsome lass', who was nevertheless quite terrified of what was to happen to her. Bill carried her away in a hansom cab to a house he had just rented in Richmond. Within minutes they married themselves by 'jumping over the broom handle'—an old Scottish custom that bound them in acceptable wedlock without the benefit of clergy. Thus Harriet, one of 'Mrs Chisholm's Chickens', became Mrs Bill Armstrong, a digger's wife. They partied until the money ran out, then sold all and headed back to the diggings. In early 1854 Bill and Harriet arrived at Jones's Gully, Campbell's Creek, near Castlemaine, 'with nothing left of their "days-of-wine-and-roses" but a tent, shovel and pick, and the spiritual gain from having been properly "churched"'.[16]

Bill and Harriet stayed together, working with a Danish digger, Claus Gronn, until Bill died from a chest complaint that had long troubled him. Gronn moved into Castlemaine, pitching his tent next to Dr Preshaw's, where Harriet found employment. She later married a prosperous brewer, and bore him many fine children—the diggings were no place for a respectable lady to be alone.

In November 1854 Caroline Chisholm visited the goldfields and was presented at a soirée held in the 'Hall of Castlemaine', a canvas-walled and roofed auction rooms built by William Hitchcock, a prominent figure in early Castlemaine society. Hitchcock introduced Mrs Chisholm with the homily that 'that lady had been staying with him for two days—would that she were to be his guest for two years', a comment which was greeted with much applause.

However, there was a degree of opposition to Mrs Chisholm's activities. Hitchcock referred to the fact that some 'persons were blaming her for bringing to the colony a class of persons not sufficiently good'.[17] Caroline Chisholm replied 'that so far from having sent out persons not sufficiently good, one man . . . had blamed her for conveying away the very cream of the English population'.[18] There were also those who accused her, a Roman Catholic, of 'endeavouring to spread the Roman Catholic religion'. Although Chisholm appeared to be the epitome of the Victorian philanthropist, and sincere in her belief that the 'gentle sex' could do much in the civilisation of the digger, there may be some truth in these remarks. Her promotion of the family as a haven for the digger, and his redemption being the hearth and home, may well have stemmed from her own strongly-held commitment to salvation.

In addressing the crowd gathered in the 'Hall of Castlemaine', Caroline remarked:

> . . . the husbands who have left their wives at home, will find that I shall follow them. There are many of them about the diggings. The other day, as I was passing along, a digger whom I approached gave a sudden start and said, 'That's Mrs Chisholm!' I acknowledged my identity. 'Oh,' he said, 'I never thought of sending for my wife until I saw you'. Now for two years that man had been digging at Castlemaine—dig, dig, digging, and yet, as he assured me, he had never thought of sending for his wife until he saw me.[19]

She admitted that:

> I know many girls get into difficulties through being discharged from one place before they have another to go to. They seek temporary

Off to the Diggings
Hand-coloured lithograph
Cyrus Mason, Melbourne 1855
(Rex Nan Kivell Collection, U2489.By Permission, National Library of Australia)

The young husband is about to leave for the diggings. With a wagon packed high with provisions, all that is left is to pack the swags and to bid farewell to his wife and child.

In the distance can be seen the flagstaff that towered over Port Phillip. (Today this rise on the northern side of Melbourne's Yarra River is still known as Flagstaff Hill.)

At times when several ships arrived in the port at the same time, the grounds on this gentle rise were literally covered with new chums camped out for the night.

> lodgings, are exposed to temptations, and generally the more innocent the girl the sooner she falls.[20]

She proposed the establishment of a series of houses along the road from Melbourne to the diggings, built to protect such young ladies who were in danger of 'falling', yet she may just as well have sought to influence those who were responsible for the way in which such girls were employed and discharged so readily.

One young lady appeared before the magistrate in Bendigo with a complaint against her employer, the owner of a restaurant and accommodation house for diggers. Having just arrived in the colony, she had been engaged in Melbourne for a position in Bendigo at 30 shillings a week and her keep. Upon arrival she discovered that she was to occupy the same room as the owner and his wife. She told the court:

Breaking the News
Oil on canvas by Sir John Longstaff, 1887
(Art Gallery of Western Australia Collection)

Noted artist John Longstaff was born in the central Victorian gold-mining town of Clunes on 10 March 1861.

Most scholars consider that this painting depicts the great mining disaster of 1882 in which twenty-two miners lost their lives trapped underground in the rapidly flooding New Australasian Mine at nearby Creswick. However, a note from Sir John Longstaff himself pinned to the wall in the Clunes Historical Museum explains that this is not necessarily so.

This painting represents childhood memories of a scene he had observed played out so many times on those early diggings—there has been a fatal accident, and the young wife fears, yet already knows, what news her husband's mate is bringing.

This typically sentimental image, of the kind popular in the Victorian age, won for Longstaff the first travelling scholarship from the National Gallery School of Victoria.

> [She] didn't like it—hasn't been used to that sort of thing, was told she would be made comfortable, and have a nice room all to herself. [That] things have been grossly misrepresented, and she wishes to return to Melbourne, but the defendant refuses to pay her unless she gives him a month's notice.[21]

The young lady, described as an 'attractive female assistant' was demanding £12 for her troubles. Magistrate McLachlan, known locally as 'Bendigo

—A Woman! A Woman!—

The sight of a woman on the diggings was quite rare in the early days, particularly a young woman, and especially one who had come to Australia without assistance from the Crown.

The following extract is from the diary of George Ogilvy Preshaw, son of Dr Preshaw, a Scottish surgeon who had migrated to Australia in 1852:

> In the month of December, 1852, my father paid us a flying visit [to our Melbourne quarters] and returned with my eldest sister, who was one of the first women on the Mount Alexander diggings. She drove up in a cart on the top of some loading, and was five days on the road. As they rode through Forest Creek the cry ran along the lead, 'A woman! a woman!' Men shouted out to their mates below, who hurried to the top, and hundreds of eyes were fixed on her the whole way from Golden Point till she reached her future home at Campbell's Creek.

Two weeks after this incident the entire Preshaw family arrived at the Forest Creek diggings, where they set up their large tent—with the Scotch Thistle flag flying proudly out in front.

From thousands of miles away even Charles Dickens noted Preshaw's presence on the field when he wrote in *Household Words*: 'We note Dr. Preshaw, of Edinburgh. He begs to intimate that he has pitched his tent at Moonlight Flat, Forest Creek . . . his tent will be distinguished by his name across an ensign flying, and a Scotch thistle on end . . .' Such was the worldwide interest in the diggings.

Claus Gronn pitched his tent alongside Preshaw, but which one of these, shown in the sketch above, is unknown.

Mac', railed at the defendant: 'And this thing to have occurred in the nineteenth century, and in a British community! Verdict for the plaintiff for the full amount!' Now in complete control of the situation, she eyed the judge, and, whimpering, remarked that she had left behind a good situation following glowing reports of Bendigo, and asked 'if something for damages cannot be added to the compensation awarded [already] for breach of agreement'.

The magistrate surveyed the lass, first with a 'searching scrutiny', then with 'wonder', followed by 'sympathetic gravity', and finally 'an unmistakable look of admiration [was] discernible in his features'. Her 'musical voice, comely appearance, lithesome figure, and tidy apparel' had done their work. 'Damages!' he exclaims, as if astounded at so moderate

Anastasia Hayes
(Prov. 12970/p0001, Unit 1. Reproduced with the permission of the Keeper of Public Records, Public Record Office Victoria, Australia © State of Victoria)

Wife of Ballarat Reform League chairman Timothy Hayes, Anastasia was one of several women who were at the heart of the Eureka rebellion.

After the dust had settled on the bloodied stockade ground, Timothy was arrested by Lieutenant Thomas Richards. Anastasia confronted Richards: 'Why didn't you come yesterday?', implying that the troops could have intervened and prevented the carnage, then added 'If I had been a man I would not have allowed myself to be taken by the likes of you'.

Always in the thick of things she assisted Dr Doyle at Father Smyth's Presbytery that night when stockade leader Peter Lalor's arm was amputated.

a request. 'Most decidedly! £10 damages!' and, turning to the police attendant, 'You will make a careful examination at once of all restaurants, and report if any are without proper sleeping accommodation for young female assistants'.[22]

While such young ladies were often at the mercy of the unscrupulous, this one had little to learn about survival. On leaving the court she received a proposal of marriage from the proprietor of a rival restaurant, and the couple were married a week later. They went on to draw to their establishment most of the customers from her previous employer.

It appears that such working-class girls were keen to make a match and free themselves from servitude as they eagerly entered into the service of their 'husbands' and their families.

On political matters the diggers were eager to press their grievances upon Mrs Chisholm in the hope that she would have influence upon the Governor, but she would not act in this manner on their behalf:

> I do not feel sympathy for any body of men who pay so little respect to their own sex as to live without wives when they can well afford to pay for them . . . what a cheer the diggers would give if the houses they go to at night were something better than the blankets which they had to creep like dogs. . .

> If I had the power to do so, I would relieve of taxes all the married men and give a bounty on all the women and children introduced into the diggers' districts. The diggers have great grievances, but they are not competent to decide on the remedy. It is impossible for them to act with discretion and judgement, huddled together as they are, in fifties listening to the evil agitator. It will be when they are really at home with their wives and families, when they live in peace and quietness, that they will best be able to tell what they want.[23]

These remarks were made only days before the battle at the Eureka stockade. It is curious to reflect that it was primarily the Irish Catholics, many accompanied by their wives, who knew very well what they wanted from the British, and that was the freedom that they had sought for centuries.

Chisholm seemed to accept the British class structure and its implementation in Australia. In fact she appeared to support the maintenance of the established social order by seeking to keep the working class happy, content and quiet in their family units, while allowing the landholders, the aristocrats, those of good quality and noble birth, to get on with the business of running things properly.

She may have been a true 'Victorian' Christian imbued with the desire to do good deeds, as many of her class did seek their own redemption through adherence to the Bible teachings ('as much as ye do for the least of these my brethren, ye do unto me'), but it was really too late. The diggings changed the way in which the working people felt about themselves; the class struggle had begun long before; and Eureka was one more battle to be fought as men, and women, sought to take their place in the new world, regardless of birth or station.

The topsy-turvey world of the diggings offered those who wanted it the opportunity to make a way for themselves.

LOLA MONTEZ(S) IN AUSTRALIA

—*The Darling of the Diggers*—

Irish-born Maria Gilbert ran away from boarding school at sixteen years-of-age to marry her English soldier-boy. However, convinced of her ability to perform and to entertain, she left her husband after five years and took her charms to the European stage, eventually taking the name of Lola Montes (Montez). Her exotic, often daring, performances captivated audiences around the world.

There appeared to be no social convention, no moral code, no social barrier that could deter this fiery young Irish lass who seemed intent on leaving her mark on the world. She became the friend of the famous, the confidante of politicians, and the lover of not just a few of the great men of her time: including Alexander Dumas, Franz Liszt and even Ludwig, the King of Bavaria.

Lola once stripped to the waist and thrust her breasts into the King's face in order to prove that her charms were all her own (after which she was granted a generous engagement to the Munich Theatre).

Ludwig eventually fell from favour and sent into exile. Lola hurriedly abandoned the European circuit and headed for New York in 1851, and then on to San Francisco and the goldfields, where she soon found a new devoted and adoring audience.

Lola became known as 'the darling of the diggers', on first the Californian, and later on the Australian goldfields. After her home at Grass Valley, California, burnt to the ground in 1855, Lola, this time, abandoned California for Australia. Her fame and notoriety would precede her.

The *Melbourne Argus* reported her arrival in Port Phillip on 22 August 1855:

> Captain Gilmore of the *Wonga Wonga*, which arrived from Sydney today, informed our shipping reporter that Lola Montez had arrived in the city under the name of Madame Landsfeld Heald.

Lola travelled from diggings to diggings.

Although Lola scandalised 'proper' citizens wherever she appeared, and there was always criticism of her abilities as a performer, the diggers on the goldfields went wild with excitement every time the curtains opened.

Her performance at the newly-refurbished Hall of Castlemaine, on 17 July 1855, re-opened the old auction rooms with yet another stirring performance of the 'spider dance'. The *Castlemaine Mail* reported that she caused 'a near riot'. She so enchanted her audience that at each performance the stage was showered with lumps of gold.

The hall was later renamed the Theatre Royal. Although it is unlikely that it was named in her honour, it is certain that Lola was the closest to 'royalty' of any who had performed on that stage.

William Craig, a digger on Bendigo describes a performance by Lola at a theatre there:

> We hear the 'town crier' ringing his bell. 'Oh yes—oh yes!—oh yes! This is to give notice to all and sundry that Lolar [sic] Montes, the late queen of Bavary, will appear in a bran' new startlin' tragedy to-night at the theatre—to be follered by a side-splittin' comedy . . . Roll up!—roll up! —roll up! God save the Queen!'[24]

When Craig took his place in the crowded theatre, he remarked on the beauty and presence of the 'star' the moment she walked on stage:

> there is no mistaking the leading 'star' when she makes her appearance. She has evidently inherited the best points of her aristocratic Irish father and her handsome Creole mother. One has only to look at her magnificent dark flashing eyes, her willowy form, the traces of former beauty, and her lithe, active movements to see that one is in the presence of a very remarkable woman, and it is not hard to believe that she should have been able to bewitch a king and cost him his throne.[25]

Craig was not, however, without criticism of her abilities as a thespian, but was enamoured of her self-control and iron nerve, especially after she was almost struck by a bolt of forked lightning that flashed through the canvas roof of the theatre, destroying part of the scenery only a few feet from where she was performing. Lola, ever the trouper, calmly announced to the audience:

> 'There is to be a little thunder and lightning in the latter part of the play . . .' The crowd loved her, rejoining with remarks such as 'Isn't she a stunner', 'Bravo Lola!', 'Oh, but you're a darlint Loly!' 'Tis a pity yez aren't some dacent man's wife!'[26]

In her spider dance Lola wore a highly-coloured costume of many petticoats, among which several black 'decorations' had been sewn. Throughout her dance, she would flail about provocatively in an attempt to free herself of the 'spiders'. This excited her rough-and-ready audiences, hungry for the sight of female form, but also bought her reputation as an artiste into dispute.

Madame Lola Montez performed her notorious Spider Dance to a most appreciative audience
(Picture Collection State Library of Victoria)

It was this dance that ensured her popularity with the Australian diggers, yet at one time she had been booed off the stage with the same show in California. Maybe the Californian diggers had witnessed the earlier performances given by 'La Petite' Susan in the Coloma theatres, who did her own spider dance and Highland fling to great acclaim.

Her lack of any real ability to adequately perform the other advertised items on her programme often drew more-than-appropriate criticism from the colonial press as well. On 19 February 1856 Henry Seekamp, the editor of the *Ballarat Times*, printed a criticism of her illustrious past in his editorial, ignoring her performance as an actress. This incensed Lola, who had suffered criticism of her performances from the press for a long time. She took her revenge on Seekamp with a riding crop. Seekamp was in the bar of the United States Hotel, next door to the Victoria Theatre where Lola was performing. He was attacked as she descended the stairs to the bar. He retaliated with his own whip, and they flailed at one another for several minutes before they were dragged apart.

Lola then set out to destroy Seekamp's livelihood. First, she charged him with criminal libel. He was committed for trial, but he paid his own bail of £300, with a further £300 surety, and in turn summonsed Lola for assault. She retaliated, and had him charged with publication of an unregistered newspaper. As Lola was very popular with the diggers and a good many of the judiciary, nobody was prepared to fight for Seekamp. This action destroyed the *Times*.

Seekamp was one of the few gaoled after the riot at Eureka; he was probably the only one never missed.

Lola retired from performance shortly after, and went on the lecture circuit, touring America and England. Although Lola had suffered criticism of her ability over and over again, from the Munich Theatre to the bar of the United States Hotel in Ballarat, and had suffered at the pens of her critics, she remained convinced of her innate ability to entertain, and, more curiously, her ability to influence political events.

It is believed that dementia, brought on by syphilis, contributed to her early demise. She died of a stroke, penniless, and alone in a New York boarding house on 17 January 1861. Letters found after she died, showed that she had been preparing a plot to capture California from the United States and to install herself as Queen of 'Lolaland'.

Neither of her two children made the effort to claim her body. Lola, who had in life captured the hearts of so many was neglected, in death, by her own flesh and blood. After a riotous life 'The Darling of the Diggers' was finally laid to rest in a pauper's grave. She was only 41 years-of-age.

CHAPTER 9

'Show Us Yer License!'

There was no more despised body of officials on the goldfields than the 'traps' [the police]. There was no more hated piece of paper than the gold license. There was no quicker way of firing resentment among the diggers than the dreaded 'license hunt', and no surer way of sending diggers running for their holes than the cry of 'Joe! Joe! Joe!'

All men on the diggings were required to hold a license and had to have the license on them at all times. The traps raided the diggings with military precision; they stretched out across the gullies and worked their

The First Commissioner Hardy Collecting Licenses and Diggers Evading
Pen and wash drawing by George Lacy, c. 1852
(Rex Nan Kivell Collection, T367. By Permission, National Library of Australia)

Diggers can be seen heading for the hills, while others hide beneath a cleft in a rock, hoping to avoid scrutiny by the traps.

Any digger found without a license on his person was immediately marched away to be chained to the logs, fined heavily, or imprisoned and set to work on the roads.

For the digger out of luck it was either a quick sprint into the trees or a week's work for the government.

The License Inspected
Watercolour by S. T. Gill, 1852,
Macartney & Galbraith, Melbourne, 1852
(Rex Nan Kivell Collection, U1006. By Permission, National Library of Australia)

This painting shows a familiar scene: a trooper checks the fortunate digger's license [fortunate that he had one], while in the background others are seen scurrying away.

The license fee was indiscriminate—it did not matter whether a person on the field was a successful digger or not, merchant, baker or blacksmith, companion or friend, all were forced to pay the same fee.

It was the over-zealous enforcement of this law—which was usually to the financial betterment of the troopers rather than the colonial treasury—that caused so much dissent, and so many attempts at avoidance.

way from one end to the other. A digger caught between the shaft and his tent without his license in his pocket would be immediately chained like a dog to other unfortunate fellows, and driven back to the Commissioner's Camp to be 'chained to the logs' until a magistrate could be found. Diggers were sent to be chained to logs or the trunks of trees, with the excuse, real or pretext, that the lock-ups were full, and often left outside all night and in all weathers.

From there, it was off to the roads for seven days. The government used errant diggers as labour to level the roads to the diggings and were always keen to have an endless supply of labourers for this important task. The diggers rightly believed that the license fees would give the administration adequate funds to provide both protection and services. The roads to the diggings were in a shocking state, and the diggers demanded that something be done. The irony was that many of them would be the very labourers providing the muscle for that service.

The government attitude was, in the first place, to levy such a heavy license fee that labouring classes would be deterred from leaving their employment and taking off for the diggings. This policy failed completely. But the license remained as a vital source of revenue to support both La Trobe's and later Hotham's inept bureaucracy. The diggers were the most heavily-taxed group in the colony, the most efficient producers of any commodity, the largest consumers, and yet aggrieved that they were totally unrepresented in the legislative body.

William Howitt states:

> . . . there is a strong feeling against the arbitrary treatment of the diggers by the Commissioners and police, and for an elective franchise—the principle of the British Constitution being grossly violated in the persons of the diggers, who are heavily taxed and totally unrepresented.[1]

Police were dispatched to any new rush almost as quickly as the diggers had opened it. While the government did little to enhance the amenity of the diggings with the funds they gathered, they certainly invested heavily in providing their own manpower to collect the taxes. The majority of troopers and magistrates treated the diggers with little regard for the intention of British law. One police magistrate fined a digger brought before him on a charge with contempt of court simply for answering when questioned. At a subscription ball where all classes were admitted, a magistrate seized a well-dressed digger and his wife. The digger had been brought up before him earlier on 'some charge', so the magistrate had the man sent to the lock-up, and refused him bail.

The troopers' eagerness was no doubt encouraged by a commission paid on all fines meted out to the diggers. Many are known to have retired from the diggings with considerable savings in their bank accounts. One fellow at Bendigo, Hermsprong by name, retired from the diggings with £15,000, a sum he had collected in only two years; over that time his salary was set at £400 a year. Hermsprong was recognised, not only for the amount he had taken but for his riding whip, which had a brass knob on its end the size of an apple. He used 'green apples' to devilish effect as he rapped the skulls of any who displeased him. He was dedicated to the destruction of the sly-grog trade, that is, any sly-grog seller who was not one of his 'supporters'. His penchant for a bribe was legendary, and he took great delight in the destruction of the property of those who were not his friends. Countless sly-grog tents operated with trooper Hermsprong's full knowledge, but they took the precaution to grease his palm well beforehand.

Hermsprong assailed one poor Irishwoman whose husband had died in a mining accident; she was left with several small children, the youngest only a few days old. Several fellow-countrymen had advised her to engage in a bit of sly-grog to support her family, promising they would give her their custom, and, knowing the power of the legendary

Diggers Licensing, Forrest Creek
Lithograph by S. T. Gill, Macartney & Galbraith, Melbourne, 1852
(Rex Nan Kivell Collection, U990. By Permission, National Library of Australia)
Diggers waiting in line to purchase licenses complained of the time wasted, sometimes for two days or more as they waited on the pleasure of the commissioners. The pace of registration angered the diggers giving them just one more reason to gripe about the government.

Irish thirst, she and her children would have been well provided for. Hermsprong charged her with the sale of grog, which she did not deny, exclaiming to her accuser, 'What your honour, was I to do?'

Hermsprong answered by ordering the police accompanying him to 'Fire that tent!' All of the children were asleep in the tent at the time, and the police refused to act on his command. Hermsprong swore at them for their 'damned nicety', leapt down from his horse, took a flaming brand from a fire in front of the tent and set it ablaze.The terrified woman had just time to rescue her baby and her other children before everything she owned was consumed. Hermsprong rode away satisfied. He was forced to leave the diggings following this incident, but it was simply one of hundreds of occasions when petulant troopers regarded the letter of the law as their excuse for 'sport'. The often arbitrary, and rigid, nature of apprehension and fine grated upon the diggers:

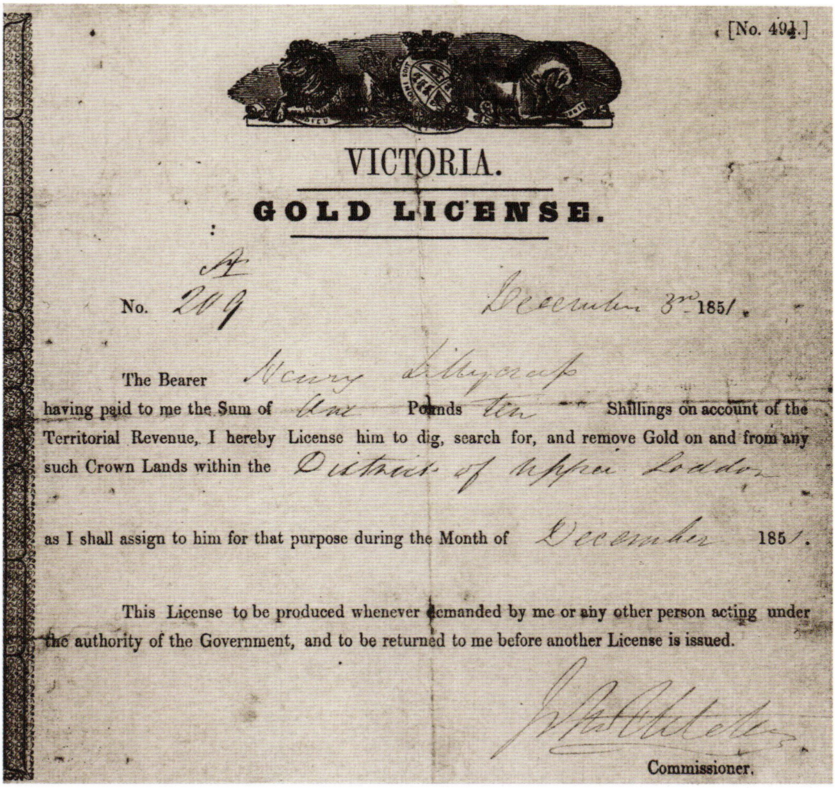

[No. 49½.]

VICTORIA.

GOLD LICENSE.

A

No. 209 December 3rd 1851

The Bearer Henry Lillycrap having paid to me the Sum of One Pounds ten Shillings on account of the Territorial Revenue, I hereby License him to dig, search for, and remove Gold on and from any such Crown Lands within the District of Upper Loddon

as I shall assign to him for that purpose during the Month of December 1851.

This License to be produced whenever demanded by me or any other person acting under the authority of the Government, and to be returned to me before another License is issued.

Commissioner.

Gold License No. 209, issued to Henry Lillecrap, 3 December 1851, at the District of Upper Loddon
(Castlemaine Pioneers & Old Residents Association Collection)

> Any one found without the license in his pocket—though he have it in his tent—is, without excuse or explanation allowed, marched to the camp, and there summarily fined £3 to £5; and if he show any reluctance or indignation at this treatment, he is, without ceremony, handcuffed and dragged off.[2]

Many recorded that, upon arriving at the diggings, they were fined before they had even started to dig for gold, even before they had an opportunity to look for and purchase a license.

One group of Americans just out from California had spent over £150 getting their goods up by bullock wagon, and each was arrested and fined before they had even had an opportunity to set themselves up. They were taken before the commissioner, who, on hearing their complaints and deciding they were honest men, paid for their licenses from his own pocket. The American diggers were able to repay him within a week from

Aboriginal Black Troopers
Watercolour by William Strutt, 1851
(State Parliamentary Library Collection)

Captain Dana parades with his squad of finely presented troopers, resplendent in their green and black uniforms, with possum skin facings and red stripes, short carbines, bayonets and swords.

At first the black troopers were the only mounted police at Ballarat. Strutt thought it a bad move to employ the Aborigines for the collection or examination of licenses because 'they could not discriminate between one piece of paper and another'.

Following Dana's death in 1852, the black squad was disbanded, with many of the troops themselves setting off to the diggings.

The native police were replaced by squads comprised of pensioned soldiers and ex-convicts from Tasmania, who were generally disliked by the diggers, 'not only for their brutality and excessively coarse demeanour, but also for their incompetence and corruption'.

the nuggets they found.This same group was dismayed to discover that they were unable to purchase land on the diggings; they had come to the colony prepared to stay and make their future there, but turned back for California soon after.

It was not long before demands were made on the government to open up the land for purchase, as well as to repeal the onerous license fees. However, the government was not at all interested in encouraging the working classes to take over the land once held by squatters, in fact the license fee had been levied with exactly the opposite in mind. But

The Forest Creek Diggings, Mount Alexander, Port Phillip
London Illustrated News, 1852
(Castlemaine Art Gallery & Historical Museum Collection)
Illustrations such as this, when reproduced in the popular papers of the time, did much to stir the adventurous soul of many an English office boy, counter clerk or wage-hand.
The idea of travel to the colonies was canvassed widely in the popular press; and gold was the currency that made the adventure possible.

the pressure of dissent and active opposition to the position taken by the government did lead to an eventual resolution.

> There was now a very large number arriving on the diggings, and the government made a charge of 30s per month for a license to dig. This was very hard as there were hundreds now on the diggings who could not get the colour, in fact not more than one in five was successful, as all the best ground had been worked. The government was very harsh. They sent out four to six constables in a company with muskets and bayonets fixed, and every man that had not got a license, even if he had not had time to get to the commissioners, which was at a place now called Castlemaine, and many poor fellows had spent every shilling to get there, for provisions were very dear, but they were all driven off the ground before these hirelings who consisted

> mostly of old hands, in other words, old convicts from Van Diemen's Land. They were fined 40s or locked up for seven days if they did not have the money.[3]

The cry of 'Joe' preceded the entry of any squad of traps who came onto the diggings with 'license hunting' in mind. The cry spread quickly from one end of a gully to the other, and unlicensed diggers would disappear down their holes like rabbits. Any left above ground without their licenses would be marched away, a bayonet at their back. The troopers were well aware that unlicensed men were hiding below ground, but were also aware that any trooper who climbed down into a shaft could well meet with a 'mining accident'.

> The zeal with which the collection of the thirty shilling gold license was proceeded with, made up at once for all accruing deficiencies. Every young man, having the requisite qualifications of incompetence and a letter of introduction, was straightaway encased in a suit of blue and silver, furnished with sword and pistol, mounted on a horse, and forthwith constituted a trooper. As a practical foil to the shortcomings of the mounted men—most of whom were exceedingly decent fellows—such as old ticket-of-leave holders from New South Wales and Tasmania as were too lazy to work, and too cowardly to steal, were enrolled as foot-policemen—'traps' as they were called by the diggers, and the name was by no means unsuitable to them. Horse and foot alike, they were despatched in hundreds on the one errand 'digger-hunting'.[4]

This system of policing was termed 'Man hunting', and the police 'Man-catchers' or 'Bloodhounds'. The diggers grew to resent the actions of the traps, and considered them guilty of 'cold-blooded, un-English, un-Christian despotism'. Howitt commented:

> No voice, however powerful or piercing, could touch the tympanum of Government; and official injustice and insolence became gigantic in their proportions, and peculation and bribery walked hand in hand.[5]

The government persisted, and as a result kindled the spark of the revolution it was at most pains to avoid. It was not long before the diggings erupted in flames.

CHAPTER 10

'Red-ribbon' Rebellion

When Earl Grey, British Secretary of State for the Colonies, warned: 'There is spirit abroad which must be carefully watched and promptly brought under control if this colony is not to parallel California in crime and disorder,'[1] he was reacting to the rumours of discontent, and open dissent, reported from the colonies.

The majority of diggers were disenchanted with rule by a despotic military, and sought justice and fair representation of their grievances from Lieutenant-Governor La Trobe.

The issue of taxation on the goldfields was at the core of most of the dissent. The license fee of 30/- a month was considered as excessive by most, but it was the corruption, oppression and disregard for the rights of ordinary men and women that brought dissent to a head.

Not all diggers on the Australian goldfields were natural-born subjects of Her Majesty Queen Victoria; and many who were had little desire to remain so. There were thousands of Irish Catholics who cared little for the niceties of English law, and saw no need to tug their forelocks to the British so far away from 'that sceptred isle'.

The diggings fast became home for adventurers from across the world—French, Italians, Greeks, Hungarians, Austrians, Germans, Jews, Russians, Balts, Americans, West Indians and Chinese had all come to Victoria looking for excitement. Very few of these had any real regard for 'Mother England', or any reason to wish to return to their own corner of a war-torn Europe ravaged by revolution. Few had any desire to live under the yoke of a dissolute military, harassed by thugs in uniform, often gaoled, frequently abused, driven in chains for glancing sideways at an officer.

There were shiploads of free Americans who, since the signing of the *Treaty of Paris* in 1783 had been free of British rule; they were well versed in matters political, having been free to stand, free to oppose, free to dissent, and used to the exercise of their hard-fought suffrage. It was the

The Government Camp, Sandhurst
Watercolour by Ludwig Becker, June 1853
(Mitchell Library, State Library of New South wales)

This watercolour was painted just prior to the 'red-ribbon' agitation in the winter of 1853.

Who knows what the two diggers are discussing here with Commissioner Panton, but by the look of the piece of paper held in his hand, the matter of the license fee was sure to be an integral part of the conversation.

The Government Camp in Bendigo was pitched on the hill to the northern side of the creek, a vantage point that overlooked the diggers' camp, which stretched for miles in either direction from Kangaroo Flat to the White Hills.

It was here in August 1853, on this flat, that the diggers assembled, then marched with flags flying, up the hill, to present the 'Bendigo Petition' to Commissioner Panton.

influence of these 'Yankee-style Red Republicans', that was disturbing to Earl Grey.

The spark of rebellion was fanned easily in such a climate; the uprising that eventually engulfed the Ballarat goldfields was kindled by La Trobe and fuelled by his own fears of such a revolution. As in California, where the discovery of gold had saved America from financial disaster, it was the toil of the diggers that La Trobe was to tax so heavily in order to save the Colony of Victoria from ruin.

The Great Meeting of Diggers

On 15 December 1851 more than 10,000 diggers assembled at the Old Shepherd's Hut on the outskirts of Dr Barker's run at Chewton in response to notices pinned to trees across the Mount Alexander goldfield, which read:

FELLOW DIGGERS!
The intelligence has just arrived of the resolution of the Government to double the license fee. Will you tamely submit to the imposition or assert your rights as men? You are called upon to pay a tax originated and concocted by the most heartless selfishness, a tax imposed by Legislators for the purpose of detaining you in their workshops, in their stable yards, and by their flocks and herds.

They have conferred to effect this; they would increase this sevenfold but they are afraid! Fie upon such pusillanimity! and shame upon the men, who [to] save a few paltry pounds for their own pockets, would tax the poor man's hands!

It will be in vain for one or two individuals to tell the Commissioner, or his emissaries, that they have been unsuccessful and that they can't pay the license fee. But remember that union is strength, that though a single twig may be bent or broken, a bundle of them tied together

3 Cheers for THE ARGUS &c.
Pen and ink drawing, unknown artist
(Rex Nan Kivell Collection, T2249. By Permission, National Library of Australia)
This rather primitive sketch records the great meeting of diggers on 15 December 1851. The note states:

> The 'Diggers' after giving 3 cheers for the *ARGUS* 3 for the *DAILY NEWS* and three groans for the *HERALD*—then separated —the great meeting at the diggings against Govermt Licenses.

> yields not nor breaks. Ye are Britons! Will you submit to oppression or injustice! Meet—agitate—be unanimous—and if there is injustice in the land, they will, they must, abolish the imposition.
> Yours faithfully, A Digger.

A report published in the *Argus* on 18 December 1851 records the spirit of the meeting as a Mr Potts addressed the large crowd:

> I see before me some 10,000 or 12,000 men which any country in the world might be proud to own as her sons. The very cream of Victoria, and the sinews of her strength ... let it be seen this day whether you intend to be slaves or Britons, whether you will basely bow down your neck to the yoke, or whether like true men you will support your rights ... the 30 shillings charged by the government is an illegal taxation, and that His Excellency has no power to tax us ... because a few men think proper to say, you shall pay, that is no reason why a body of men such as I now address, should accede to such extortion.

Following the Great Meeting the miners resolved to refuse to pay any license fee at all. Captain Harrison, Dr Richmond and Mr Plaistow—were delegated to go to Melbourne and press the diggers' claims on Governor La Trobe. La Trobe's response was to send a further 130 troops to Forest Creek.

On arrival on the goldfield the 99th Regiment (made up of army pensioners) found themselves outnumbered 200 to one. They were met with derision, and were unable to take control by their show of arms. La Trobe was eventually forced to capitulate, and the license fee remained unchanged.

William Howitt writes:

> ... the most glaring sign of the fatuity of a Government, is its unconsciousness of its own weakness, or the power of those whom it seeks to control ... but the most fatal error which a Government can commit, is to teach its subjects its utter inability to compel them, if they choose to resist; except it be of setting them an example of injustice and rapacity.

If La Trobe was unable to learn from his mistakes of 1851, his successor, Charles Hotham, was determined to repeat his errors of judgement three years later. The consequences were to change the colony forever.

The Great Meeting of Diggers
15 December 1851 – from *Ham's Five Views of the Gold Fields of Mount Alexander and Ballarat, in the colony of Victoria*, Thomas Ham, Melbourne, 1852
(Collection, Allport Library and Museum of Fine Arts, Hobart)

This was the first of the many meetings that were held across the goldfields in protest at the license fee that was proving a hardship for many diggers, and also in protest at the behaviour of the police and troopers who benefited from the fines levied on the diggers.

One police inspector, a former blacksmith turned law-enforcer, whose arm once 'used to smite iron, now smote men', was forced to retire from the Bendigo diggings after two years of protest at his over-zealous force in upholding the law.

The behaviour of the police who profited from the arrest of the diggers, who were free of constraint by the government, were a law unto themselves, creating more unrest than they seemed prepared to prevent.

The diggers' protest may have caused the government to rethink the issue of the license fee, but until military rule was abolished the goldfields remained a hot-bed of sedition.

The diggers were not, as a body, a lawless lot; they simply felt that they were being treated unfairly, and that the troopers, who received a commission on all the fines extracted by the arrest of the diggers, were over-zealous in their prosecution of the law.

William Howitt complained of this on his arrival in Bendigo:

> ... once there, with weary limbs, and empty pockets, before we could dig up a grain of gold the police were down on us for £1/10 shillings each for licenses. We did not object to the license, that was quite just and fair; but we thought it hard to be dragged off to the camp at a

Left: *George Edward Thompson*
Thompson was a leader of the Anti-Gold-License Association that formed in Bendigo on 3 June 1853.

Right: *W. D. C. Denovan*
A persuasive orator, Scots-born Chartist, former school-master, W. D. C. Denovan also led the Bendigo diggers agitating for removal of La Trobe's hated license fee.

> moment's notice, and expected to pay before we had had a single day allowed to get the means.[2]

David Tulloch added his opinion:

> While jealous of their rights, and prepared to withstand oppression, they [the diggers] were not desirous to evade any just claim of the Government; they were willing to submit to *equitable* taxation.[3]

But the government could only see the 'milch cow' that the diggings had become. Mrs Gilbert, wife of the Gold Commissioner at Bendigo, told Howitt (who recalled it in his letter of 25 September 1852) that diggers had been arriving in Bendigo at the rate of 5000 to 6000 a week, with issues of licenses increasing in equal proportion. She said that 'at that Digging [Bendigo], a few months ago, the monthly licenses were 6000, then 8000, then 10,000, and now they are 20,000'.[4]

The deposits in the coffers for the benefit of the bureaucracy were enormous, and all the government of the day had to do was to sit back and watch the money pour in. Or so they thought. Those making the deposits were increasingly demanding that the government put something back into the colony at large.

Masthead of the Gold Diggers' Advocate and Commercial Advertiser, 22 July 1854
(Picture Collection, State Library of Victoria)

The Advocate, published in Melbourne in the early days of the goldrush, was filled with advertisements for tents, tools and tucker: in fact, everything the digging party would need for a successful expedition to the goldfields.

The Advocate was a vocal supporter of the movement for diggers' rights; this empathy is expressed best in the design of the shield shown supported by a pair of diggers. The shield is divided into quarters showing the pick and shovel, the cradle, and the pan, representing
labour; as on the diggers' flag—a purse for nuggets is displayed in place of the bundle of faggots.

Here individual success is celebrated rather than unity, and the whole is crowned with the kangaroo and a rather oddly-shaped emu, celebrating Australia.

The motto of the newspaper reads 'Labour founds Empires; knowledge and virtue exalt and perpetuate them'. It would appear that such noble sentiments never reached the ears of the Governor.

Little was done to make safe or even slightly comfortable access to the diggings, police oppressed rather than protected, diggers were unable to purchase land and invest in their future in the colony. The government and the squatters held control of the land and did their best to keep the workers without opportunity. However, the diggers began to sense a power of their own—the power of common rights, of unity, of equality, of suffrage—and they soon demanded these rights.

Dissent grew apace. The Anti-Gold-License Association was formed in Bendigo in June 1853. The leaders: George Thompson, Dr Jones, and an Irish-born American, 'Captain' Edward Brown, sought to represent the concerns of the 23,000 diggers and their families on that goldfield to the government.

By 3 August a petition of more than 5000 signatures, and 30 metres in length, was signed by the diggers and taken to Melbourne to be presented to Governor La Trobe. The diggers must have moved pretty sharply among the men to collect so many signatures in only four weeks.

On 13 August 1853 more than 10,000 diggers (although Howitt suggests a figure closer to 4000) assembled at View Point, a central point close to the camp at Bendigo, to greet the delegates on their return from

Artists' impression of the Digger's Banner, based on Howitt's description in Land, Labour and Gold.

Melbourne. The meeting was excited, and at times agitated; those gathered represented the great number of nations on the field at that time.

March on the Bendigo Camp

A fife and tambourine had led a parade from the White Hills to View Point. First were the Irish behind a green and gauzy banner of great length, then came the Scots, the Union Jack, and the revolutionary flags of France and Germany, the Germans carried the *schwarz-rot-und-gold* [black, red and gold] flag of the German revolution, then came the American Stars and Stripes, followed by flags of various smaller countries, some with original designs.

William Howitt followed the procession to View Point, where a tent and bunting awaited the speakers. In the centre of the clearing flew the diggers' flag:

> The flag showed the pick, the shovel, and the cradle,—that represented labour. There were the scales,—that meant justice. There was the Roman bundle of sticks,—that meant union: altogether,—all up at once. There were the kangaroo and emu,—that meant Australia.[5]

The diggers' flag had been designed by a Mr Dexter, a china painter from Devon, who had learned much from his time spent among French 'Red Republicans', and deemed it an honour to have been able to render his talent to the cause.

There were those who decried the Union Jack and supported the cause of revolution, but they were countered by the loyal response of most of the crowd, who called for three cheers for the British flag. The diggers may have had a grievance with their Governor, but they were not prepared to stand by as others attempted to revile the very 'bosom of the grand old mother-country which had suckled and raised him to man's estate'.[6]

Association delegate George Thompson leapt to his feet and cheered the British ensign, 'which had led the way to the pre-eminence of England all over the world, and to the liberty they were that day enjoying'.[7]

Poster calling diggers to assemble in protest at W. D. C. Denovan's Monster Meeting in Bendigo.
26 August 1853

Despite the diggers' enthusiasm, the petition fell on deaf ears. In response to the Governor's inaction the diggers resolved once again to resist his tax. They agreed to offer no more than ten shillings when licenses next fell due.

About this time it was reported that Sir Charles Fitzroy, the Governor of New South Wales, had decided to abolish the license fee in that colony. La Trobe wrote a letter to Fitzroy, which was published in the newspapers, strongly advising against such action. Fitzroy ignored La Trobe's entreaty.

This brought the situation to a head. On 27 August another meeting was held at View Point. This time a much larger procession, led by two pipers, gathered. The diggers at this meeting again agreed to pay no more than ten shillings a month, to present themselves to the authorities on the appropriate day and, if the ten shillings were refused, to offer themselves to be taken into custody.

As a symbol of this defiance they took to wearing a red ribbon in their hats, to show that those who wore the ribbon would no longer tender the old fee. The so-called 'Red-ribbon Rebellion' was born. The wearing of the ribbon became so common that supplies of red flannel, a popular material used in the making of diggers' shirts, all but dried up.

La Trobe was indecisive in quieting the dispute. A number of soldiers and cannons were dispatched to Bendigo, yet the diggers remained steadfast: 'firm and resolved . . . used no idle threats, or military parade'.[8] They carefully stayed within all other aspects of the law.

At Waranga the Commissioners foolishly arrested several men for refusing to pay the full license. Fully-armed diggers marched in a body upon the Camp, and forced the release of their mates.

Following this news the Governor hurried to the Legislative Council, and 'in a speech replete with indications of terror, proposed at once to abandon the license-fee altogether'.[9] Then he placarded the goldfields with conflicting messages. Two placards bearing the same date, 1 September, bore different messages, the first from the Governor who told the diggers the new laws were before the legislature and that fees due for that month were waived, the second from Chief Commissioner Wright, who stated that, although laws were before the Legislative Council, the last law was still in force, and that diggers should pay as usual.

The diggers' representatives once again sought clarification from the government, which then acquiesced, reducing the fee to £1 a month, £2 for two months or £8 a year, adding a registration fee on all businesses and a gold export duty. The diggers had won some concession from government, but not all were happy with the result.

After continued public protest against Governor La Trobe he was recalled to England in May 1854. He sailed away from a colony in debt, a bureaucracy in decay and a citizenry in revolt. La Trobe left Victoria indebted to the British banks for £1,000,000, and more than one-quarter of that sum could not be accounted for. Under La Trobe's administration hundreds of petty officials had been enriched at the expense of the citizens, the taxes extracted from the diggers diverted into the pockets of the police.

The Arrival of Hotham

La Trobe's successor, Charles Hotham, was received enthusiastically by the diggers at first. They feted the new governor, and his wife on their first visit to the goldfields. At Castlemaine the diggers met his carriage some miles from the camp, removed the horses, and pulled the entourage with jubilant manpower towards Forest Creek. They were overjoyed that the

Gold license instructions:

The Bearer, ...,
having paid to me the Sum of One Pound, Ten Shillings, on account of the Territorial Revenue, I hereby License him to dig, search for, and remove Gold on and from any such Crown Land within the .... District, as I shall assign to him for that purpose during the month of .... 18..., not within half-a-mile of any Head station.

This License is not transferable, and to be produced whenever demanded by me or any other person acting under the Authority of the Government, and to be returned when another License is issued.

The following regulations were printed on the back of the license:

Regulations to be observed by the Persons digging for Gold, or otherwise employed at the Gold Fields.

1. Every person must always have his License with him, ready to be produced whenever demanded by a Commissioner, or Person acting under his instructions, otherwise he is liable to be proceeded against as an Unlicensed person.
2. Every Person digging for Gold, or occupying land, without a License, is liable by Law to be fined, for the first offence, not exceeding £5; for a second offence, not exceeding £15; and a subsequent offence, not exceeding £30.
3. Digging for Gold is not allowed within Ten feet of any Public Road, nor are the roads to be undermined.
4. Tents or buildings are not to be erected within Twenty feet of each other, or within Twenty feet of any creek.
5. It is enjoined that all Persons at the Gold Fields maintain and assist in maintaining a due and proper observance of Sundays.

The above list of regulations pertain to the use of a Gold License, including instructions on how close tents can be erected to one another, and a reminder to observe the Sabbath.

new Governor was keen to see at first hand the state of the diggings, and they were anxious to impress upon him their hard work, their enterprise and the richness of the field. They may have overplayed their hand a little when Hotham was amply rewarded with nuggets in his dish after they had led him to try his hand at prospecting—from a 'salted' shaft.

Hotham returned to Melbourne with the impression that the diggings were occupied by an enthusiastic population: industrious, cheerful, and above all patriotic. Uppermost in his mind was the crippling debt left to his colony by the excesses of the La Trobe administration. He mistakenly looked to the diggers for the funds to bankroll his bureaucracy. The license fee remained the easiest method of raising funds; rule by military the surest way of enforcing compliance. La Trobe's legacy to Hotham was the unrest that simmered throughout his years in office, and the conflagration that was shortly to engulf the entire colony.

THE BENDIGO PETITION

[TO:]
HIS EXCELLENCY CHARLES JOSEPH LA TROBE ESQUIRE LIEUTENANT GOVERNOR OF THE COLONY OF VICTORIA &C.
The Humble Petition of the Undersigned Gold Diggers and other residents on the Gold Fields of the Colony **Sheweth** That your petitioners are the loyal and Devoted Subjects of Her Most Gracious Majesty Queen Victoria the Sovereign Ruler of this Colony one of the dependencies of the British Crown

That in the present impoverished conditions of the goldfields the impost of Thirty Shillings a Month is more than Your Petitioners can pay as the fruit of labour at the Mines scarcely affords to a large proportion of the Gold Miners the common necessaries of life

That in consequence of the few Officials appointed to issue Licenses the Diggers Storekeepers and other residents lose much time at each Monthly issues in procuring their Licenses

That the laborious occupation of Gold digging and the privation attendant on a residence on the Gold Fields entail much sickness and its consequent expenses on Your Petitioners

That in consequence of the Squatter Land Monopoly a large proportion of Successful Diggers who desire to invest their earnings in a portion of land are debarred from so doing

That newly arrived Diggers must lose much time and money before they become acquainted with the process of Gold Mining

That in consequence of Armed Men (many of whom are notoriously bad in character) being employed to enforce the impost of Thirty Shillings a Month there is much ill feeling engendered amongst the Diggers against the Government

That in consequence of the non-possession by some of the Miners of a Gold Diggers License some of the Commissioners appointed to administer the Law on the Gold Fields have on various occasions Chained non-possessors to Trees and Condemned them to hard labour on the Public Roads of the Colony—

A proceeding your Petitioners maintain to be contrary to the spirit of the British Law which does not recognize the principle of the Subject being a Criminal because he is indebted to the State.

That the impost of Thirty Shillings a Month is unjust because the successful and unsuccessful Digger are assessed in the same ratio

For these reasons and others which could be enumerated Your Petitioners pray your Excellency to Grant the following Petition

First. To direct that the License Fee be reduced to Ten Shillings a Month

Secondly. To direct that Monthly or Quarterly Licenses be issued at the option of the Applicants

Thirdly. To direct that new arrivals or invalids be allowed on registering their names at the Commissioners Office fifteen clear days residence on the Gold Fields before the License be enforced

Fourthly. To afford greater facility to Diggers and others resident on the Gold Fields who wish to engage in Agricultural Pursuits for investing their earnings in small allotments of land

Lieutenant-Governor Charles Joseph La Trobe
Engraving from the *Picturesque Atlas of Australasia*, 1888
(Private Collection)

Fifthly. To direct that the Penalty of Five Pounds for non-possession of License be reduced to One Pound

Sixthly. To direct that (as the Diggers and other residents on the Gold Fields of the Colony have uniformly developed a love of law and order) the sending of an Armed Force to enforce the License Tax be discontinued

Your Petitioners would respectfully submit to Your Excellency's consideration in favour of the reduction of the License Fee that many Diggers and other residents on the Gold Fields who are debarred from taking a License under the present system would if the Tax were reduced to Ten Shillings a Month cheerfully comply with the Law so that the License Fund instead of being diminished would be increased.

Your Petitioners would also remind your Excellency that a Petition is the only mode by which they can submit their wants to your Excellency's consideration as although they contribute more to the Exchequer than half of the Colony they are the largest class of Her Majesty's Subjects in the Colony unrepresented.

CHAPTER 11

The Battle at Ballarat

Karl Marx wrote of the diggers' agitation and the continuing protest that led to the battle at the Eureka Stockade on 3 December 1854 as a 'revolutionary movement of the workers'.

Marx made his observations from afar. Such an interpretation obviously suited his political ideology—a body of working men rising together to overthrow the ruling class, which if successful, would have been a major fillip to the cause of universal class struggle and revolution.

While there is some verity in this view the diggers at Ballarat did not play by standard revolutionary rules. While there certainly were many disaffected diggers who did harbour truly revolutionary ideals, for most their resistance was rooted in economic reality and a distaste for arbitrary and perverse 'justice'.

A report to Governor Hotham found that 'foreigners formed a larger proportion among the disaffected than among the miners generally'. This simply supported his belief that most loyal diggers would not do such an 'un-British' thing as to seriously consider revolt.

> Nursed in intrigue, the foreigners, who had been members of secret societies in Europe, were conspiring with the worst class of the Irish on the goldfields, and no vile art was wanting among the desperadoes whom Italy, Germany, and France had yielded to the Australian mines.[1]

There was a belief that the 'rebellious element of Ireland, who thought to fright the British Isles from their propriety in 1848 [The Young Ireland Movement*] were represented in some strength', and it was probably justified.

---

* *The Young Ireland Movement*
Dissatisfied with Irish political leader Dan O'Connell and the slow rate of progress over the question of Irish self-determination, the Young Ireland Movement was formed in 1842. The new movement included wealthy land-holders such as Smith O'Brien, journalists John Mitchell, the radical James Fintan Lalor and the hot-head Thomas Meagher.

The Eureka Slaughter, 3 December 1854
Watercolour by Charles Doudiet
(Ballarat Fine Art Gallery Collection)

The goldfields did have all of the elements of serious social unrest, if not actual revolution, thrown together in a unique environment. There was little diversion to hold the interest of such a large body of energetic, excited and politically aware young men, other than hard labour and

---

The movement echoed European romantic nationalism and desired a collective consciousness for all Ireland.

Young Ireland believed in 'physical force politics' to free the Irish from the bondage of English landlords, but the movement disintegrated after the failed insurrection of 1848, after which several of the leaders were transported to Van Diemen's Land.

English digger William Craig, who had travelled to Australia on the same ship as Eureka Stockader, the Irish-born Peter Lalor [the younger brother of James Fintan], later recalled in his memoir, *My Adventures on the Australian Goldfields*, that Lalor:

> never tired of descanting upon the wrongs of Ireland . . . was a strong believer in the use of physical force for redressing her wrongs.

James Fintan Lalor, died from an attack of bronchitis in 1849. His naturally poor health had been exacerbated by his incarceration by the British after the failed revolt.

A monument raised to honour him near his birthplace in Queen's County [now Laois] bears this inscription:

> Ireland her own, and all therein,
> from the sod to the sky.
> The soil of Ireland
> for the people of Ireland.

hard drinking. The constant calls to take control of their own destinies fell on eager ears.

Prelude to Battle

For months dissent and resistance had been growing across all the Victorian goldfields. The story was the same everywhere; protest meetings were being held from Waranga to Bendigo, Forest Creek to Ballarat. Resistance to license fees, revulsion at the random and oppressive digger hunts, objection to the privilege assumed by capricious and dissolute troopers on 'the Sacred Camps', were common on all the diggings.

However, it was the failure of deep mining on the Eureka field, where no lead had 'bottomed out' for over five weeks, that put increased pressure on the diggers around Ballarat when demands were made to pay the monthly license fee.

13 September 1854: The desperate attempt by the government to force compliance with the law, and bring order to the goldfields, by the instigation of twice-weekly license checks, may well mark the date when the determined struggle for liberty really began.

While there had been meetings protesting against the license fee across all the diggings—and some among the diggers had been pressing for a physical response—it was the brutal murder of Scottish digger James Scobie, on the Eureka field, and the response of the Ballarat authorities that followed, that changed the diggers' mood from lawful petition and deputation to direct action and rebellion.

The Death of James Scobie

7 October 1854: Scottish digger James Scobie had spent the day celebrating the arrival of his old friend Peter Martin to the goldfields. Making their way home to Scobie's tent the pair came upon the Eureka Hotel. Scobie tried to gain entry to the hotel by banging on the door, waking up Bentley the owner. They were told to go away, whereupon the already inebriated Scobie attempted to kick the door in. A brief altercation followed, and Scobie made some unfortunate remarks impugning the reputation of the owner's wife, who, awakened by the banging on the door had joined her husband in the darkened bar.

Scobie and Martin staggered off into the night. Only fifty yards or so from the Eureka they were attacked from behind. Bentley, his wife,

Dry Diggings, Gravel Pits, Ballarat
Watercolour by Charles Doudiet
(Ballarat Fine Art Gallery Collection)

> I think the practical miner, who had been hard at work, night after day, for the last four or six months, and, after all, had just bottomed a shicer, objected to the tax itself, because he could not possibly afford to pay it. And was it not atrocious to confine this man in the lousy lock-up at the camp, because he had no luck?
> —Raffaello Carboni

and their employees Farrell, Mooney and Hance surrounded Scobie, knocked him to the ground and kicked him to death. Martin, also badly beaten,was able to scurry away, protected by the dark that descended over the diggings like a blanket.

It was not long before the news of this brutish attack spread across the diggings.

9 October: An inquest was held into the death of James Scobie, but, much to the disgust of the diggers, an open verdict was returned.

10 October: The following day Johann Gregorious, the Armenian servant of the Catholic priest Father Smyth, was abused and arrested by police for not being in possession of a license. Gregorious, who was crippled, protested that, as the servant of the priest, he was not in need of a digging license. The troopers were simply not interested. Gregorious was forced to march to the Camp by Officer Lord.

Gregorious was fined £5, but not for the original charge of being without a license. Commissioner Johnstone changed the charge to assaulting a trooper in the execution of his duty, as he feared he could not justify the original in the face of the prevailing sentiment on the goldfield. The effect was much the same.

It must be noted that the population on the Eureka diggings were largely Irish Catholic. Father Smyth was held in high regard, and any attack on his servant would be seen as an attack on the much-admired young priest. Any attack on the priest was also seen as an attack on the Church, and on the Irish themselves.

The cronyism, ineptitude and sheer corruption of the goldfields administration was plain for all to see and the treatment of Gregorious simply added to the anger of the diggers over the handling of Scobie's death.

Every digger on the Eureka field was convinced that James Bentley, the publican of the Eureka, an ex-convict with close connections to the corrupt magistrates' court, was guilty of Scobie's murder but Bentley's associates on the magistrates' bench, let him walk free. This simple act of obvious collusion literally set the diggings aflame.

17 October: A meeting was held near the spot where Scobie died, to try to find a way to have the case of his death, and the subsequent acquittal of Bentley brought before 'other and more competent authorities'. After this meeting several of Commissioner Rede's troopers, who had been watching the protest, moved across to the front of the Eureka Hotel to protect Bentley, who feared some form of retribution by the diggers. The sight of the troopers, who appeared to be guarding the very source of their current discontent, brought the situation to the boil.

A young lad threw a stone at the lamp in front of the hotel. The sound of breaking glass was the catalyst that fired the agitated assembly and they began to tear the Eureka apart.

A fire, lit in an adjoining bowling saloon, quickly spread until both buildings were engulfed in flames. The police lent Bentley a horse. He galloped away to the protection of the Camp.

His escape, aided by the troopers, was proof enough to the diggers of collusion within the Camp to justify their anger at the goldfields administration and authority of government.

Governor Hotham believed that those who took part in the events

Burning of the Eureka Hotel 17 October 1854
Watercolour by Charles Doudiet
(Ballarat Fine Art Gallery Collection)

Doudiet's eyewitness depictions have only resurfaced since 1966. Unknown for over one hundred years, they were discovered in a collection of papers in Canada and brought back to Ballarat by public subscription.

His primitive, yet remarkably detailed, style provide the best pictorial record of the fateful events that changed the course of governance for ever in the Colony of Victoria.

of 17 October were preparing to 'overawe' him, and that he must show them 'that they could not take the law into their own hands', however, he responded to the diggers' demands with the arrest of Bentley, Farrell and Hance, and he ordered an investigation into the affair by Magistrate Sturt and two other members of the bench.

Although James Bentley had served time on both Norfolk Island and in Van Diemen's Land, he had support from John O'Shanassy and F. P. Stevens; from the manager of the Bank of New South Wales, Alex Willis; from the Superintendent of Her Majesty's Hulks in Port Phillip; and from two auctioneers in Geelong: all of whom agreed to his fitness to hold a publican's license. He was also supported by John D'Ewes, Senior Magistrate and Chairman of the Licensing Bench in Ballarat, from whom he had obtained the license for the Eureka.

Bentley had a notorious reputation for the running of 'a slaughter-house', as the hotel was known among the diggers. It was the biggest hotel on the Ballarat field at the time, and was well known for its strong-

—Chartism—

The ideals of the Chartist movement were the background against which the demands of the Eureka rebels were set. There were many men on the diggings who had carried these ideals with them from the old country and saw the new colony as the ideal place to test their mettle. They sought to bring change where society could begin anew and the goldfields were a fresh canvas upon which bold strokes could be made.

Chartism was a working-class movement begun in England whose principal aim was to gain political franchise and better working conditions for the ordinary worker.

The People's Charter was drafted in 1838 and made six demands: Universal Suffrage, Secret Ballot, Annual Elections, Payment of Members, No Property Qualification for MPs, and Equal Electoral Districts. Three petitions presented to the English parliament in 1839, 1842 and 1848 failed to achieve their aims.

Australia had seen ordinary workers transported for attempts to improve the lives of the workers. In 1834 Sydneysiders had turned out to witness the arrival of George and John Loveless, Thomas and John Standfield and James Harriett, a small group of agricultural labourers from Tolpuddle in Dorset who had attempted to establish a farm labourers' union. However, their attempt was an affront to the establishment who were perfectly content to run the country as a personal fiefdom, so they were arrested, convicted and transported to New South Wales.

'The Tolpuddle Martyrs', as they were known, were another link in the chain of discontent that ultimately led to Eureka. George Loveless had pleaded at the time:

> We are uniting to preserve ourselves, our wives and our children from utter degradation and starvation, we have injured no man's reputation, character, person or property.

armed men who were not afraid to use their muscle if the occasion arose. John Farrell was also an ex-convict, and had made his mark as a Crown Prosecutor in the Court of Petty Sessions in Ballarat and as a Chief Constable in Castlemaine. Tom Mooney worked as roustabout and nightwatchman at the hotel, and Hervey Hance was in charge of the till.

The only barrier between felons and enforcers in those days seemed to be the Bench, and people seemed to move freely from one side to the other. The game of law seemed to be the same for all players, the colour of the uniform and the braid on the shoulders, or lack of it, was the only thing separating the one from the other.

25 October: A number of Father Smyth's parishioners met at the Roman Catholic chapel on Bakery Hill.

Even though the officers of The Camp were quite capable of corruption, the digging fraternity were not altogether without blame. The Irish Catholics had largely hijacked the argument for reform that had begun with the birth of the Red-ribbon Movement three years earlier in Bendigo. At Ballarat the 'Hibernian element' was eager to avenge centuries of mistreatment by the British Crown. Scobie's death was simply the catalyst for the revolutionary zeal that had been smouldering on the diggings since 1851. Hotham seriously believed that 'foreigners' were largely to blame for the agitation; however, the largely Irish band of dissidents who fought at Eureka on 3 December were to prove otherwise.

17 November: A report of the inquiry into the Bentley affair was released, and it recommended that D'Ewes be dismissed from his position. It found that he was closely connected with, and indebted to, publicans on the field and had given false evidence.

18 November: Bentley, Farrell and Hance were convicted of manslaughter and sentenced to three years' imprisonment, with hard labour on the roads. It was on the evidence of Bentley's man, Tom Mooney, who had responded to a reward of £500 offered for information on Scobie's death, that the case was proved.

In the face of this evidence Hotham still despatched a further 450 troopers to Ballarat, with the instructions to Rede to 'use force whenever legally called upon to do so, without regard to the consequences that might ensue'. He demanded from Rede the arrest of those responsible for the burning of the Eureka Hotel.

23 November: Several diggers were arrested for this offence, but after the dismissal by Magistrate Sturt of the diggers Balderstone, Stuart, MacIntosh and Van der Byl, three unfortunate others, Andrew McIntyre, Thomas Fletcher and Henry Westerby, were the only men brought to trial.

The case against them was proved; even though admittedly they were present at the fracas, they were not solely responsible for the fire. A fourth man, Carey, was selected for trial but never brought before the magistrate (curiously, the fact that he was an American appears to have given him exemption from colonial justice).

John Basson Humffray
Pastel drawing by Thomas Flintoff, 1859
(Picture Collection, State Library of Victoria)
Moral force advocate and diggers' leader. As those who promoted direct action took charge of the protest, Humffray withdrew into the background—he favoured debate over violence.

The Ballarat Reform League immediately voted to demand the release of the 'three martyrs to British injustice'.

The League's demands were again refused by the Governor. It was the word 'demand' that so incensed Hotham, he advised Humffray, Kennedy and Black that 'I must take my stand on the word demand'. They reminded him of the royal prerogative of pardon that he, as the representative of the Crown, was empowered to give. They also referred to the pardon allowed to the American citizen Carey, but were to learn that it was a petition by the American Consul that had secured his release.

The League's delegates, while imploring Governor Hotham to show leniency in the case of the three diggers were unaware that reinforcements for the 12th Regiment were already on their way.

A Diggers' Reform League had been proposed to represent all of the diggings, but by 11 November the anger that followed Scobie's murder, and the ineptitude of the justice system to deal adequately with his killers, forced the Ballarat Reform League into being.

Its main proponents were Henry Holyoake, a London chartist; George Black, a well-educated Englishman who published the *Diggers' Advocate*; and the more moderate moral-force exponent, Welshman J. B. Humffray. There were present at these early meetings those who favoured a more energetic form of protest. The German, Frederick Vern, promoted 'red republicanism' and Tom Kennedy, the Scottish chartist, was in favour of direct and physical action. The Ballarat Reform League adopted a platform far more extreme than that proposed at earlier meetings. Black, Humffray and Kennedy were sent to Melbourne to put the demands that the Gold Commission be disbanded, the license fee abolished, manhood suffrage introduced, and a raft of other matters to put before the Governor.

—Raffaello Carboni—

The flamboyant Italian-born writer Raffaello Carboni was a keen observer who played a significant role in the Eureka uprising.

Blessed with blazing red hair and prominent beard, the Italian revolutionary placed himself at the centre of the debate over the diggers' resistance to the license fee. He was, however, at pains to ensure that he was not considered a red republican and that it was the license issue that was at the centre of his and the diggers' dissent.

Popular among the diggers, educated and able to speak several European languages Carboni acted as a conduit between men of different backgrounds. Although he was in the thick of things right from the beginning he tried to remain one step aside from the actions of the rebel protagonists.

Yet it was Carboni who stood with Peter Lalor and Frederick Vern when the call for all men on Ballarat to stand together in defiance of the government was first heard.

Although not in the stockade at the time of the attack Carboni was arrested later in the morning at the London Hotel where he had been attending to the wounds of his injured comrades. He was sent for trial with all the other diggers' leaders. After their acquittal he was one of nine diggers elected to the local Ballarat Court to adjudicate on mining affairs.

Disappointed by the act of a government rising up against its own people, Carboni, who was at heart an Italian patriot, returned to his homeland after only four years in Australia. It was in Italy that he wrote his memoirs and published *The Eureka Stockade* in 1855, while the memory of those exciting days on the diggings were still fresh in his mind.

Ever the one to put himself at the centre of great causes, Carboni worked with the Garibaldi forces for the liberation and unification of Italy until he died in 1875.

DOWN WITH THE LICENSE FEE!

DOWN WITH DESPOTISM!

"WHO SO BASE AS BE A SLAVE?"

ON

WEDNESDAY NEXT

The 29th Instant, at Two o'clock,

A MEETING

Of all the DIGGERS, STOREKEEPERS, and Inhabitants of Ballarat generally, will be held

ON BAKERY HILL

For the immediate Abolition of the License Fee, and the speedy attainment of the other objects of the Ballarat Reform League. The report of the Deputations which have gone to the Lieutenant-Governor to demand the release of the prisoners lately convicted, and to Creswick and Forest Creeks, Bendigo, &c., will also be submitted at the same time.

All who claim the right to a voice in the framing of the Laws under which they should live, are solemnly bound to attend the Meeting and further its objects to the utmost extent of their power.

N.B. Bring your Licenses, they may be wanted.

PRINTED AT THE "TIMES" OFFICE, BAKERY HILL, BALLARAT.

Down with the License Fee!
Poster, November 1854
(Public Record Office Collection Laverton)

This poster was placarded across the Ballarat diggings, calling all those on the field who wished to voice their protest to meet on Bakery Hill at two o'clock on 29 November.

The meeting was to greet the delegates Humffray, Kennedy and Black on their return from Melbourne, and to press once again for the abolition of the license fee and the release of the three prisoners who had been convicted for the destruction of the Eureka Hotel.

On 16 November 1854 Governor Hotham established a Royal Commission to inquire into concerns on the goldfields, but just one week later, and before the Reform League delegates had even reached Melbourne, he dispatched all available troops to Ballarat. On Monday, 27 November, the Governor agreed to receive the deputation from Ballarat. The Ballarat diggings were placarded with posters calling for a meeting on the 29th to hear the report of their delegation. However, it appears that the diggers were already resolved to burn their licenses. The Ballarat Commissioners' Camp was barricaded with bales of hay and bags of oats, and the military seemed none too confident about the outcome of the next few days.

Governor Hotham believed, as did his Commissioners on the field, that the rebels were 'foreigners and Irish'. This may well have been true of this little corner of the vast Victorian diggings, but the troubles had been brewing for more than three years.

The Government Camp, Ballarat, 1854. Troops' Arrival from Melbourne
Wood engraving by Alfred Clint, from a sketch by S. D. S. Huyghe.
Published in the *Ballarat Star*, 1870
(By permission, National Library of Australia)

Just as La Trobe had done at Bendigo three years earlier, Hotham replied to the diggers' petition by sending more troops onto the offending goldfield. This action also proved to be counter-productive, achieving the exact opposite to what was desired.

As G. W. Rusden had remarked, on all the diggings there were a large number of men filled with revolutionary zeal, and countless others had a particular axe to grind with the British Crown. One such man was Dublin-trained engineer Peter Lalor who had family connections to the radicalised 'Young Ireland' movement, and had previously held a claim next to Scobie. The Irishman from Queens County, Lalor, was a decent fellow who despite his background had decided to leave politics at home and take the world as he found it when he emigrated to try his luck on the diggings. Yet his pedigree would not be denied; he was to rise to prominence at this time when his self-respect and righteous indignation would not allow him to stand by any longer.

Troops despatched by Hotham entered the Ballarat diggings on Tuesday, the 28th. They marched in with bayonets fixed and were met with hoots of derision. As they passed through the Eureka lead they were pelted with stones, carts were overturned, and a drummer boy inadvertently shot; he later died from the wounds sustained in that frivolous skirmish. In revenge, the troopers drew their swords and flailed into the fray in an attempt to recover both government property and their dignity.

This action of the hotheads at Eureka angered the Reform League delegates who were, by this time, in Melbourne, as it had simply moved the Camp into battle mode and whetted an appetite for revenge. They returned to Ballarat on 29 November, only to find the situation had deteriorated after the debacle of the previous day. At a mass meeting, held on Bakery Hill, the Eureka flag was raised for the first time. The meeting was addressed by Peter Lalor, one of the founders of the Reform League, and licenses were consigned to a great bonfire set by Frederick Vern.

30 November: Commissioner Robert Rede ordered one more license hunt as he attempted to show the diggers who was in command. Rede believed that the government must crush the movement at Ballarat if it were to control this and other goldfields. Rede had told a digger that morning that 'we will stand no more of this nonsense'. As the troopers rode out they were again pelted with stones, hooted and abused. They fired a volley over the heads of the diggers, and received several shots in reply. Half a dozen prisoners were taken.

The action of the troops this day bought the immediate future into sharp focus. Just before noon on the 30th Rede arrived at the Gravel Pits, where he called on the diggers there to present their licenses. Lalor, Raffaello Carboni and their mates had gone to their shafts earlier in the morning. The flamboyant Italian Carboni was thinking of calling it quits for the day when he heard the cry go up—'The traps'. Peter Lalor later recalled :

> I was working in a shaft at Eureka 140 ft deep, Timothy Hayes at the windlass, when suddenly the news spread that the diggers were being fired on at the gravel pits.[2]

Lalor was quickly hauled to the surface, and he rushed to the scene. When Rede saw the Eureka mob hurrying up the gully, he read the Riot Act and called for reinforcements from the Camp. The angry crowd dispersed.

Later in the afternoon, as if by some unheard signal, crowds began to assemble at Bakery Hill, where, in the absence of the Melbourne delegates, Lalor again addressed the meeting:

> I looked around me; I saw brave and honest men, who had come thousands of miles to labour for independence. I knew that hundreds were in great poverty, who would possess wealth and happiness if allowed

—A Family in Dispute—

In Ireland, Lalor's father had represented Queen's County in the House of Commons, 1832-35. He had led the Leix farmers in a campaign of resistance to the paying of tithes to the established Church. He had also organised a system of 'defensive resistance' using pitchforks and pikes to defend local farmers against eviction until tithes were abolished in 1838.

Lalor's brother, James Fintan, who featured prominently in the failed 1848 rebellion, was planning an armed uprising up until his demise in 1849. He had devised a design for 'fortified circular encampments' to defend Irish insurgents against attack by the English; this may have influenced Peter in the construction of the Eureka Stockade.

Although Peter had determined to leave the troubles of old Ireland behind when he emigrated to the colony, when strife began he could not deny his destiny. It was from this background that he made his principled stand against the government.

Digger's leader Peter Lalor
Lithograph by Ludwig Becker, 1856
(Rex Nan Kivell Collection NK1398, National Library of Australia)

> to cultivate the wilderness which surrounded us. The grievances under which we had long suffered, and the brutal attack of the day, flashed across my mind; and with the burning feelings of an injured man, I mounted the stump and proclaimed 'Liberty'.
>
> I called for volunteers to come forward and enroll themselves in companies. Hundreds responded to the call . . . I then called to the volunteers to kneel down. They did so, and with their heads uncovered, and hands raised to Heaven, they solemnly swore at all hazards to defend their rights and liberties.[3]

At this meeting at 4 pm on 30 November 1854 Peter Lalor stepped up on a tree stump beneath the billowing Southern Cross flag, and into his place in Australian history. The diggers knelt as one, on the dusty ground,

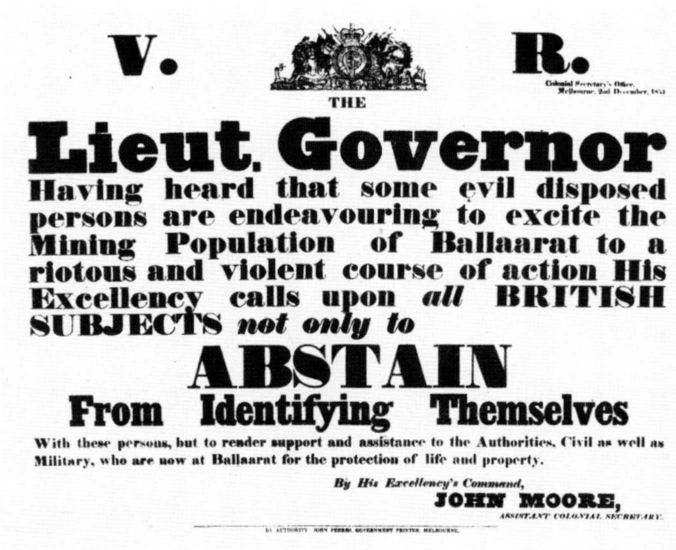

V. R.

Colonial Secretary's Office,
Melbourne, 2nd December, 1854

THE

Lieut. Governor

Having heard that some evil disposed persons are endeavouring to excite the Mining Population of Ballaarat to a riotous and violent course of action His Excellency calls upon *all* BRITISH SUBJECTS *not only* to

ABSTAIN

From Identifying Themselves

With these persons, but to render support and assistance to the Authorities, Civil as well as Military, who are now at Ballaarat for the protection of life and property.

By His Excellency's Command,

JOHN MOORE,

ASSISTANT COLONIAL SECRETARY.

BY AUTHORITY: JOHN FERRES, GOVERNMENT PRINTER, MELBOURNE.

Notice placarded across the diggings, 2 December 1854
(Public Record Office Collection, Laverton)
This notice, dated one day before the battle at Eureka, indicates the paranoia of the government at that time. Hotham acted decisively to bring the diggings to order, to show the diggers who was really in charge. What a pity for him that his actions proved exactly the opposite.

placed their hands over their hearts and chanted together the diggers' oath:

> 'We swear by the Southern Cross to stand truly by each other, and defend our rights and our liberties'.

Over the next two days a thousand diggers began the construction of a stockade on the Eureka field. The roughly circular encampment was about an acre in area, and barricaded on three sides by a rude construction of pit logs thrown together in a higgledy-piggledy manner. There were also several tents within the enclosure.

3 December: At dawn on the morning of 3 December 1854 government troops attacked the stockade. It was a Sunday morning. As work on the shafts was prohibited on Sundays, it is fair to surmise that most diggers had taken some relaxation the previous evening and were well asleep at that early hour; a dawn raid was the last thing they would have expected. In fact, very few were actually at the stockade, and those who were, were in little condition for battle.

Swearing Allegiance to the 'Southern Cross'
Watercolour by Charles Doudiet, 1 December 1854
(Ballarat Fine Art Gallery Collection)

The Eureka Flag flew over the stockade for the first time at this impromptu meeting on 30 November when the Diggers' Oath was also first proclaimed:

> 'We swear by the Southern Cross to stand truly by each other, and defend our rights and our liberties'.

The attack was a complete surprise. The battle was short and bloody, leaving 22 diggers and six government soldiers dead or dying. The action of some troopers after the battle had ceased was barbaric; bleeding diggers were bayoneted where they fell. Tents were set alight without any attempt made by the troopers to remove the wounded within. Lalor's left arm had been shattered by a musket ball, and he lay wounded in a shallow shaft beneath a pile of logs. After the dust had settled, he was smuggled away by Father Smyth to the Presbytery, where his arm was amputated. Anastasia Hayes, wife of one of the rebel leaders, was at the Presbytery and assisted in the operation.

Commissioner Rede issued the following proclamation from the Government Camp at Ballarat on the afternoon after the battle:

> Her Majesty's forces were this morning fired upon by a large body of evil-disposed persons of various nations, who had entrenched

The Storming of Eureka Stockade, 3 December 1854
Watercolour by J. B. Henderson
(Dixson Galleries, State Library of New South Wales)

This was painted soon after the battle at Eureka, and Henderson shows the battle from the perspective of sympathetic diggers.

The diggers are shown as a loosely disciplined motley of amateur soldiers, who are falling before the onslaught of an organised, practised and fearless military force—suffering is shown here, not glorious or heroic deaths, but simply wasted lives.

> themselves in a stockade in the Eureka, and some officers and men were killed. Several of the rioters have paid the penalty of their crime and a large number are in custody. All well-disposed persons are earnestly requested to return to their ordinary occupations, and to abstain from assembling in large groups, and every protection will be afforded them by the authorities. GOD SAVE THE QUEEN!!!.[4]

Funerals for the dead were held all the following day. On the night of 4 December soldiers fired into several tents where 'illegal' lights were showing, with the loss of three more lives. It seems that Rede's promise of protection counted for nothing. The *Argus*, 4 December (obviously typeset and 'put to bed' before news of the previous day was broadcast) offered this opinion:

The Eureka Flag, after the battle
(Ballarat Fine Art Gallery Collection)
After the dust had settled over the bloodied battle ground, trooper John King volunteered to tear down the ensign. King cut it away with his bayonet and trampled it into the dust, where he bayoneted it yet again.

This original flag has been kept in the Ballarat Gallery for more than 100 years.

For a long time the flag was viewed with some suspicion, not venerated but treated as a curiosity, not displayed but simply draped across a wooden trestle in a gallery storeroom. Snippets were taken from time to time and given as mementoes to various visiting dignitaries or curious celebrities.

It is now regarded as an Australian icon—a genuine historical artefact that has no other equal in Australian history. Although ownership of the remnant flag has long been in dispute—the descendants of the Ballarat Reform League prosecute their argument for ownership against the gallery and the descendants of the King family—the flag is now hanging in a darkened room in the Ballarat Fine Art Gallery, with Doudiet's watercolours of the battle displayed alongside it.

that a very active part is taken in the present disturbance by natives of other countries . . . if we are doomed to engage in a sad and serious struggle, let us at all events fight it out amongst ourselves!

This is still an English colony, with English laws, English habits, and English sympathies! If we do fight, let the encounter be an English one, conducted upon English principles, and in an English spirit! . . . we trust that rumours of their identification with the movement may be un-founded; and that the leading men of their several nations will

> exert themselves to the utmost to retain them in their proper position of neutrality. Let them dig our gold and welcome, but they should abstain from interfering in our national disputes.

Martial law was declared in Ballarat on 5 December with Major General Sir Robert Nickle in command. The following day the *Argus* reported that:

> No further intelligence arrived last night from Ballarat. Up to one o'clock yesterday all was quiet in that locality, but an opinion prevailed among many people, well able to judge, that the calm was the result not of defeat but of a cool determination to attain a certain object.

Aftermath

William Denovan, one of the main agitators on the Bendigo goldfield, was on his way to Ballarat with Henry Holyoake, a Ballarat representative who had been in Bendigo giving an eyewitness account to his compatriots there. They got as far as the Guildford Arms Hotel beyond Castlemaine, where they stopped for the night. It was here that they received news of the battle and defeat of the diggers' stockade at Eureka. A large meeting gathered at Castlemaine on 9 December condemning military rule. Red ribbons, accompanied by mourning bands, were worn by the diggers who agreed to stand together, defiant in their refusal of the license fee. Hotham's resolve to defeat Eureka had only hardened the resolve of the diggers right across Victoria.

Denovan turned back for Bendigo. A trooper shadowed him all the way. Denovan strode into Bendigo in red shirt and white trousers, a scarlet scarf given to him by an admirer at Castlemaine flying at his neck. He was immediately recognised, and cheered all the way into the centre of the camp. However, the Bendigo diggings remained calm. The popularity of the Assistant Commissioner, Joseph Panton, was in stark contrast to the high emotion at Ballarat. Although feelings towards the government were high on all of the diggings, Forest Creek, McIvor and other diggings more closely allied with Bendigo were not all that eager to broadcast their support for the Irish at Ballarat.

Although the movement was inclusive of all the nationalities who came together under the Southern Cross, the predominance of the Irish among those who defended the stockade led contemporary commentators to conclude that it was a purely Irish, or Catholic, protest, whose main aim was to win independence from British rule.

Hotham began to justify his actions, and in his request to the Secretary of State for a grant of secret service money he insisted:

> secret societies everywhere exist . . . the French Red Republican, the German political metaphysician, the American Lone Star Member and the British Chartist here meet not to dig gold but to agitate, overturn the government and seize the land.[5]

Bendigo Goldfields Commissioner Joseph Panton
Portrait by Batchelder & Co., 1867
(Picture Collection, State Library of Victoria)

Panton was only 24 years-of-age when he took the posting to the Bendigo diggings.

Although not a military man he was well-educated and had the facility to judge the measure of any man. His even-handedness, fairness and integrity when dealing with the diggers on Bendigo helped him keep a lid on the protest there.

If the British had been more inclusive of the dispossessed and less inclined to the promotion of established social orders to the exclusion of almost all else, they may not have felt the need to rule with military force. The Americans certainly had little love for England, but were in no mind to attempt to overthrow the government. The Irish Americans may have held Britain to blame for the potato famine and the loss of 1,000,000 to the shores of America, but with that emigration they were free of the landlord class. Neither group had any reason to continue the struggle in Australia. However, few were prepared to be treated as 'base as slaves'.

Hotham certainly regarded the foreigners on the goldfield as more than influential, but it is difficult to guess whether he thought of the Irish as foreign. Certainly, adherence to the creed of Catholicism would have been regarded by him as foreign enough, if not downright seditious.

Several of the leaders of the Reform League had stepped back when they had felt that the agitation was veering away from 'moral force',

Reward poster, 18 December 1854—for information leading to the apprehension of the diggers' leaders Peter Lawlor [sic] and Henry Black
(Ballarat Fine Art Gallery Collection)

This poster calling for information that may lead to the arrest of Lalor and Black, uses remarks made by them on or about 13 November as the 'treasonable' trigger from which charges could be laid.

Lalor and Black avoided capture at Eureka, and were sheltered by sympathisers and well-wishers until well after those sent to trial were acquitted.

The rewards offered had no impact at all. No self-respecting digger on any goldfield would hand over their leaders into the hands of the police, the troopers or the government.

and entering a 'forceful action' phase. Humffray had withdrawn, as did other 'moral force' leaders, and Lalor stepped in and filled the vacuum.

The passwords, 'Vinegar Hill',* instigated by Lalor at the stockade represented a partisan political view commensurate with the 'lick in the lug' philosophy.

Commissioner Rede was to remark just before 3 December: 'the license is a mere watchword of the day . . . a mere cloak to cover a democratic revolution'. The British-dominated bureaucracy was ever fearful of rebellion by those they sought to subdue; they had expressed the same views when it seemed that the Californian rush was about to cost them control over Oregon.

It was not only the citizens of Ballarat who showed concern after the events of Sunday, 3 December. The following petition from the citizens of Geelong was sent to Hotham—it would appear that the threat of military rule and continued agitation against such rule would do more to destabilise the wider community than to serve it:

> To His worship the Mayor of Geelong—Sir,—we, the undersigned inhabitants of Geelong request that you will convene a public meeting, to petition His Excellency Sir Charles Hotham at once to set aside the

* Vinegar Hill refers to a disastrous engagement during the Irish uprising of 1798. After the decimation of the English military by a body of armed peasants at Oulont Hill, near Wexford, the peasants were soundly defeated at Vinegar Hill. The rebel leaders were arrested, convicted and transported to Van Diemen's Land.

The Trial on 22 February 1855
(Picture Collection, State Library of Victoria)

One hundred and twenty men were arrested following the defeat of the diggers at the stockade. Only thirteen were brought to trial in Melbourne, charged with treason.

Of these, Thomas Dignum, Timothy Hayes, John Manning, William Molloy, John Phelan and Michael Tuhey [sic] were of Irish descent.

They were brought before Chief Justice Sir William Beckett, as was the Italian Raffaello Carboni, and the African American, John Joseph.

The contemporary engraving published in *The Age* newspaper, 10 March 1855, shows those brought to trial together in the dock.

They are from the left:

1. Timothy Hayes
2. James McFie Campbell
3. Raffaello Carboni
4. Jacob Sorenson
5. John Manning
6. John Phelan
7. Thomas Dignum
8. John Joseph
9. James Beattie
10. William Molloy
11. Jan Vennick
12. Michael Tuhey
13. Henry Read

> present licensing system of the diggings; convinced as we are that all the troubles and bloodshed that menace this colony originate in the manner in which such system is carried out. We publicly profess our loyalty to the throne, and our intention is to support the law; but our hearts bleed for the sufferings of our fellow-colonists at the diggings.

The *Mount Alexander Mail* of Monday, 11 December, carried a report of the 'greatest meeting that ever was held in Castlemaine' which 'took place on Saturday last'. After this meeting, held only a few days after the fall of the Eureka stockade, the *Mail* reported:

> That as the legislature have taken no satisfactory steps to redress the grievances of the residents on the Goldfields, this meeting protests against the injury done them, and resolves to take out no more

The Acquittal of all Prisoners
Engraving from *Illustrated Australian News*, 1887
(Picture Collection, State Library of Victoria)

Jan Vennick, one of the diggers arrested and charged with treason after the battle at Eureka is lifted above the crowd, following his acquittal.

The juries refused to convict any of those brought before the courts. They did however manage to convict Henry Seekamp, the former editor of the *Ballarat Times*, who was charged for inciting the rebellion and jailed for the crime of sedition.

Lalor was never brought before the courts. He was taken into hiding where he remained until all of his compatriots had been freed.

In the aftermath of the whole affair both Lalor and Humffray were elected to the Victorian parliament, where they continued the push for further reform of the goldfields administration. Carboni was appointed to the post of mining warden—a popular choice among the diggers.

> licenses for gold digging, and to quietly abide the consequences; and as it is necessary that the diggers know their friends every miner agrees to wear as a pledge of good faith, and in support of the cause, a piece of red ribbon on his hat, not to be removed until the License-tax is abolished.

Denovan also addressed this meeting, wishing to encourage Castlemaine to unite with Ballarat, Bendigo and the Reform League, and to continue the fight against Hotham. The spark of rebellion that had begun at Forest Creek in December 1851 was not going to be allowed to be extinguished. The 'Red-ribbon' Rebellion was about to join with the spirit of Eureka, and set its course to deny the Governor his taxes yet again.

Of the 120 diggers arrested after Eureka the courts brought only thirteen to trial. The charge of treason was fearful, yet the jury set each man free. The American negro, John Joseph, was tried first and acquitted; he was carried from the court on the shoulders of the crowd. Carboni and Hayes were next to be acquitted.

The Crown law prosecutors advised Hotham that it would be wise to drop further trials, as it was obvious that the jury was intent on freeing each and every man.

Hotham replied that if the juries would not do their duty, he could see no reason for failing to do his. After ten men were set free, Hotham gave up. The case against the 'Eureka rebels' was no longer worth pursuing.

Although there was a reward of £500 for his arrest, Lalor never stood before a judge. Protected by sympathisers, of whom there were many, it was only when an amnesty was granted to all participants in the 'uprising' that he was free to emerge. The diggers had won a great victory over an inept government; they won the right to vote in the new legislative assembly, which was formed in 1855; and Peter Lalor won the right to represent them in the colonial parliament.

The license fee was abolished and replaced with a Miner's Right for an annual fee of £1, and an export levy on gold. This Right gave the diggers title deed to their claims, allowing them to establish permanent dwellings, and a permanent sense of community. Commissioners were replaced with mining wardens, and military rule was abolished on the goldfields.

Hotham lived for only one more year; he died on 31 December 1855. He had been a naval officer of distinction who had inherited an outmoded system already in decline, and an increasingly vocal community demanding to be free. Victoria had been his undoing.

CHAPTER 12

A Law Unto Themselves

Countless stories are recorded in first-hand accounts of the dangers of attack by bushrangers on the roads to and from the diggings.

The simple fact was that 'new chums' fresh from the streets of London, or the green fields of Ireland were walking through the darkened forests, carrying all they owned with them, and it was too great an opportunity for the hundreds of Vandemonians who had come to Victoria. Many an old lag was to make his fortune without ever lifting a shovel.

Polish digger Severyn Korzelinski, while on his way to Mount Alexander, was accompanied for a short distance through the Black Forest by a rather 'well-dressed man . . .with pistols and a revolver in his belt.'[1] He turned out to be a bushranger who eventually took his leave after he discovered that Korzelinski and his party were Polish. He remarked before he galloped away: 'I wouldn't have wasted so much time on you. It's well known that you Poles never have anything'. This was usually true, as most middle Europeans were refugees from their war-ravaged homelands, bringing little with them to this new country.

Most eyewitness accounts of the diggings refer to bushrangers as one of the greatest worries when travelling. Because of this, few chose to travel alone, often teaming up with a bullock driver or others who knew the route and its dangers.

Bushrangers, escaped convicts or men of low character had been active in the region for many years. In fact, when Captain John Hepburn first passed through the area in 1838 he discovered the remains of a convict who had been buried in the sand where two creeks came together [at what is now the town of Castlemaine]. Hepburn recalled later:

> On the brink of the waterhole at the junction of the creeks known as Barker's and Forest Creeks I buried the skull of a prisoner of the Crown who was murdered by his mates after absconding. It was dug

Capture of Bushrangers at Night by Gold Police
Watercolour by George Lacy, c. 1852
(Rex Nan Kivell Collection, R4113. By permission, National Library of Australia)
What a surprise to be so rudely awakened, even the mongrel straining on his leash did not make enough noise to warn these 'wild boys' of the arrival of the goldfields police.

> up by the natives twice, and the third time I buried it in the dry deposit in the waterhole.[2]

Escorts were established to carry the gold from the diggings to the Treasury in Melbourne, yet the government took no responsibility for any loss incurred on the journey. The escorts were heavily armed, but although attacks were frequent most of the gold got through.

It was the lone digger who was easy prey for those with evil intent. Korzelinski remembers seeing ragged skeletons tied to trees on lonely tracks through the forest. Bushrangers would attack lone travellers, taking all they had and leaving the unfortunates to the ants, flies, mosquitoes and other bush creatures. What a miserable end for the unwary or foolish 'new chum', and what a salutary lesson for all those who thought they could go it alone.

On the Ballarat Road, 19 December 1852

Frank McCallum, alias Captain Melville [not to be confused with George Melville] and his companion, William Roberts, held up two diggers, Thomas Wearne and William Madden, on the Ballarat road. Melville relieved them of £33, but gave back £10 as it was close to Christmas and he didn't wish to deprive them of an enjoyable holiday in Geelong. Melville and Roberts made their way on to Geelong, taking what they could from other travellers on the way. They were apprehended on Christmas Eve after they were discovered in a brothel. They had a long list of crimes for which they were wanted, including murder and robberies on the Ovens diggings.

On 3 February 1853 Melville was sentenced to 32 years in gaol for his crimes. He was sent to the hulks in Port Phillip Bay, where he was found strangled in his cell in August 1857. Roberts also got 32 years, and was sent to another hulk, the *President*. He was released on a ticket-of-leave on 19 January 1864.

McIvor Escort Robbery, 20 July 1853

The McIvor Escort was held up fourteen miles out of Kyneton in central Victoria on its way from the McIvor [Heathcote] diggings. The escort was attacked in broad daylight by a large band of bushrangers. They escaped with 2230 ounces of gold.

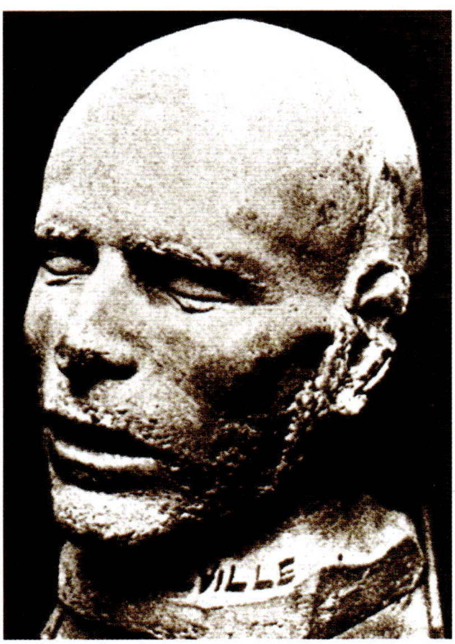

Death mask of George Melville
This cast was taken after the bushranger George Melville was hanged in the Old Melbourne Gaol on 3 October 1853.

Melville was the leader of the gang that robbed the McIvor Escort on 20 July. There are various reports of this daring robbery. Polish digger Korzelinski records:

> during the battle between the immobilised escort and the bushrangers, six members of the escort and two bushrangers were killed. The bushrangers left the field victorious, with 3,000 ounces of gold. I heard later that an expedition of about fifty settlers and merchants went after the bushrangers, surrounded them and caught them, recovering part of the booty.

The details of the number shot differ with each telling, but one thing is certain: that the bush telegraph carried such news far and wide, and no doubt the daring deeds grew a little each time the story was retold.

McIvor Diggings, 25 July 1853
(Picture Collection, State Library of Victoria)
This drawing of diggers gathered around an auctioneer's tent was made only a few days after the attack on the McIvor Escort by a large band of thieves.

A 'digger's intelligencer', a method of advertising, or posting notices, for seeking old friends, or selling goods etc, can be seen on the tree at the centre of the engraving.

This is a lithographic copy of an earlier drawing by Edward La Trobe Bateman, from a year previous, and may have been published as a way of illustrating one aspect of the McIvor robbery.

It took some time for the police to track down the robbers but they were all eventually captured, and three of the band were hanged before a large crowd in Melbourne.

George Melville [shown opposite] took so long to die that the hangman had to pull down on his legs 'with considerable force before life was extinct'.

A reward was posted offering:

> £250 for the apprehension and conviction of the parties who robbed the McIvor Branch of the Escort—and a further sum of £250 for the recovery of the stolen property, or a proportional sum, for the recovery of part thereof.

Most of the gang were captured as they were preparing to leave the country. Only £2501 10s. in gold, notes, sovereigns and bankdrafts was recovered, suggesting that most of it had already been taken out of the colony. Some of those caught committed suicide before being brought to justice; only three of them were tried, convicted, and sent to the gallows.

Hold-up of the Gold Escort [A Bush Hold-up]
Pen and wash drawing by William Strutt, c. 1855
(National Library of Australia Collection)

One of the victims of the hold-up later described his attackers:

> . . . you might see them starting on a campaign, on the great roads leading out of Melbourne to the Mines. There are a pair of them, well mounted, and wrapped up in great coats, they have a quiet reserved air, and keep a little aloof from the main line of traffic. They always go armed with loaded revolvers; but these are kept concealed.[3]

The bushrangers [William Atkins, George Wilson and George Melville] were executed before a large crowd on Monday, 3 October 1853. Melville's wife took his body and displayed it, decorated with flowers, in the window of an oyster shop in Bourke Street, Melbourne, where they had been living. This added attraction brought hundreds to the shop out of morbid curiosity. Whether it did much for business is unknown, but after that ghoulish display the bodies of those executed were buried within prison walls.

The threat of such punishment did little to deter the determined bushranger. So many old lags were abroad in the bush, and so many had suffered such indignities from transportation, floggings and deprivations of all kinds, that the long arm of the law held no fears for them.

Such felons were past redemption and often past caring; they had been taught that their own lives held little value, and they cared little for the lives of others. John Chandler's diaries* record an encounter with some poor unfortunate travellers who had the misfortune to make the acquaintance of a notorious bushranger:

> In the morning we saw some who had been stuck up; they were camped on the road. Captain Moonlight [sic] and the others had taken all their money, revolvers, ammunition, and whatever they wanted, leaving them without money to buy provisions.
>
> He stuck up every one along the road, and the troopers seemed to keep well out of his way. It was not far from this place where they robbed the escort a year or two before, and killed some of the troopers.
>
> We unloaded and got safe back with our money. I put my money in a leather bag and when we camped, I dug a little hole in the ground and put the bag into it, and then drew my dray wheel on top, keeping some in my pocket so as not to raise suspicion, for if they thought you planted it, they would have shot you in a moment.
>
> Moonlight was captured soon after, and he committed suicide in gaol.[4]

'Mad Dan' Morgan

Morgan kept a butcher's 'shambles' at Barker's Creek, near Castlemaine. He was often seen in the town, accompanied by his white bulldog. He was arrested only once in all his long bushranging career, for the robbery of a hawker on the Castlemaine goldfields in 1854.

---

* There may be some confusion in this report by Chandler about the identity of the particular bushranger.

Andrew Scott, alias Captain Moonlite, did range the Victorian goldfields; he robbed the London Chartered Bank at Mt Egerton in Victoria of £1000, after befriending, and tricking the young local bank agent 18-year-old Ludwig Brunn.

Frank McCallum, alias Captain Melville, also made a nuisance of himself around the Victorian diggings, and it is recorded that he strangled himself with a neckerchief in his prison cell in August 1857. The other Melville, George, robbed the McIvor Gold Escort, and he did die on the gallows.

It does seem that Chandler in writing his diaries has confused the Captains, the Moonlites and the Melvilles, and attributed this crime to poor old Andrew Scott although he was not active for at least another decade.

What is in no doubt is that those on the road were well aware of who was about, who to look out for, and who to avoid.

The niceties of formal introduction may well have been eschewed once the bullets started to fly.

MORGAN, THE BUSHRANGER. — SEE PAGE 10.

Left: *Andrew George Scott a.k.a. Captain Moonlite*
(Police Records Victoria Collection)

Andrew Scott was probably schizophrenic. He was well-educated and well-liked, and made friends easily, particularly of impressionable young men. At Mt Egerton, in Victoria in 1869, he practised as a lay preacher, and as an engineer, then robbed the bank.

He requested that after his execution in Darlinghurst Prison on 20 January 1880 his body be laid in the same grave as his young accomplice James Nesbitt, but the authorities refused. 115 years later he was exhumed from Rookwood cemetery and buried alongside Nesbitt in Gundagai.

Right: *Morgan, the bushranger*
Wood engraving by Samuel Calvert
(National Library of Australia Collection)

Morgan earned the nickname 'Mad Dan' because of his seemingly wanton brutality and unpredictable nature—one moment charming, the next viciously brutal.

He was sentenced by Judge Redmond Barry to twelve years' hard labour, the first two to be spent in irons. He always protested his innocence of the crime for which he had been convicted, and on his release on a ticket-of-leave in 1860 he began a long and bloody campaign of revenge against the police and the society that had incarcerated him. He ranged far and wide, and clocked up a huge number of heinous crimes that were attributed to him. He was eventually surrounded by police and killed in a shoot-out at Peechelba Station on the Ovens River on 9 April 1865.

After photographers and artists made a record of his corpse a ghoulish mutilation followed: the head was severed at the request of the Coroner, Dr Dobbyn, who wanted it for scientific research; locks of his hair were souvenired; and his facial skin and hair flayed from the flesh for Police Superintendent Cobham so he could 'peg it out and dry it like a possum skin'; his scrotum was removed for use as a money pouch. The police were disgusted by such unseemly souvenir hunting.

The public treated Morgan in death as poorly as he had treated those whom he had murdered. He was a curiosity, feared in life, and humiliated in defeat.

Bank of Victoria Robbery Ballarat, 16 October 1854

Four digger mates walked into the Bank of Victoria on Bakery Hill, and, with unloaded pistols, held up the clerk at the counter. They walked out with 350 oz gold and about £14,300 in banknotes.

Henry Garrett, a stonemason from Geelong, and diggers Henry Marriott, Thomas Quinn and John Boulton had planned the robbery the previous day in their tent at the Gravel Pits. The robbery was bold and brazen, and went very smoothly for them; they then divided the money and the gold between them, and went their separate ways. Garrett went south immediately, boarding a ship bound for England; Quinn and Boulton went to Melbourne, where they sold their share of the gold to the London Chartered Bank; Marriott stayed in lodgings in Ballarat. It was not before long that their daring cheek bought them undone. Quinn and Boulton returned to Ballarat, where Boulton went back to the Bank of Victoria and attempted to draw a draft on London for £1,450. He tried to use some of the money he had stolen, was identified, delayed, and captured.

It was one down and three to go, and the police rounded up Marriott and Quinn very soon after. By this time Garrett was 'safe' in England, but the Victorian police traced him there. The story goes that he was bailed up by Detective Henry Webb in the streets of London when Webb used the Australian bush cry of 'coo-ee' [others suggest Webb simply yelled out 'Garrett']; either way, Garrett gave himself away, and was brought back to Australia where he received a ten-year sentence.

When he was released on a ticket-of-leave in 1861, he travelled to the New Zealand goldfields, and was soon up to his old tricks. Garrett was considered by many to be the first New Zealand bushranger.

Black Douglas

One name featured prominently in the records of many a traveller on the roads to and from the diggings, and that name was Black Douglas.

A Butcher's Shambles nr. Adelaide Gully at Forest Creek
Lithograph by S. T. Gill, Macartney & Galbraith, Melbourne, 1852
(Rex Nan Kivell Collection, U991. By Permission, National Library of Australia

It is not hard to imagine that the character depicted could well be Morgan with his bulldog by his side. Castlemaine pioneer Walter Wilson recalled seeing Morgan in the town:

> I knew Morgan well by sight . . . on Sundays he used to visit the Robert Burns Hotel. He had invariably a white bull-dog with him, and it and its master seemed a sulky pair.[5]

Castlemaine Pioneers Hughes and Ottey recalled the first time they walked the track to Mount Alexander:

> . . . on the second day we entered the Black Forest, noted then as the haunt of the celebrated 'Black Douglas'.[6]
>
> . . . before we started next morning we heard of bushrangers, Black Douglas and his gang were about, and as the majority of us were armed we felt pretty plucky . . . I think if anyone had looked black at us we would have done a bit of shooting, but if, on the other hand a revolver had been pointed at us, I have my doubts of the pluck holding out.[7]

Douglas was a powerfully-built negro who had jumped ship at Port Phillip. He and his bushranging band made their headquarters at Alma, near Maryborough. They were supposed to be working on the diggings, but made their gold by stealing from tents and shops. This was easy work, as tents were left untended during the day and the shops at night. They would create a disturbance in front of a shop late at night and, when the owner came to see what was going on out front, others would slit the rear canvas wall and help themselves.

Owing to a cost-cutting measure and the resultant reduced presence of police on the goldfields, diggers were eventually forced to band together in mutual protection societies, just as their digger brothers had done in California years before. At Alma they took the law into their own hands. One night they surrounded Douglas and his cronies, tied them up, and burnt their tents. Douglas put up a good fight, but was overpowered. He was sent by cart to Maryborough, but several hundred miners, taking no chances, escorted him there.

There are several versions of the demise of Black Douglas. Severyn Korzelinski recorded that Douglas was taken from Maryborough to Melbourne, and hanged. Richard Thimbleby, a digger at Diamond Gully near Castlemaine, recalled that Douglas was captured in 1855 at Fryer's Creek, where he was taken into the hospital at the Castlemaine Camp [Thimbleby was himself in the hospital with 'brain fever' after sticking his head in a bucket of water to cool down]. He wrote in his letter to *The Castlemaine Pioneers and Old Residents* that Isaac George, the hospital warder, keen to take a look at the notorious bushranger, had left the door to the small wooden building unlocked, and Black Douglas disappeared. From the same collection of letters another wrote 'that notorious robber, Black Douglas' was chained to the logs at Pennyweight Flat alongside sixteen other diggers who had been apprehended for being without a license.

Yet another claimed that Douglas was apprehended following an unsuccessful series of raids on groups of diggers who were taking their gold to Melbourne. The diggers were well prepared for such a raid; they had replied to Douglas's intentions with muskets and pistols. Douglas and his band were taken by troopers the following day while attacking a roadside inn. This report states that Douglas was 'sentenced to fourteen years but is impossible to confirm as records of his trial and punishment have long since disappeared'.

Whether hanged or shot, captured or chained to the logs, Douglas seems to have at least captured the imagination and incited the fears of countless travellers on those lonely roads. The name 'Black Douglas' was feared by all who entered the Black Forest and his demise the stuff of legend.

The Eugowra Escort Robbery NSW, 15 June 1862

The Lachlan Escort was held up by Frank Gardiner and his gang near Eugowra, 27 miles from Forbes. When the coach slowed to pass some bullock drays at the edge of the roadway, the gang of eight men, all with blackened faces and wearing red serge shirts, appeared alongside. One of the gang shouted 'Fire', and a volley of shots splintered the walls of the coach. The horses took fright and bolted, capsizing the coach. Three of the police guard were wounded in the brief exchange of fire, others took to the bush for refuge. The gang escaped with gold boxes containing 2717 oz gold, £3700 in cash, and several mailbags. The haul was worth over £14,000.

Gardiner had some notorious accomplices that day: Johnny Gilbert, Harry Manns, John Bow, Alexander Fordyce, Dan Charters, Johnny O'Meally, Charles Darcy, and the charismatic Ben Hall. The news of the robbery—it was the biggest and boldest holdup in Australia's history—caused a sensation. Gardiner escaped north with Ben Hall's sister-in-law, Katherine, the wife of settler John Brown. They opened a store in Aphis Creek, Queensland where he went straight—for a time. In fact, while he was there he was so well regarded that local diggers left their finds with him for safe-keeping. In March 1864 the police, following a trail left by Katherine, finally tracked him to Aphis Creek. On 17 May 1864 Frank Gardiner was sentenced, at last, in the Central Criminal Court in Sydney to a total of 32 years.

Gardiner served only ten years before the government reviewed the harsh sentences dealt to those at this earlier, tougher period of colonial rule. He was pardoned by

'Bold Ben Hall'
Cart de visite by Freeman Brothers, Sydney, 1863
(Mitchell Library Collection, State Library of New South Wales)

25 year-old Ben Hall had a cattle farm near Wheoga, a wife and a young son, when he was arrested with Frank Gardiner on suspicion of a wagon hold-up near Forbes.

He was held in gaol for a month before the charges were dismissed. When he returned to his farm, he discovered that his wife had run off with a policeman, his house was burnt and his cattle gone.

He took his revenge on the roads around Forbes until he was killed on 6 May 1865. His body was riddled with between fifteen and 30 bullet holes.

Bailed Up
Oil on canvas by Tom Roberts, 1895
(Art Gallery of New South Wales Collection)

This painting was inspired by both a story Roberts had heard when he was painting his famous *Shearing the Rams* at a sheep station near Inverell, NSW, and reports of the Eugowra robbery. Roberts decided to create an imaginary image of an event from the 'wild colonial' days.

Inverell's Cobb & Co. coach driver, 'Silent-Bob Bates', had been held up by the notorious bushranger Captain Thunderbolt in the 1860s. His retelling of the story, in his typically laconic style, was the inspiration for the relaxed attitude of the bushrangers and the occupants of the coach.

For accuracy, Roberts painted the landscape background on the Eugowra road near where the escort had been attacked.

Roberts had a platform constructed by the side of the road where he was able to work 'plein-air' in comparative comfort.

The finished painting never met with approval from the colonial authorities who thought that Roberts' depiction of the casual attitude of the bushrangers who seemingly have attacked this coach as if they are all on a pleasant outing together in the bush, combined with the response of the young lady in the coach who is obviously captivated by the charm of her 'attacker', did little to show the real terrors of such an event and the criminal behaviour of the so-called 'Lords of the Bush'.

Henry Parkes in 1874, but was exiled to China. He sailed as far as Hong Kong, hopped on an American ship, and landed in San Francisco.

Ironically, it was in San Francisco that vigilante groups had formed only a few years earlier to rid that town of the 'Sydney Ducks', the notorious groups of 'old lags' from Australia in the rough'n'ready days

Left: *Frank 'Darkie' Gardiner*
(Private Collection)

Gardiner rode onto the Kiandra goldfields in 1859 on a stolen horse. There he ran a butcher's shop, selling meat to the hungry diggers. He found it easier to steal his meat than buy it, and was eventually arrested for cattle duffing in January 1861. He stood before the magistrate, was bailed, and absconded from the district in May.

His derring-do and spectacular robberies gave him the status of folk legend; after many adventures he was eventually imprisoned, pardoned and deported.

His was exiled to China but absconded yet again, and ended up in California, where he apparently settled down and ran a saloon in San Francisco.

Right: *Johnny Gilbert*
(Private Collection)

John 'The Canadian' Gilbert was a dashing young man who knew the Kellys, rode with Gardiner and Ben Hall, and is immortalised as 'Jack Marsden' in Rolf Boldrewood's classic novel *Robbery Under Arms.*

He was killed by police on 13 May 1865, and lies buried on a hillside near Binalong, NSW, in what was once the police paddock.

of that Californian province. Times must have changed. Gardiner, under the assumed name of Frank Smith, set up in business and opened a saloon, the Twilight Star, on Kearney Street. There are several versions of Gardiner's demise: the most romantic in a 'penny-western' setting is that he was shot in a gambling fight in Colorado, another less so, that he died from pneumonia in 1904.

Gardiner, Gilbert and Hall had all been at Lambing Flat (Young, New South Wales) in the heart of the Riverina district of central New South

The Way Her Majesty's Mails & the Public Protectors Are Served in New South Wales
Hand-coloured lithograph, Paul Jerrard & Son, for Messrs Newbold & Co., London, c. 1860, from *Sketches of Australian Life and Scenery*, after a drawing by S. T. Gill
(Rex Nan Kivell Collection, U2820. By Permission, National Library of Australia)

Wales where 'not less than five hundred of the most notorious thieves, forgers, foot-pads, gamblers, horse-stealers and escaped convicts' had gathered on those remote diggings.

It is no surprise that this group of hot-heads, so far away from the reach of the law, was almost uncontrollable when they decided to take action against the Chinese in 1861. The notorious scoundrels, Gardiner, Gilbert and Hall, who revelled in their notoriety, were eventually hunted down, one by one, and shot, imprisoned or deported.

Gilbert lies in a lonely grave near Binalong, shot at the age of 25 by police. Hall, aged 28, shot by police who had been led to his bush hide-away by his former friend, black-tracker Billy Dargin, lies in Forbes cemetery.

Lynch Law & Larrikins: The Wild Colonial Boys

One of the greatest fears on the Australian goldfields was that the diggers would adopt the American style of summary justice, known as

Diggers of Low Degree
Lithograph by S. T. Gill, H. H. Collins & Co., London, 1853
(Rex Nan Kivell Collection, S170. By Permission, National Library of Australia)
There were plenty of unsavoury characters on the goldfields. Other diggers were wise to keep their eyes open and their powder dry.

'lynch law'. The Californian goldfields had been well out of the reach of the law; as a consequence the diggers there took it upon themselves to dispense their own brand of rough justice. Many an unfortunate miscreant was taken and strung up, with few questions asked.

Vigilante groups had formed in the Californian seaports to deal with the criminal element that had washed up on their shores. Prominent among them were scores of old lags from Van Diemen's Land and ex-convicts from Sydney, none of whom had any respect for either life or the law.

Miscreants from New South Wales earned the nickname 'Sydney Ducks' and roving gangs of escapees from the antipodean colonies soon fell foul of the Californian vigilantes. Summary justice was meted out to a few old lags unlucky enough to be in the wrong place at the wrong time; several swung from the gallows beam as an example to others.

The first trial and execution by the vigilantes in San Francisco was carried out on 10 June 1851. John Jenkins, from Sydney, was arrested after he stole a safe from a store on the wharf. He was captured, tried and strung up at two o'clock in the morning, on the same night that his crime had been committed. He was given little time to reflect on his crime, but was allowed a cigar and a shot of brandy before he felt the noose around his neck.

At this time California was governed by politicians to the east of the Rockies. The United States was a democratic republic, whereas Australia was still under military rule. It must have been a pleasant surprise for 'Australians' to find such a freewheeling democratic society, but then a shock to discover how swift and decisive was American summary justice when the citizens took control of their own safety.

Just as in California, crime on the Victorian diggings was rife and the police so incompetent that protection committees were formed, and swift justice dealt to those who offended. Murder, robbery, horse stealing, claim jumping, hold-ups, shootings and beatings were common. The prudent diggers stuck close to one another, and kept their powder dry, just in case they were called on to defend themselves.

W. H. Wilson wrote on 26 September 1890:

> One Sunday night, while the five of us were lying down in the same tent, we heard footsteps coming towards us, the opening was thrust aside and a man stepped inside with a revolver in his hand and said 'Bail up!' An old soldier was lying near the opening and sang out:– 'He's a bushranger!' and seized the intruder by the legs. This sudden act threw the scoundrel, and as he fell his

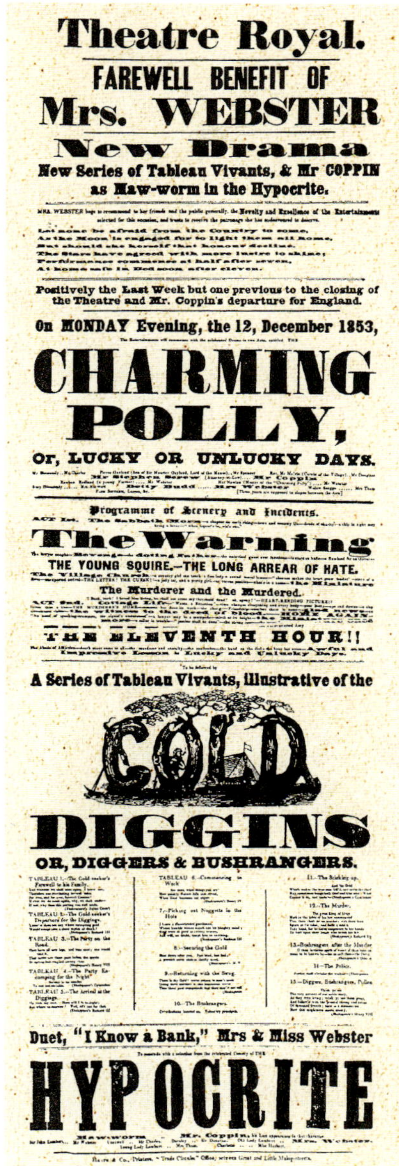

Theatre Poster, 12 December 1853
A full evening of entertainment is promised on this Monday night at Melbourne's Theatre Royal.

Well down the programme is offered a *Series of Tableau Vivants, illustrative of the Gold Diggins*—a series of short plays which begin with: The Digger's Farewell to his family; then Travelling to the diggings; On the road; Camping Out; Arriving at the diggings; Digging for nuggets; Heading back to town with a full swag; Attack by Bush-rangers; Sticking-up; A Murder and dealing with the Police.

When told together these little incidents reflected the common experience of all who took the same path. The bushranger attack and its consequences, must have been so common to have made up almost half, and probably the most dramatic half, of the play.

> revolver flew out of his hand and on to my stretcher. We secured the fellow with rope, whipped him and kicked him almost to a jelly.[8]

Judge Barry, in sentencing the felon to 15 years, complained of the brutal treatment meted out to the unfortunate miscreant. The old soldier replied that 'the next time he saw a bushranger he would kill him if he could'.

Beatings of this kind were common, yet there is only one instance where an American-style lynching has been recorded. A Vandemonian was captured by diggers after he had killed his partner when they were divvying up their gold. Although he pleaded to be taken to the Commissioner for trial, he never made it. He was taken and strung up

The First Trial and Execution in San Francisco (California) on the Night of 10th of June at 2 o'clock (1851)
W. C. K. (artist), Justh, Quirot & Co. (lithographer & publisher)
(Rex Nan Kivell Collection, S10127. By Permission, National Library of Australia)

The caption to this lithograph reads as follows:

> John Jenkins, a Sidney [sic] man, entered the store of McV on long Wharf in the evening of 10th of June & carried off a safe. After he was captured he was brought to the corner of Sansomie & Bush Sts. where he was tried by a jury of the highest respectability, and condemned to hang.
>
> The execution took place on the Plaza on the same night at 2 o'clock.
>
> Immediately after sentence of death was passed upon him he was asked if he had anything to say, he replied: No, I have nothing to say, only I wish to have a cigar & brandy & water, which was given him.

to the nearest tree. More than 4000 diggers gave the murdered man a solemn burial, then cut down his killer, threw him in a hole, and covered him with dirt.

It seems that the crime of stealing from a mate was the worst of all possible offences, against the ideals of mateship, dependence and trust, born on the goldfields. There were many other incidents where diggers nearly met their Maker at the end of a rope:

BOURKE STREET WEST IN THE FORENOON.

Bourke Street West in the Forenoon
Wood engraving by Frederick Grosse from *Australian News for Home Readers*, 24 March 1864
(Rex Nan Kivell Collection, S920. By Permission, National Library of Australia)

The diggings brought all kinds together, and there were plenty of young men, full of vigour, bursting with high spirits and pockets filled with gold, who wanted to do nothing more than to spend both their energy and their money—and most of all to impress anyone who cared to watch their antics.

William Howitt commented rather disparagingly of the goings-on in the streets of Melbourne:

> The whole street swarms with diggers and diggeresses. Men in slouching wide-awakes with long untrimmed hair and beards, and like navvies in their costume. Some have horse-whips in their hands, and are looking at the exploits of other diggers on horseback with a knowing air.

Although the engraving shown does not necessarily depict bushrangers or criminals in action, yet the 'wild colonial boys' illustrated here care little for the niceties of society or for the arm of the law.

This same freewheeling, devil-may-care, larrikin streak has always been part of the Australian character, where every man is equal as long as he has enough money to prove it.

> . . . we wandered about Forest Creek. We had not gone far before a digger with a pistol in his hand shot by us; he was followed by an immense mob, hooting, yelling, and screaming, as only a mob on the diggings can. It was in full pursuit, and we turned aside only in time to prevent ourselves from being knocked down in the confusion. 'Stop him—stop him', was the cry. He was captured, and the cry changed to, 'String him up—string him up—it's useless taking him to the police-office'.

When asked of the mob what the man had done the reply was that: '[He had] shot a man in a quarrel at a grog-shop'.

The mob continued to howl for justice:

> String him up—string him up—confront him with the body, . . . at this moment the firmly secured and well-guarded culprit passed by, to be confronted by the dead body of his adversary. No sooner did he come into his presence than the corpse found his feet, 'showed fight', and roared out, 'Come on', with a most unghostlike vehemence.[9]

It appears that the pistol shot had simply grazed his forehead, and no serious injury was sustained. The fugitive took advantage of the lull in the proceedings, and 'declared that the wounded man had been robbing him'. The tables had now turned, and the 'dead man' took to his heels and disappeared into the bush.

Although there were many who would have been prepared to shoot first and ask questions later, a large number of practising lawyers offered swift recourse to the protection of the law when it was desired. The legal system in place on the goldfields may have frustrated the diggers for most of the time, but it must have also saved many from an unlawful demise.

The Escorts

Gold was carried from the diggings to the Treasury by way of armed escort. One of the most remarkable was the escort under the command of the redoubtable South Australian Chief of Police, Alexander Tolmer, who carried huge amounts of gold from the Victorian diggings back to the Adelaide Treasury. Tolmer battled against swamps, floods and bandits as he opened up the overland route.

Much of the gold Tolmer carried was won by South Australian diggers who consigned their nuggets back to the South Australian Treasury,

Gold Escort attacked by bushrangers
From *The History of Australasia* by David Blair. Published by McGready, Thomson & Niver, Edinburgh, 1873
(Rex Nan Kivell collection, NK3449. By permission, National Library of Australia)

Daring robberies made for exciting news in the days of gold in the same way that such escapades, and their protagonists, feature prominently in the popular media of today.

Although published in Edinburgh some twenty years after the event this lithograph, including a misplaced exotic palm-tree, recalls the murderous attack on the McIvor Escort in July 1853. More than eighty years after the attack, the *Argus* newspaper [22 February 1936] was still arguing over the details; where one journalist had written: 'the escort turned and fled without firing a shot', adding, 'from behind [a] mia-mia six men emerged, each armed with a double--barrelled gun' and all wearing 'overcoats of uniform make and colour', another writer had observed that:

> Eleven ex-convicts formed an ambuscade on a narrow section of the road just beyond the Campaspe crossing. As the horses carrying the gold came on with three troopers riding on each side a volley ran out from a screen of boughs and foliage. Four troopers fell and the other two replied from a distance till their ammunition was exhausted. They then went for assistance. One bushranger placed a pistol against the breast of a fallen trooper and shot him through the lungs. All the troopers recovered, though the bushrangers left them for dead.

Whatever the details; the story, and the subsequent, but foiled, attempt by the robbers to escape with all their loot on the ill-fated *Madagascar*, was just the sort of narrative to excite the public imagination.

Postscript: On that voyage out from Port Phillip on 23 July 1853, the 835 ton, full-rigged frigate *Madagascar* disappeared without trace carrying more than 60,000 ounces of gold, a large cargo of Australian wool, passengers and crew.

Dangerously Suspicious
Lithograph by S. T. Gill, 1852–3
(Mortlake Library Collection, State Library of Victoria)
A pair of ruffians wait by the side of the track ready to greet any unwary digger heading back to Melbourne with pockets filled with gold.

which at the time gave the diggers a higher price for their gold than could be gained in Melbourne.

In fact there was such a severe shortage of sterling left in Adelaide after half of the population had taken off for the diggings, that South Australia was almost bankrupt. The South Australian Government Assay Office began to mint its own coins under the Bullion Act, which they believed allowed them to exercise the Royal Prerogative of Coining if 'urgent necessity exists'.

The first escort from the diggings was despatched to Adelaide in November 1851 carrying 94,000 ounces of gold.

In January 1852 the first escort to Melbourne arrived at the Gold Offices in William Street. There was great excitement as three heavily laden drays drew up to discharge their precious cargo. Each dray carried two boxes of gold, each of which had to be carried into the office by six men. After only three months since the declaration of the goldfields at Mount Alexander that week's deposit at the gold office was 105,000 ounces. The following day almost all of the staff of clerks and draftsmen in Hoddle's Survey Office resigned and set off to try their luck at the diggings.

In July seven drays, 17 foot soldiers and six troopers delivered 83,582 ounces to Melbourne. Between May and December 1852 the South Australian Escort carried 224,220 ounces out of Mount Alexander and a further 363,384 ounces were taken to Melbourne.

The escorts were constantly in danger of attack from bushrangers who lurked along every highway waiting for an unguarded moment.

The McIvor Escort, carrying gold from the diggings east of Bendigo, had been robbed of 2230 ounces on 20 July 1853 and on 15 June 1862 the Lachlan Escort had been attacked near Eugowra, 2717 ounces and £3700

Arrival of the Gold Escort in Melbourne
Watercolour by William Strutt
(State Parliamentary Library Collection, Victoria)
Carrying the chests into the Treasury, Spring Street; from sketch taken from nature in 1851 [*sic*].

in cash was taken. There are numerous other reports of the escorts coming under attack on the roads, yet the huge amount of gold carried compared with the small amount stolen indicates that the escort remained the safest way diggers could get their gold to the Treasury.

CHAPTER 13

The Celestials

'Rule Britannia! Britannia rule the waves!
No more Chinamen allowed in New South Wales!'
—cry heard across the New South Wales diggings

'No Chinese – Roll Up! Roll Up!'
—cry heard at Lambing Flat, 30 June 1861

The industrious Chinese had always been ready to supply much-needed labour wherever there was demand. In California, as on the Australian east coast, the Chinese had sold their labour well before the discovery of gold.

On 2 February 1848 the brig *Eagle* landed the first ship-load of Chinese workers in San Francisco. They had sailed to California not to dig for gold but to till other fields. It was much the same story in Victoria. One hundred and fifty Chinese labourers had been working for the squatters around Port Phillip long before the gold rush, but once the discoveries were known they too joined in the rush to the diggings.

In both California and Australia the Chinese applied their muscle to the goldfields with as much energy as any other man, and at times with more diligence and a level-headed dedication that was often wanting in the Europeans.

By 1850 tens of thousands of Chinese were in California, yet an official census taken in March 1854 counted only 2000 in Victoria, although in that year thirty-seven shiploads had landed in Australia. In 1855 sixty-one ships disembarked their human cargo. By the end of 1855 Victoria enacted legislation to curb Oriental emigration. The Victorian government imposed a levy of £10 per head on each Chinese arrival, and limited the number to one Chinese per ten tons of shipping.

The *Act to Make Provision for Certain Immigrants*, proclaimed on 24 October 1857, was a purposely created device to halt Chinese immigration.

Chinatown, Creswick, c. 1894
Oil painting by Percy Lindsay
(Percy Lindsay, Chinatown, Creswick, c. 1894, oil on canvas, 30.8 × 46.0 cm, Collection: Art Gallery of Ballarat. Gift of Enid Gourley and Molly Elder)

Forty years after the first rush was all but over many Chinese remained on the diggings, although their rough shacks built in the early days appear, in this painting by Creswick-born artist Percy Lindsay, quite a bit the worse for wear by the end of the century.

After the gold had run out the Chinese turned readily to market gardening; they excelled in furniture manufacture, became merchants, importers and exporters—integrating themselves into all aspects of Australian society.

There are few goldfields towns in Australia today which do not recognise the legacy of their enterprise today, few towns whose citizens do not count among them generations of Australian-born, almond-eyed descendants of 'The Celestials' who stayed.

Along with restricted entry into Victoria, the Act also empowered the government to collect a fee of £4 from all Chinese working and living in the colony. This did not stop the flood of Chinese migration; ship-owners simply sailed a little further west and landed their cargo in South Australia. By the end of 1857 more than 14,000 Chinese had landed at Guichen Bay, near Robe in South Australia, and made their way overland to the diggings. The Act had failed in its intention.

The Victorian government sought to put pressure on South Australia and New South Wales to agree to similar legislation. South Australia fell into line, but New South Wales left the gates open for cheap 'coolie' labour.

The Chinese still poured into Australia, this time through New South Wales, and by the end of the 1850s their number had grown to

Off to the Diggings – Flemington near Melbourne
Watercolour by Samuel Brees, c. 1856
(Picture collection, State Library of Victoria)

An almost-unbroken line of Chinese diggers pass the Flemington Hotel, heading for the Mount Alexander diggings near Castlemaine. This scene can be contrasted with images of Europeans making the same journey, where, although many banded together for mutual protection it was essentially 'every man for himself'.

The communal enterprise of the Chinese can be seen in this drawing, each man taking his turn, making his progress along with every other person, moving purposefully towards their collective goal. It was this sort of behaviour that separated the Chinese from others, and they were resented for it; as well as for the difference in their eating habits, their religion, their clothing, their bamboo hats, their pigtails, their opium smoking, their hard work, their diligence.

The following description from the *Annals of Bendigo* describes a Chinese Camp, 'of over 1000 souls', that stretched along Bridge Street near the Bendigo Creek:

> The village was of an oblong form, through the centre of which ran one main street, consisting of between fifty and sixty buildings . . . there were a number of cross and back lanes, all very narrow . . . the streets and lanes were kept pretty clean, but in some of the back slums there were disgusting and unwholesome collections of rubbish and filth, and the attempts which had been made at drainage had been very defective so much so that most of the drains had become a highly offensive nuisance.
>
> An inspection of the various dwellings was extremely interesting. There were gambling-houses, joss-houses, eating-houses, and smoking-shops, as well as private habitations. A cook-shop was of considerable size, a novel description of building, being a tent of two stories, and an inspection of the arrangements occupied some time. Cooking operations on an extensive scale were being carried on the ground floor and in the adjoining kitchens. Tables were laid out in the lower story, and the upper one seemed devoted to persons of the bettermost class.

In an attempt to control what he thought were evil practices among Chinese men Governor Hotham had demanded from the Consuls in Chinese ports that an equal number of Chinese women migrate with the men, and proposed an extra tax on 'single' male migrants that would be levied on the shipowners who carried them.

However, there were only two Chinese women in the Colony of New South Wales, and only one is recorded on the Bendigo diggings. The Governor believed that almost 40,000. Considering how poorly they were treated by both the government and the Caucasian diggers, it may seem surprising that they continued to come. For them it was not a great colonial adventure, they came as a form of indentured labour, working for labour-supply contractors, paying off their debts against their earnings. This type of contract arrangement was described by Sir Henry Parkes, who himself had little affection for the Chinese, as 'nothing short of slave labour'.

Reports at the time suggested an almost unbroken line of Chinese, carrying their goods slung from bamboo poles across their shoulders, that stretched from South Australia to the central Victorian diggings. One observer recalled: 'They were winding across the plain like a long black mark, and as I passed them every one behind seemed to be yabbering to his mate in a sing-song tone'.

On the early diggings, when gold was plentiful, the Chinese were largely left to themselves. They were industrious, working together in gangs and sharing all they had. They worked the poorer ground left abandoned by the European diggers, who were ever ready to rush away to new finds. The Chinese picked meticulously over these untended claims, often recovering more gold than was ever taken by the previous owner.

It was when the easy gold became scarce that the Chinese began to be openly resented by the Europeans, especially those who tried to return to their abandoned claims, to find them being worked successfully by the 'Celestials'. It was not long before the European diggers sought to reclaim the territory they believed belonged to them.

Chartist William Denovan, the diggers' leader at Bendigo, was foremost in showing his discrimination against the Chinese. In July 1854 he had attempted to bring the diggers at Bendigo together *en masse* to drive the Chinese from that field. He had chosen 4 July for the expulsion,

---

the Chinese indulged in sexual practices of the darkest kind, and was fearful that all-male emigration would corrupt the youth of the colony. He believed that:

> the goldfields will be trained in vice and profligacy, and the moral growth of the colony blighted.

Yet the Chinese fascinated the Europeans. They offered a taste of the exotic and the unusual. In their camps all sorts of recreational services were on offer, from prostitution [they employed European girls] to the pleasure of the pipe.

From the *Annals of Bendigo*:

> Opium smoking seemed to be carried on in almost every shop and dwelling, and, truth to say, there was the smell of opium everywhere and in everything throughout the whole encampment . . . Several men were seen overcome by the narcotic, apparently in a deep and quiet sleep.[1]

Diggers savour the delights of Chinatown
The Chinese provided plenty of diversion for the European diggers, for most it was an exotic trip into forbidden pleasures.

but after he was called to a meeting with Lachlan MacLachlan [Bendigo Mac], an authoritarian Police Magistrate on the Bendigo diggings, he withdrew, acting to avoid the planned confrontation.

It appears that Denovan, although carried away with the power of his own oratory, had been made aware that he had unleashed emotions among the diggers that were less than desirable. The Chinese, fearing an assault on their camps, had posted armed sentries. Denovan soon became concerned for his own safety, and it was up to him to defuse the situation. He posted this public notice across the diggings:

> Brother Diggers,
> as a FALSE REPORT has appeared in the Columns of the Advertiser injurious to my personal liberty, relative to the Chinese question, I call upon the Digger throughout Bendigo to refrain from taking steps against the Chinese on the 4th of July.
> A MONSTER MEETING,
> — Wm D. C. DENOVAN

Pigtail Petitioners

The Chinese were resented for the style of their dress, their culinary tastes, their cultural habits, their pigtails, their religious rituals—in fact, the Europeans found them easy to revile for almost any reason at all.

Quang Chew, a prominent Chinese, spoke passionately in defence of his countrymen in an address to the Governor in 1855:

> Wherefore have we Chinese, humbly disembarked upon your pleasant shores, given just cause for your anger? . . . Why should our gardeners, cooks, animal trainers, conjurers etc. etc. see themselves driven away when they could become such useful members of the colony? The whole question is this: Will it be unwise to allow 20,000 Chinese to come to Australia? Will it be necessary to send back whence they came those who arrive from so far and who are all such respectful people?[2]

On 4 July 1857 a group of disgruntled miners decided to rid the Buckland River diggings, near Beechworth in north-eastern Victoria, of the 'Oriental menace'. They attacked the Chinese camp: they swept through the gorge, smashing and burning as they went; they destroyed tents, stores and even a joss house, as they drove the Chinese into the river.

It is not known how many lives were lost in this attack, but several Chinese died of exposure as they were forced to remain in the chilly waters of the Buckland until police arrived from Beechworth.

As was the practice in California, Australian diggers also took great delight in parting the Chinaman from his pigtail; it was the ultimate insult and relatively easy to achieve, while having a long-lasting effect on the victims. Following the Buckland River riot it was recorded that some diggers even kept pigtails as trophies, and some pigtails were said to have had large bits of skin and skull still attached.

Although the Chinese were resented by most Europeans, the perpetrators of the Buckland River riot were brought to trial. However, only three were convicted of the crime of unlawful assembly, and one of riot. All three served prison terms of nine months only. Such punishment was no deterrent to the active discrimination against the Chinese, which continued right across the diggings.

On 27 July 1857 the diggers at Golden Point near Castlemaine attempted to drive the Chinese from that goldfield. Just as on the Buckland River, the diggers destroyed goods belonging to the Chinese, jostling any

MR. W. D. C. DENOVAN.

Digger's leader W. D. C. Denovan
Denovan was a vocal agitator on the Bendigo field. He had expressed his opinions on the miner's license at every opportunity, as well as his opinion on the 'Chinese question'.

He had been on his way to Ballarat to pledge the support of the Bendigo diggers in support of the Eureka protest, but the Stockade had fallen before he arrived. On his return to Bendigo, wearing a red ribbon fluttering in the breeze as he made his way along the creek he was feted as Bendigo's own 'Eureka' hero.

Denovan also agitated against the Chinese, but when things started to get out of hand in Bendigo he was prompted to defuse the situation.

After Eureka he was prevailed upon by the Chinese leader in Bendigo to carry their petition for equal rights to the Governor. Although at first refusing, he changed his mind. He later became a defender of the rights of the Chinese in much the same way as he had fought for the European digger.

who resisted. Hundreds rushed to join in, shouting 'Down with the Chinese—expel them from the goldfields'. They were hoping to 'encourage' the Chinese on Golden Point to move out to join other larger Chinese camps at nearby Pennyweight and Moonlight Flats, leaving Golden Point to the Europeans.

Although the British government had previously signed a treaty with the Chinese Emperor to protect its citizens abroad, the Australian diggers were in no mind to honour that treaty.

The authorities sought to impose any legal means to drive the Chinese away. A 'capitation tax' was imposed on them [this was later to become a residence tax], and this impost proved a heavy burden for most of them.

On the Bendigo diggings the first of the Chinese Residents' License tickets were issued at the beginning of 1858, but by May only 165 Chinese had paid the fee and held the piece of paper that gave them the right to remain. Several were arrested, but over 1000 Chinese demanded that either the detainees be released or they be arrested also, as they, too, could not afford the newly imposed tax.

Denovan must have had quite a change of heart. He became one the Chinese diggers' biggest supporters in their fight to have the discriminatory 'residency' taxes lifted. He assisted in the presentation of a petition, signed by the Bendigo Chinese, to Sir Henry Barkly.

Revival of the Fine Old Australian Sport of License-Hunting
Melbourne Punch, 1854
(Private Collection)

The caption to this contemporary cartoon reads :

> Up here all of us, and especially our jurymen, are looking forward with great pleasure to the prospect of a good Chinese hunting season.
>
> Under the proposed new laws the sport will gain much extra éclat, by being carried on with official sanction and patronage, and will not as hitherto, merely by sufferance. I send you an anticipatory sketch by a local artist.

The troopers are depicted here up to their old tricks. After Eureka and the disappearance of the license fee, the sport of digger hunting had also disappeared. Now, with the introduction of the residence tax, the troopers could pick up where they left off.

The petition, which Denovan first declined to carry to Melbourne on behalf of the Chinese, read:

> That your petitioners are anxious to be placed on the same footing of social liberty as all other alien races living on the goldfields.
>
> That your petitioners, although they strive to be industrious and economical in their habits, find great and daily increasing difficulties to obtain sufficient means whereon to subsist. That their average daily earnings do not exceed half a dwt [pennyweight] of gold per man, out of which they are now required to pay over and above their share in export duty on gold the sum of £4 each man per annum, in the shape of special taxes to the revenue, a sum which your petitioners regret to inform your Excellency they are no longer able to pay.
>
> Your petitioners have, therefore, hastened to throw themselves at the feet of your Excellency, and to implore your protection.

Chinese Camp, Beechworth
(Burke Museum Beechworth Collection)
Chinese business establishments line the road on the Beechworth diggings.
The left side of the road, shown here, was known as 'The Canton Camp', the right as 'The Peking Camp'.
These 'hotels' were open to all who had the money to spend within, and were frequented by both European and Chinese alike.
The first flag reads 'Sun Quong Goon Hotel', the second, 'Wye Kee Hotel' and the third, 'Hang On How Hotel'.
The Peking Camp was demolished only five years after this photograph was taken, when the Beechworth Lunatic Asylum consolidated its 'reserve' for agricultural use.

The *Mount Alexander Mail* reported that the Chinese in Castlemaine had been given 24 hours to pay the tax. Only one man paid. Although the gaol was too small to hold them all, over one hundred were arrested and held in the Camp. The same action took place on the Spring Creek diggings near Beechworth.

Denovan wrote to the *Bendigo Advertiser* on 22 May 1859:

> I am as much opposed to extensive emigration of Chinese into this colony as ever I was, but it does not necessarily follow that . . . I should be in favour of maltreating those already here . . .[3]

Obviously buoyed by this seemingly reconciliatory note, the Chinese asked again, and Denovan, always keen to put himself in the middle of the action finally agreed to take their petition to the Governor.

Behind the resentment lay the prejudice that stems from the difference in culture between the 'Christian' majority of Europeans and the 'pagan' minority of the Chinese. This difference was tolerated until economic factors entered the equation. Sir Henry Barkly added this critical opinion of the Oriental diggers:

> The Chinese, because of total dissimilarity of habits and ideas obstructed the miners, whose dislike grew with envy and jealousy; others condemned the Chinese because they were, like many others, sojourners who contribute little to the permanent settlement or prosperity of the colony; still, others including the Statesman and the Christian, viewed with extreme anxiety these all-male immigrants, pagans in religion, and addicted, as was loudly asserted, to unnatural practices.

The Europeans assumed that the lack of females amongst the Chinese encouraged practices frowned upon, even illegal in British law. Everything was up for close scrutiny, even the peculiarities of the Chinese barbershop attracted interest. The *Annals of Bendigo* regarded even the most domestic of practices as worthy of critical attention:

> The operation of shaving in one of the numerous Barber shops was an event of much interest. From the peculiarity of the manipulation, and the strangeness of the instruments employed . . . the eyebrows and

Sun Loong, ceremonial dragon, Bendigo
(Author's photograph)

Although the Chinese were at times treated harshly by the European diggers, they remained very civic minded in all of their dealings on the goldfields.

The thousands of Chinese stuck together, worked and played together; they banded together for cultural reasons as well as for self-protection.

Many had travelled from the same village in the same province, and remained connected by history, or a family or community bond. Very few travelled with female company, and many Chinese were to marry European wives, staying and making their future in Australia.

On public holidays in both Beechworth and Bendigo the Chinese paraded through the streets of the towns they had adopted, raising money for local charities.

The Chinese of Beechworth raised donations from spectators of their procession, which was in turn donated to the Ovens Hospital and Benevolent Home for the Aged.

Curiously, many of the old diggers who would benefit in turn from the generosity of the Chinese would have been the same diggers who had actively protested against their presence on the goldfields.

Left: *Boxing Day Procession, 1895, Ford Street, Beechworth*
(Burke Museum, Beechworth Collection)

Right: *John Chinaman*
Watercolour by Harold John Graham, c. 1882
(Rex Nan Kivell Collection, R9866/57. By Permission, National Library of Australia)

> even the eyelashes were trimmed, . . . the cheeks, the ears, the throat . . . and the operation was twice gone over with different razors.[4]

The Protection Ticket enactment of the previous year was superseded by a residence tax of £4 per annum. The government was not so cynical that it could allow a tax to remain with the title of 'Protection Ticket', when it did little to protect the Chinese at all. The residence tax was hard on the poorer Chinese who, like the diggers at Eureka only five years earlier, began to organise resistance to this imposition with the help of professional agitators connected to Chinese secret societies. Notices were seized that were to communicate the message:

> Caution. After this no Chinese would allow to take out the Residence Ticket, if they do they will be punished by apprehension to the Sze Yip Club House severely, without pardon.
>
> If a Chinese may be arrested by having no ticket we will with the exertion of our strength help him and find him all the expenses during the time of his being kept in the prison.
>
> —£200 reward for killing the headman.[5]

The goldfields of Australia, Ballarat
Wood engraving published *London Illustrated Times*, 8 July 1865, after a watercolour by George Rowe
(Rex Nan Kivell Collection, U4951. By Permission, National Library of Australia)

JOHN ALLOO'S CHINESE RESTAURANT, MAIN ROAD, BALLAARAT. 1853

John Alloo's Restaurant, Ballarat
Lithograph by F. W. Niven & Co., from a sketch by S. T. Gill, 1853, from W. B. Withers, *History of Ballarat*, 1887
(City of Ballarat Fine Art Gallery Collection)

The Chinese generally built their camps well away from the Europeans. They created small townships of tents and huts, huddled together with very little space between them.

Although the Chinese always presented themselves as clean and tidy, the fronts of their dwellings always kept with pride, the alleys that ran between them at the rear were often filthy and vermin-infested.

This was just another aspect that added to the resentment of the Chinese by other diggers, giving them yet another reason to demand that the Chinese be forced out.

—The Coolie—

The word 'coolie' comes from a merging of two Chinese words: *koo* meaning 'to rent' and *lee* meaning 'muscle'—to rent muscles, to work.

In Chinese culture the labourer ranks higher than the merchant class but below scholars and farmers. The labourer is respected and free to choose his own employment.

The term 'coolie' was applied as a pejorative, meaning 'bonded labourer', which is understandable, as many who came to Australia worked in this manner.

In Castlemaine the Chinese offered rewards for the murder of several of their own headmen who were suspected of collusion with the authorities over the enforcement of the tax.

It appears that one such fellow, Ah Coy, had been running protection rackets, deceiving his countrymen with the lie that opium trading was a capital offence, and demanding £1 a week as danger money for engaging in this trade. He seems to have been caught up in the wave of ill feeling that was sweeping through the Chinese camps.

The Chinese Rise in Protest

Like their European 'brothers' the Chinese soon banded together in protest. They formed their own organisation—United Confederacy of Chinese—to represent themselves in the same way that the diggers had rallied under the Southern Cross flag to protest for their rights on the Eureka diggings. The Chinese again sent delegates to Melbourne to request exemption from the residence tax of £4 per head that the government had levied against them. They argued that the tax was only justified if it covered the expenses of the protectorate on the goldfields, however they certainly felt that they were not getting much protection for the fee that they were charged.

Disputes between the European diggers and the Chinese continued to fuel the rage that burnt across the diggings from Victoria to New South Wales. The governments of both colonies, while appearing to abide by the letter of the law and attempting to keep the peace, seemed eager to provide the kindling for an eventual conflagration. Yet, among all of the disquiet, discrimination and dissent Chinese continued to land on Australia's shores.

Might Versus Right
Watercolour by S. T. Gill, c. 1862
(From Dr Doyle's sketch book / John Thomas Doyle & Samuel Thomas Gill, c.1862–3. State Library of New South Wales Collection)

A party of boisterous European diggers attack a group of Chinese, dragging one from his shaft by his pig-tail.

This watercolour by Gill was intended for inclusion in a lithographic sketchbook, a collaboration between Gill and amateur watercolourist Dr John Thomas Doyle. The project was never completed although more than 50 watercolours [from both artists] were produced.

'Roll-Up' at Lambing Flat

It was at Lambing Flat, near Young in New South Wales, that the worst instance of violence against the Chinese took place. The government had stationed soldiers from the 12th Regiment, accompanied by a squad of artillery, on the diggings following continuing attacks against the Chinese beginning in December 1860, when vigilante groups had driven Chinese diggers from the Lambing Flat field. In the months between December and the July of the following year two Chinese had been murdered, and hundreds of others attacked, yet the government had taken the view that the situation was under control, and the troops were pulled out on 24 May 1861.

Just one month later, on Sunday, 30 June, the diggers, under the umbrella of the Miners' Protection League, and marching to the strains

The Lambing Flat Flag
(Author's photograph)

The flag carried on 30 June 1861 at Lambing Flat (Young), NSW, was a tent-fly that had been expertly painted by a digger on the field. The flag bore a white cross on a brilliant blue ground. Five stars were also painted, one in each quarter and one at the centre of the cross, which, although diagonal, was reminiscent of the Southern Cross flag flown at Ballarat only a few years earlier.

Each corner of the elegant design was embellished with golden decoration, and the words 'No Chinese—Roll Up, Roll Up' formed a typographic border around the blue square, and was fringed with gold.

The decorated tent-fly was more in the style of trade banners carried by unionists than that of a true flag. It required two men to support its weight when the miners rallied behind it on the march to the Chinese camp.

of a 'military' band, swept into the Chinese camp, carrying a banner bearing the stars of the Southern Cross and the words 'No Chinese—Roll Up, Roll Up', destroying all before them. This report is from the *Illustrated Sydney News* of 5 August 1861:

> . . . meanwhile matters were approaching a crisis: fifers and drummers were obtained, and flags bearing sentiments were hoisted. Fire-arms and other weapons were procured; public-houses and booths were rushed, and plenty of Dutch courage imbibed. All these precautions were considered necessary by thousands of brave men [?] in order to successfully attack a few hundred defenceless Chinese.
>
> The poor Asiatics made scarcely any resistance. All who could do so secreted their gold, and many of them lost their lives for refusing to tell where it was; others who were not quick enough in getting out of their holes and drives were buried alive in them—just for fun; and such of the tents and goods as were not appropriated by the civilizers were collected in heaps and burned, and thus the work of murder and robbery went bravely on.

Troops were called to Lambing Flat from surrounding districts, and three men were eventually arrested for inciting riot. The diggers demanded that their mates be freed, and attempted to release them from the police lock-up. They fired at the police horses and the police fired back, dropping one digger in his tracks, shot straight through the head. As at Beechworth, the Europeans arrested seemed to escape the full weight of the law—at Lambing Flat only one digger was gaoled.

Barricade at Clunes

On 9 December 1873, following a dispute over wages and hours of labour between miners and the proprietors of the Lothair mine at Clunes in central Victoria, it was reported that Chinese labourers were to be brought into Clunes as strike-breakers or 'scabs'. Once the news was abroad, the miners gathered together and determined to 'resist the invasion'. Telegrams sent on 8 December said that the Chinese were aboard five coaches being sent up from Ballarat and from Creswick. More than 1000 miners assembled with their wives and children at the junction of the Ballarat and Clunes roads, about one mile from the town. Fire bells rang the alarm incessantly, and a barricade was erected across the road. The miners waited all night, and it wasn't until about 8 o'clock the following morning that the first coach came into sight. A storm of stones and bricks rained down upon the coaches, and the miners charged, assaulting the Chinese on board. The persistence of the miners and their wives forced the police guard to withdraw, and the coaches turned back to Ballarat.

Once the miners had achieved their aim, the district returned to its 'former quietude'. This was the first time in Australia's history where violence and resistance was the solution to a labour dispute. Their action was condemned:

> . . . the successful attempt to resist the law, and to prohibit by force of arms the exercise on the part of the employers of their unquestionable right to get labour where they pleased, caused a great shock to the public feeling of the colony, and it was felt that a very objectionable example had been set, and a dangerous precedent established.[6]

The miners and their wives had fought a 'great battle' to save their jobs and livelihoods, they had stood up to the bosses, had stared into the barrels of the troopers' guns, never flinching, not backing away from the fray, and once again the poor Chinese were the victims. What was in essence a working-men's struggle, labour against capital, became another chapter in the ever-expanding chronicle of the Australians' distrust of the Chinese.

This event was celebrated for many years with a victory ballad composed to celebrate the great day where the people of Clunes rose up to defend themselves:

Disturbances at Clunes, Miners Resisting the Introduction of Chinese Labourers
Wood engraving by Samuel Calvert, *The Illustrated Australian News*, Ebenezer and David Syme, 31 December 1873
(Picture Collection, State Library of Victoria)

The diggers' hero, Peter Lalor, who had fought so hard for the rights of the miners in 1854, was partially responsible for the troubles at Clunes. As director of the Lothair Mining Company he had refused the miners' demands that they be allowed more than a single day off per week from digging. This refusal sent the workers to strike for fourteen weeks.

Lalor's attempt to break the strike by bringing Chinese miners from Ballarat caused the riot.

Mother Bailey was in front,
The Chows were driven back
With her apron full of stones,
All a-quiver and a-quake,
Determined if she could
With Larner* and his escort
To break some of their bones.
Following in their wake.

While the Chinese were eager to take their place in goldfields society, they never escaped this kind of constant harassment.

---

* Sergeant Larner was the leader of the small band of police who had escorted the coaches to the Clunes barricade.

In the first barrage of rocks he had been hit on the head, and fell from his horse. With blood streaming from his wound, he leapt on to the barricade and thrust his pistol into the chest of one miner, who did not flinch in his own defence.

The Chinese Invasion, Northern Queensland
Wood engraving, *Illustrated Australian News*, 2 July 1877
(Rex Nan Kivell Collection, U5302. By Permission, National Library of Australia)
In Queensland the Chinese were treated just as poorly as they had been on other fields during the 'roaring days'.

The Chinese continued to arrive in Queensland in large numbers even after the easy alluvial gold ran out. They were already suffering constant harassment on every goldfield, but the continuous migration caused the angry and resentful European miners to attempt to drive them all from the diggings yet again.

Towards the end of 1868, after the European diggers began to fall back upon earlier abandoned diggings around Gympie, the cry of 'Roll Up, Roll Up' was heard again. Just as had been done on earlier diggings in Victoria and New South Wales, the Queensland diggers swept through the camp at Chinaman's Flat in an attempt to drive the Chinese from the field. Although the Chinese were considered by the *Gympie Times* to be 'orderly and harmless . . . and we presume there can be no objection to them', the diggers were looking first for a 'Mongolian' scapegoat on which to vent their anger.

In Tambaroora, near Mudgee in New South Wales, as a lark, a gang of Chinese had been sold the lease to a mining claim that in fact belonged to a group of European diggers. Two of the diggers who actually owned the claim had been in the town for several days on a spree. When they returned to their claim, they found their shafts filled in and a number of Chinese busily mining where their claim once was. The diggers were shocked to discover that their mates had been murdered by the Chinese who had collapsed the shafts burying their bodies. They gathered together a mob of other diggers, and took their revenge on the Chinese.

In the face of such open discrimination the Chinese gradually retreated to the towns, using their muscle to win riches in other ways.

Chinese Quarter, Ballarat
Wood engraving, published *Illustrated Australian News*, 18 July 1868
(Picture Collection, State Library of Victoria)

They established laundries, restaurants, and market gardens, and, although few Chinese women accompanied the men to the goldfields, they were prominent in the importation and supply of prostitutes for the pleasure of the European miners. In San Francisco, as on the Australian diggings, to 'See the world' meant a trip to Chinatown where an oriental morality could be freely enjoyed. Wherever the Chinese went, their so-called 'pagan' habits infuriated 'Victorian', conservative, Christian moralists and confirmed their prejudice against them.

Yet there were still new goldfields being opened up, and still plenty of opportunity for those with muscle for hire. The discovery of gold in Queensland led to a mass migration to the north, and the same old problems followed.

Swift 'justice' for the Chinese

A group of diggers on the Queensland goldfields, at the height of Chinese troubles there, became very suspicious of one storekeeper after half of their gold had been stolen:

> A meeting was held and suspicion fell upon a Chinaman who kept a general store . . . it was arranged that half a dozen of them visit his store the next morning and overhaul it . . . every cask, sack, box and

Honour Board, Chinese Society, Mt Alexander
(Castlemaine Art Gallery and Historical Museum Collection)
This carved honour board commemorates the good works of one Chinese leader, and is signed, at the left, by a number of his grateful students.

> article of clothing in the place was closely examined . . . [as nothing] could be found . . . the Chinaman become more bold, shrugged his shoulders and [even complained] of the treatment he and his goods had been receiving.
>
> Not being able to find the lost gold, the men were determined to have something to take with them . . . looking around they saw a great many German sausages hanging from the roof . . . 'Let's have one of these saveloys each, Joey,' said one of the men . . . 'Half one of these big 'uns is enough for me,' said Joey, and whipping out his knife he divided it in two on the counter.
>
> The moment he put his knife through the skin, out poured the gold.[7]

The storekeeper, Ah Silah Joy, ran from the shop, chased by the irate diggers, who quickly apprehended him:

> They dragged him back to a clump of trees near the camp . . . his pigtail was cut off, and his hands tied behind his back with it. He was made to stand on top of a bucket with his back to a tree. His ears were nailed fast to the tree and the bucket kicked from under his feet.[8]

Ah Joy was left hanging in this manner until police arrived the following day.

In Breach of the Law

The Chinese were frequently before the courts, usually charged with trying to dispose of spurious or adulterated gold or for stealing.

Chinese Burning Towers, Beechworth
(Author's Photograph)

These towers are typical of those built in almost every cemetery across the goldfields where Chinese gathered.

After the attack on the Buckland River, the Chinese fell back into Beechworth, and set up a large community there. The burning towers were built in 1883 in the local cemetery that holds the remains of 2000 Chinese who never returned to their homeland.

Contrary to popularly-held opinion, cremations were not held in the burning towers. Paper tokens were burnt, gifts of food and wine were placed within, the purpose being to sustain the departing spirit on its journey to Heaven, carried on the smoke of the paper prayers. Firecrackers were exploded to frighten any devils away.

Many a young larrikin had a good feed of pork, washed down with rice wine, after the funeral party had departed.

On the Bendigo diggings in February 1857 three Chinese were charged with 'occupying Crown Lands without being licensed to do so'.

Although they were let off with a warning, the magistrate, 'Bendigo Mac', felt that it was about time an example was made of some of the Chinese. Before long another Chinese, the unfortunate Ah King, came before him, charged with stealing four hats from a store in Bendigo; he received a three months' sentence.

Another, Ah Yan, was sentenced to six months for the theft of five panama hats. Ah Tong and Ah Chang were both sentenced to one month each for stealing seven pairs of 'trowsers' from Campion's Store in Pall Mall, Bendigo.

Some Chinese even had a go at bushranging, but were not all that successful. In New South Wales in 1859 a large, stout Chinese bailed up a Mr Ball, from Cathcart, and demanded he hand over his money. Ball took to the assailant with a whip, and chased him away.

Another unlucky fellow who had bailed up several people in the Mudgee district shot the policeman who came to capture him. The policeman survived, and escaped to a nearby farmhouse where he raised the alarm. The 'Oriental bushranger' was eventually captured and hanged.

Chu Ah Luk was one of the few Chinese hanged in Victoria. He had killed his fellow-countryman, Ah Pud, in a store at Campbell's Creek. Poor Ah Pud had simply asked Chu Ah Luk for 10 shillings that he was

Chinese Merchants at Gulgong, New South Wales, c. 1870
(Mitchell Library NSW, Holtermann Collection)
After the riot at Lambing Flat, Governor Cowper placed restrictions on the Chinese in New South Wales, and some were even refused miner's licenses.

The resourceful Chinese soon found other means of survival. As merchants they were usually successful, some became restaurateurs, some market gardeners, some herbalists. Many married, raising Chinese–Irish Australians.

owed, but when he refused to pay Ah Pud threatened to take his clothes from him. Chu Ah Luk stabbed Ah Pud, and fled. He was captured in Ballarat, brought back to Castlemaine, and hanged.

Considering the large number of Chinese on the goldfields the incidence of crime was actually quite small, and was usually for offences such as stealing chickens or clothing; mostly for the simple reason that many Chinese were destitute. The *Bendigo Advertiser* reported in 1858 that 'there is in reality more actual distress among the Chinese population than is generally supposed'. When crime occurred among the Chinese themselves it was usually dealt with according to their own customs.

Also, considering the treatment the Chinese had received at the hands of the Europeans it is a testament to their fortitude that so many remained in the goldfields' towns where they developed good solid businesses, where many married and raised families. In a lot of instances the Chinese took young Irish girls for their wives. Freed from 'service' the Chinese offered these working-class girls a standard of living they could not expect from any other match, both groups being considered less than equal to the ruling 'British' classes.

The Chinese left a legacy that has persisted for over a century. They, like the diggers at Eureka, forced change, as they too demanded their rights in the new egalitarian society born of the diggings.

CHAPTER 14

The End of the Roaring Days

As the alluvial gold ran out across the goldfields and the creeks no longer flowed with nuggets, mining companies were formed as investors rushed to finance the shift to deep-lead exploration. The wild, frontier days of the goldrushes gradually disappeared.

The Australian traditions of independence and mateship forged on the diggings entered a new era, with miners organising to protect themselves once again from exploitation, not from the government but this time from the 'bosses'; the investors and speculators whose decisions, often made by businessmen sitting far away in comfortable London offices, ensured the viability, or the extinction, of the diggers' livelihood.

The 'red republicanism' so feared by Earl Grey metamorphosed into collectivism as mining unions became established. The workers did not forget the hard lesson of Eureka when they had joined together to fight under the Southern Cross flag.

Some of the settlements that had sprung up on the alluvial fields flourished with deep-lead mining while others were forced to change direction. The landscape was soon dotted with towering poppet-heads as miners dug deep into the earth in search of the quartz reefs and gravel beds far beneath the surface. Thousands of once-free, independent, diggers became employees. Their lives, once spent in the sun with the creeks swirling at their knees, were now confined in dark and airless shafts as they blasted and drilled away at the gold-bearing quartz. Ironically, many diggers who had fought so hard for the right to be free from autocratic overlords were now chained to the mine owners and the promise of a weekly pay packet.

The incessant thump and hammer of the massive quartz-crushing plants thundered day and night from Castlemaine to Kalgoorlie, stopping only on Sunday. When the mines ceased at midnight on Saturday an eerie quiet fell across the field; many were unable to sleep in the deathly

Sandhurst from Camp Hill, 1886
Oil on canvas by James Edwin Meadows
(Collection, Bendigo Art Gallery)

Essex-born Meadows was a popular, and successful, artist who specialised in traditional scenes of rustic laneways and rose-covered, thatch-roofed cottages.

Although he travelled extensively throughout Britain seeking inspiration from the beauty of the southern coastline in particular, and had spent some time in Venice, he never travelled to Australia. Yet, he painted two large and surprisingly accurate canvases of the pre-eminent goldfields centres of Ballarat and Bendigo.

Commissioned by colonial authorities the paintings were first exhibited in the Victorian pavilion of the Colonial and Indian Exhibition in South Kensington [London] in 1886.

The exhibition theme was 'Progress' and the paintings of the well-laid out colonial centres of industry and enterprise, with their proud public buildings, broad and bustling, tree-lined boulevards and generous parks were fine examples of the superiority of progress in the British colonies.

Meadows worked from photographs, maps and plans of the buildings and streetscapes and although there are some inaccuracies in his description of the lay-of-the-land both paintings are remarkable for their accuracy.

silence, and were relieved when the roar took up again at midnight on Sunday to mark the beginning of the new working week.

The rush to the diggings in 1851 had been a great colonial adventure, but as the alluvial gold had all but played out by the end of the 1850s, and great centres such as Ballarat, Bendigo and Bathurst settled into domesticity, the later rushes to the north and to the west were born of different economic climes.

Ballarat: The Lucky City

Common usage has shortened the official spelling of Ballaarat to Ballarat.

The original name is taken from the Aboriginal word meaning a grassy, well-shaded spot on the bank of the creek—'a resting place'. How inappropriate this meaning became after the influx of diggers in 1852. What had been described before the rush as one of the prettiest spots imaginable soon resembled the site of a great battle, with craters and holes littering the landscape.

When they first arrived on the diggings inexperienced 'new-chums' rushed from place to place seeking the easy gold, the gold that lay in the creeks, or glistened in the gravel beds. A rush would lose its appeal as quickly as it had begun: when another rush was on, diggers simply abandoned the claims they had in favour of any new patch of ground where others professed to have found the latest rich source of gold.

The troubles that besieged Ballarat in the early years before Eureka had largely stemmed from the lack of alluvial gold after the first rush had passed. When Cornishmen arrived in their hundreds in 1852 and found the diggings all but deserted, they put their experience in the Cornish tin-mines to work, and tunnelled deep into the earth.

Ballarat from the Black Hill, 1868
Wood engraving by Robert Bruce, from *Illustrated Australian News*, July 1868
(Rex Nan Kivell Collection, S2399. By permission, National Library of Australia)

MINING OPERATIONS AT THE BLACK HILL, BALLARAT.

Mining Operations at the Black Hill, Ballarat
Engraving by Robert Bruce, Ebenezer and David Syme,
from *Illustrated Australian News*, 18 July 1868
(Picture Collection, State Library of Victoria)

The truth was that the real wealth at Ballarat lay deep beneath the surface in the ancient gravelled streams that were long buried. The newly arrived professional miners saw those who remained were still getting gold as they dug deeper and deeper into the clay, following the creek-bed lines.

Shafts over 100 feet deep were dug through the waterlogged ground until bedrock was struck. Some of the shafts were so rich they soon became known as 'jewellers' shops', and the second rush to Ballarat began. The three main leads at Ballarat—the Eureka, Gravel Pits and the

Arrival of the Geelong Mail, Main Road, Ballarat, May 2nd 1855
Watercolour by S. T. Gill, 1880
(City of Ballarat Fine Art Gallery Collection)

Canadian—were described by W. B. Withers as 'the Golden Trinity that made Ballarat famous throughout the civilised world'.

When English novelist Anthony Trollope visited Ballarat in 1872 he wrote:

> It struck me with more surprise than any other city in Australia. It is not only its youth . . . but that a town so well built, so well ordered, endowed with present advantages so great . . . and the like should have sprung up so quickly with no internal advantages of its own other than gold.[1]

J. C. Patterson also described the Ballarat township only a decade after the first discovery, praising the community that had grown with enterprise into respectability:

> the money that in other mining districts took the form of unbottomed shafts and unfinished drives—of machinery built to be thrown down again, and mines only now being brought to paying point—built long lines of handsome streets, erected foundries, flour mills, and breweries and brought into cultivation such large tracts of territory that while Ballarat claims to excel Bendigo as a goldfields, the country

Ballarat, 1886
Oil on canvas by James Edwin Meadows
(James Meadows. Ballarat, 1886, oil on canvas, 30.8 × 46.0 cm. Collection: Art Gallery of Ballarat. Presented, 1887)
A companion piece to his painting of Bendigo in 1886, this painting of Ballarat was also commissioned for the Colonial and Indian Exhibition in South Kensington, London. Painted from maps, plans and drawings sent to him in London, Meadows could have had no knowledge of the local topography and has failed to show the steep incline to the east of Lydiard Street.

> around it aspires to be regarded as the leading agricultural district of the colony.
>
> It has supplied itself with the machinery for its own mines; it produces the implements with which its own fields are tilled; it grinds its own corn, and brews its own beer . . . the result of all this is well-directed energy, and the local circulation of the stores of gold obtained from the deep gutters, has been a sound and healthy trade in Ballarat itself.[2]

Patterson's 'well-directed energy' may have been a reminder to the contemporary reader that Ballarat had not always directed its energies where good and loyal citizens should, that there was a stain on the character of the town that hardwork, enterprise and patriotic loyalty would eventually erase:

> . . . there is an abundance of employment at fair wages, for all who are willing to labour, and the still unexhausted alluvial in the shallow

> gullies affords a living to the weak and unskilled, and to the swarms of Chinese to whom Ballarat East is being rapidly abandoned.[3]

The company mine, its managers and shareholders, may have held the key to the future, yet, in Ballarat, the 'Eureka' spirit lived on.

Opposite: *Speculators on 'The Corner' at Ballarat*
Engraving from *Picturesque Atlas of Australasia*, Sydney and Melbourne, 1888
(Private Collection)

'The Corner' was an open-air stockmarket. Equal to the New York Stock Exchange in its day, more stock was traded here than anywhere else in Australia.

— Notable Nuggets —

The Canadian [1319 oz]
Canadian Gully, Ballarat—31 January 1853
D. & J. Evans, J. Lees, W. Poulter & W. F. Green

Lady Hotham [1177 oz]
Dalton's Flat, Ballarat—8 September 1854
McDonald, Irwin, Cock, Radcliffe, McPhillamy, Day, Lyons & Bryant

Un-named [1011 oz]
Canadian Lead, Ballarat—2 January 1853
Gough, Sulley & Bristow

The Welcome Nugget [2195 oz]
Ballarat—15 June 1858. Red Hill Gold Mining Co.

Kohinoor [834 oz]
Ballarat—August 1860. Kohinoor G. M. Co.

Lady Don [606 oz]
Ballarat—12 November 1866. Lady Don Co.

The Welcome Nugget was found at Bakery Hill by Richard Jeffrey, working with the Red Hill Gold Mining Co., a company formed by twenty-two Cornish miners.

At the time of its discovery the Welcome Nugget was the largest piece of solid gold found anywhere in the world. It measured 20 inches long, 12 inches wide and 8 inches thick, and weighed 2195 oz. The morning after its discovery, the miners carted the Welcome Nugget in a wheelbarrow through the streets of Ballarat to the Treasury (where the Art Gallery now stands). The lucky diggers were followed by a large crowd amazed at the sheer scale of the horsehead-shaped golden lump resting in the barrow.

Visitors paid a shilling to see it before the Ballarat gold-buying firm Wittowski Bros bought it for £10,500 and sent it to England for display in the Crystal Palace. Purchased by the Royal Mint in November 1859 the Welcome Nugget was finally melted down for sovereigns.

SPECULATORS ON THE "CORNER," BALLARAT.

O'FARRELL: THE FAILED ASSASSIN

Henry James O'Farrell was another of the vengeful sons of Erin who wrote their name into the history of Ballarat.

This red-faced and excitable Dubliner, who spent his afternoons at 'The Corner', had been a hay and grain merchant when he came to Ballarat in the 1850s. A shrewd investor, he bought cheap and sold dear, but eventually he saw the value of his stock holdings in Ballarat mines collapse.

However, he continued to buy and sell, and then to drink, mostly to drink, and began to spend most of his afternoons at the bar of Royal Craig's Hotel. He eventually left Ballarat.

It was in Sydney on 12 March 1868 that O'Farrell made his mark in history. Prince Alfred, Duke of Edinburgh, second son of Queen Victoria, had just enjoyed a picnic at the Sailors' Home at Clontarf, and was about to watch a corroboree when O'Farrell stepped from the admiring crowd and shot him in the back.

The prince fell to his knees crying, 'Good God, I'm shot. My back is broken.'

As a Mr Vial, a Sydney coachbuilder, grabbed O'Farrell from behind in an attempt to take the gun from him, another shot was fired, striking bystander George Thorne. The crowd turned in search of the assailant, and attacked Vial, whom they thought was the would-be assassin. They soon discovered their mistake, and the mob moved against O'Farrell yelling 'Hang him, lynch him'; and almost beat him senseless. A sailor found some rope, threw it over a tree and called for O'Farrell to be hanged on the spot. The police managed to rescue him from the angry mob; his clothes had been ripped to shreds, and he was carried, bruised, bleeding and unconscious, to the steamer *Paterson* anchored nearby. The prince survived. He was carried to his tent where doctors from HMS *Challenger* and the *Galatea* treated him immediately—the bullet had struck his braces,

Henry James O'Farrell
Photograph by Montagu Scott, c. 1868
(David Scott Mitchell Collection, State Library of New South Wales)

O'Farrel [sic] in Darlinghurst
Pencil drawing attributed to Viscount Francis Charles Needham Newry, c. 1868
(R6193. National Library of Australia Collection)

which deflected it past his spine and into his abdomen, missing all vital organs.

O'Farrell was sent to trial charged with the attempted assassination of the young prince. He was convicted, and executed at Darlinghurst gaol five weeks later.

It would appear that O'Farrell was just another among scores of defiant Irishmen who seemed to forgive the English for nothing, and like so many before, and after, was prepared to die in the belief that his action could redress the wrongs he believed had been done to the Irish nation.

EMINENT ARTISTES OF THE GOLDFIELDS

—Gill, Strutt and Thatcher—

Samuel Thomas Gill

Samuel Thomas Gill is the most recognised of all the artists who recorded life on the diggings. He was born at Perriton, in Devonshire in 1819 the son of a Baptist minister and schoolmaster. His early training with W. J. Hubard's Profile Gallery taught him skills of drawing and observation that became the hallmark of his works on the goldfields.

Samual Thomas Gill
(La Trobe Library Picture Collection, State Library of Victoria)

The Gill family migrated to South Australia in 1839 and it was there that S. T. began to seek commissions for his portraits and was commissioned to record the homes of the squatters, and the streets, of early Adelaide.

Before long he joined the rush to the diggings, where he captured the very tenor of all life there—the fights, the troopers, licensing tents, diggers on a spree, diggers' weddings, destitute and disappointed diggers, from Forest Creek to Bendigo, Ballarat and Eaglehawk.

Gill's drawings are the most human and often the most humourous of all images made at the time, yet his life was filled with pathos.

Like his image of the 'unlucky digger', Gill took to the bottle and gradually fell on hard times. Alone, destitute and drunk, 61-year-old Gill collapsed and died, from a rupture of the aorta, on the steps of the General Post Office in Melbourne on 27 October 1880.

The *Herald* reported his sad and lonely death and described Gill as one 'who [had] once occupied an opulent position . . . has of late been in reduced circumstances'. The *Argus* described him as 'one of the notables of the land of gold'.

Charles Robert Thatcher. The Diggers' Minstrel

Born in Bristol in 1831 Robert Thatcher was destined for a life on the stage. Having been taught the flute as a child, sixteen-year-old Thatcher set off for London to try his luck. He began playing in various theatre orchestras, for dramatic performances and vaudeville acts, and it was on the London stage that Thatcher was introduced to the style of popular entertainment known as 'The Music Hall'.

Concert Room, Charlie Napier Hotel, Ballarat, June '55. Thatcher's Popular Songs
Watercolour by S. T. Gill, 1855
(rex nan kivell Collection, r8789. By permission, National Library of Australia)

In this watercolour by his contemporary S. T. Gill, Thatcher is shown on stage in the Charlie Napier Hotel on the Ballarat diggings.

Thatcher recycled popular melodies adding new lyrics in which he, like Gill, also saw the humour in the daily round. As was typical of his day Thatcher satirised the petty goldfields bureaucracy, who in their earnestness made life difficult, and unneccesarily complicated, for the average digger who would prefer to be at their claims than waste their time dealing with the often capricious demands of an over-bearing government.

Like so many others Thatcher was seduced by the promise of easy pickings in the goldfields, and in 1852 he joined the throng and sailed aboard the *Isabella* bound for Port Phillip.

Having little luck at gold-digging Thatcher decided to polish up his flute and fall back on his old trade. He first found a job with the orchestra at the Royal Victoria Theatre in Sandhurst [Bendigo], and it was here, between performances, that he filled in by singing new words to popular tunes. He soon became the most popular satirical performer on the goldfields stage.

Although he was thought the cleverest of all the contemporary song writers, not everybody found him amusing. The Bendigo newspaper considered his 'clever sarcastic songs' to be 'really good', yet Thatcher was in and out of battle as those he lampooned often took issue with him.

He performed widely over all the diggings, including those in New Zealand, then retired to London in 1867. He established himself in the West End as an importer of curios, scouring Europe, Japan and China for goods and souvenirs. He died, from cholera, on one such trip to Shanghai in September 1878.

The Keen Eye of William Strutt

Colonial artist William Strutt arrived in Hobson's Bay on the Culloden in July 1850. He was descended from a long line of accomplished artists—his father, William Thomas Strutt, was a noted miniaturist, and his grandfather, Joseph Strutt, an artist and author who had illustrated his own works, *Dresses and Habits of the English People* (1796–99) and *The Sports and Pastimes of the People of England* (1801).

Strutt had studied in Paris, but the stress of his early occupation as an engraver had caused him severe eyestrain and near-breakdown. He travelled to the colonies hoping that the outdoor life would improve his health.

William Strutt
(Collection: State Parliamentary Library of Victoria)

The Route to the Diggings
Liardet's Four-in-hand Coach, the 'Eclipse', making a trip to Ballarat
Watercolour by William Strutt, 1851
(Collection: State Parliamentary Library of Victoria)

A party of adventurers make out for the diggings, on foot, bullock dray or pushing hand-carts before them as Sandridge hotel-keeper Wilbraham Liardet, who provided a coach service for 'tourists' to the diggings, rides in comfort to take in the sights.

Golden Point, Ballarat, 1851. Taken from the west.
Sketched on the spot by William Strutt, 1851
(Collection: State Parliamentary Library of Victoria)

At the time of Strutt's arrival, the established publisher and engraver, Thomas Ham, was under contract to the Victorian government. Ham Bros had engraved Melbourne's corporate seal, the first postage stamps, various maps and currency notes for various banks.

Before Strutt's arrival there were no illustrated newspapers in Australia, but his arrival in July coincided with the first issue of the *Illustrated Australian Magazine.* Ham Bros had announced their intention to publish an illustrated magazine, and Strutt's abilities and experience gained him a position as illustrator soon after he stepped onto colonial soil.

Strutt's legacy of superbly drafted images of early Melbourne, his portraits of important figures and his drawings of the diggings, seem as fresh today as they must have been 150 years ago.

'BOLD' BENDIGO

When William Tulloch visited the Bendigo diggings he described the already well-established community he saw there straddling the creek:

> In fact, Bendigo is a large city, where a population of 40,000 lives in tents and huts instead of houses. Almost every tent has its large fire place and chimney, constructed of logs, at one end of it . . . It is curious to see the various rude constructions of these huts and chimneys.
>
> Some huts are built of solid trunks of trees, laid horizontally—in fact, the log-huts of America reconstructed here . . . you may generally distinguish the abodes of the native of Ireland, by their picturesque resemblance to the cabins of the Green Isle, being more remarkable for their defiance of symmetry than any others.

At one time it was possible to scoop up pannikins of gold from the Bendigo Creek, and gold was even found trampled into the mud at the little stockyard by the creek on the outskirts of Fenton and Gibson's run, but it was after this alluvial gold had all but petered out that Bendigo really came into its own. Mining companies were established to raise the funds to dig deep into the earth.

Fighting for Bendigo

With the establishment of deep-lead company mining Bendigo settled into domesticity quickly and there were any number of stalwart citizens of the growing municipality who fought to create a glorious Victorian city worthy of its reputation as a great centre.

Scottish chartists such as W. D. C. Denovan, enlightened administrators like Panton and zealous law enforcers like the notorious Police Magistrate Lachlan McLachlan—all fought to build Bendigo into a thriving, modern community that would endure past the heady days of the gold rush.

Police Magistrate of the Bendigo district from 1853 ('Bendigo Mac'), was a stern disciplinarian whose credo seems to have been taken from the saying 'desperate evils require desperate remedies'. He was often censured for the rigour, severity and clear discrimination with which he administered the law of the day. He had also cause to censure Denovan when W. D. C. over-stepped the mark on the matter of the Chinese expulsion.

Once an officer with the Van Diemen's Land police force, 'Mac' had considerable knowledge of the criminal classes, and knew the history of many of the old lags who came before him in his Bendigo court. McLachlan could accuse a prisoner brought before him:

Hustler's Reef, Sandhurst
(La Trobe Library Picture Collection, State Library of Victoria)

> 'I know you, you scoundrel, your name's so-and-so; you were at Norfolk Island in such a year;' . . . of course the prisoner would be at quite a loss to account for the police magistrate's knowledge of his past career.
>
> If the charge was trivial, 'Mac' would turn to his favourite henchman . . . 'Sergeant Richards, see that this ruffian leaves the district within 24 hours; if not bring him here again'.[4]

As Bendigo rid itself of the remnants of the bad-old days of the rush it settled into a thriving 'modern' manufacturing and mining centre. With tons of gold still below the surface, and the capacity to extract it, great wealth was returned to investors in the Bendigo mines. Based on this wealth, the town grew apace—line after line of giant steel poppet-legs were strung out across the landscape as Bendigo, 'Bold Bendigo', living up to its namesake, tried never to lose the fight for gold.

Eaglehawk and the North

In 1856 a storeman found himself stranded about 60 miles north of Bendigo in the granite country around Mt Hope. Fearing that his goods would spoil and he would lose his investment, he started the rumour that he had found gold there. When the news of this 'bogus' find reached Bendigo

Left: *'Bendigo Mac'*
From the Annals of Bendigo, original photograph by Benjamin Pierce Batchelder
(La Trobe University Bendigo Library Collection)

Right: *Christopher and Theodore Ballerstadt*
The Ballerstadt brothers sold their claim on the Victoria Reef, Bendigo, to George Lansell, later known as the 'Quartz King' of Bendigo. Lansell built his mansion, 'Fortuna', on the site of Ballerstadts' original house.

Ballerstadts' was one of the first claims to have been worked on Bendigo.
(Picture Collection, State Library of Victoria)

GOLD DIGGERS USING A 'PUDDLING MACHINE' AT BENDIGO.

Gold Diggers Using a Puddling Machine at Bendigo
Wood engraving by Walter Mason, J. R. Clarke, Sydney, 1857
(Rex Nan Kivell Collection, U822. By Permission, National Library of Australia)

Eagle Hawk Gully, Bendigo
Watercolour by S. T. Gill, c. 1852
(Bendigo Art Gallery Collection)

Eaglehawk was a fiercely independent community to the north-west of Bendigo, on the very edge of the rolling hills and deep gullies where gold was once readily found. Beyond Eaglehawk the country becomes harsh—gravelly, flat, with iron-hard black-trunked trees and devilishly hot in the blistering months of summer.

another rush started. It was in the height of summer, and this hoax cost the lives of fourteen diggers, who perished in their haste to be the first to stake out a claim on Mt Hope.

In Eaglehawk, the surface gold soon ran out. In 1855, rich quartz reefs were located deep beneath the gullies. The mines continued to work, their batteries filling the valleys around with mountains of grey sand, until the last, the South Virginia, closed in 1950.

Back Creek, Bendigo looking towards Epsom, 1860
Watercolour by S. T. Gill, 1860
(From Dr Doyle's sketch book / John Thomas Doyle & Samuel Thomas Gill, c.1862–3. State library of New South Wales Collection)

William Thompson
Oil on canvas by Thomas Earl, 1850
(Courtesy National Portrait Gallery, London. NPG 4191)

This striking portrait of William 'Bold Bendigo' Thompson was painted just one year before the rush to the goldfield, that was to adopt his name, had begun.

Post Office, Sandhurst, Victoria, in the 1850s
Watercolour, artist unknown, c. 1855
(Rex Nan Kivell Collection, r3642. By Permission, National Library of Australia)

This first Post Office stood beside the creek that runs through the heart of Sandhurst [Bendigo].

Towards the end of the century this muddy track had been developed into a grand Victorian boulevard—it's name Pall Mall, famous for its gentlemen's clubs, taken from one of London's most prestigious addresses.

Macpherson's store, Bendigo
Watercolour, artist unknown, c. 1858
(Rex Nan Kivell Collection, nk206. By Permission, National Library of Australia)

THE QUARTZ KING: GEORGE LANSELL

George Lansell arrived in the Bendigo district from Echunga, in South Australia, in 1853. He was a candlemaker by trade, who, with his brother, established a butchery, store and soap factory at Bendigo's View Point.

After the first alluvial rushes had begun to fade and companies established to finance deep mining, it was Lansell's unfailing faith in the value of these deep Sandhurst reefs that eventually made him the richest man in Bendigo. At one stage it is recorded that he was making £1000 per day from his investments in, and often sole ownership of, a large number of mines.

With the proceeds of his favourite, the 'Big 180' (right), which at one time was the deepest mine in Victoria, bottoming out at just over one kilometre, he built the mansion 'Fortuna' in Chum Street, Golden Square—a three-storeyed Italianate mansion, built on the site of the Ballerstadts' original property. It was one of the most extravagant homes in the colony, and set among one of the most appropriately named districts on the goldfields.

In 1879 Lansell left Bendigo and travelled to England. He may have been escaping from an unhappy first marriage to a chronic and, at times, abusive alcoholic, Bedelia Mulganney. George left her in their St Kilda Road mansion, where she died on 20 September 1880, aged 38. He established himself in the Grand Hotel, Charing Cross, London, in company with his housekeeper, Edith Basford, a young widow from a respectable Bendigo family.

George and Edith at home
(Q.C Binks Collection)

Lansell's favourite the 'Big 180'
(Bendigo Regional Library Collection)

New Chum line of reef, Bendigo, c.1875
Photograph by Nicholas Caire
(National Library of Australia collection)

Sandhurst in 1862
Oil on canvas by Thomas Wright, 1862
(Collection: Bendigo Art Gallery)

The Bendigo diggings sit in a wide dished landscape surrounded by low, tree covered hills. This was verdant, gently rolling country, just right for grazing, watering and washing sheep—before the days of gold.

This painting shows that only a decade after the first rush Bendigo has gained some substantial architecture. All Saints, the Anglican church, its roof rising beyond the group of trees left around the Government Camp Reserve; the large buildings fronting Pall Mall contrast sharply with the crude miner's huts and tents that still dot the landscape. The ubiquitous goats graze from this vantage point on Gravel Hill to the east of the township. St Killian's Church is on the extreme right, with some buildings lining Bridge Street just visible beyond.

Above: *The 'Discovery of Gold [at Bendigo]' memorial*
Sculpted by C. Douglas Richardson
Sculptor Charles Richardson and an assistant work on the monument to the discovery of gold in Bendigo which was installed in Pall Mall at the junction with Bridge Street in 1901.

Richardson was one of the most gifted sculptors working in Australia at the time. Born in Islington, London in 1853, his parents migrated to settle in Portland, Victoria, where his uncle Thomas Elliott Richardson was both Presbyterian minister and editor of the *Portland Guardian* newspaper.

Charles studied at the School of Design in Carlton and at the National Gallery of Victoria, where along with his fellow classmate Tom Roberts successfully petitioned for the establishment of life-drawing classes. In 1881 he enrolled in the Royal Academy of Arts in London sharing digs with Roberts and fellow sculptor Bertram Mackennal. Richardson was regarded as an important member of the Heidelberg School, showing paintings in the 1889 9" × 5" exhibition of Australian Impressionists but his style of neo-classical allegory fell from favour in the 20th century.

Opposite: *The Pioneer Gold Discoverers of Bendigo, Early Days—From the Annals of Bendigo*
Bendigo was justly proud of its achievements. It had grown into a bustling city that had extracted more than 450 tons of gold, making it the quartz-mining capital of the world.

Those who had been lucky, or provident, or both, also felt justly proud of what they had become. Many ordinary working-class men and women had the wealth to live like lords. In the substantial buildings they left, they showed they were intent on making sure that their names were recorded for posterity.

This illustration shows aspects of digging life, a reminder of the pioneering days: *(clockwise, from top)* Off to Bendigo, Issuing Licenses, A Whim, The First Shaft at Bendigo, The Gold Escort, Hut and Store at the Mines, Washing Off, Deep Sinking, Puddling; (*centre*) Horse Puddling Machine, and Digger Hunting 'Joe Joe'.

The Pioneers are *(1st row, from left)*: Edward Pepprell, Walter Sandbach, Patrick P. Farrell, James Mouat [aka 'Bendigo', see p.244], William C. Coleman, Abraham Motherwell, John Paton, William Stewart, Joshua Norris, George M. Newman, William Sandbach, (*2nd row*) Frederick Fenton, Henry Frencham, Margaret Kennedy, William M. Johnson.

Edith became the second Mrs Lansell on 12 August 1882—he was 57, she 27—and their first son, George Victor, was born two months later.

In leaving Bendigo Lansell may also have been escaping the wrath of the Bendigo mining community who, although he had led the movement to reduce miners' wages, were incensed that he had let his mines on the New Chum Reef flood, creating a domino effect, closing other mines and throwing hundreds out of work. As a result Bendigo's mining industry went into a rapid decline.

In a desperate bid to restore its fortune the civic leaders of Bendigo prepared a beautifully illuminated petition containing 2,628 signatures, which was sent to London requesting Lansell's return. Many believed that he had some mystical power over the Bendigo mines, and were delighted that, on his triumphal return to his 'kingdom', Bendigo once again began to flourish.

After his death in 1906, Lansell's employees received a parcel of shares in his mines, and trust funds were established to support widows and orphaned children of Bendigo miners. In death, as in life, George Lansell was the benefactor of those who had helped make his great fortune.

Koch's Pioneer Co. quartz crushing machinery, Sandhurst
American & Australasian Photographic Company
(State Library of New South Wales Collection)

Ore-crushers such as this were dotted all over the Bendigo landscape. The noise from the multi-head stampers was deafening as heavy steel heads were lifted by the steam-driven camshaft and dropped, time and time again onto cartloads of gold-bearing ore.

The crushed rocks, ground to fine sand in this process, were washed away; any gold was trapped in the rivulets of the corduroy beds shown at the left of the photograph. These were big buildings, long, tall and wide; their chimney stacks stood like sentinels, their poppet legs like mechanical beasts, the cacophony from the stampers—the hammerings of hell. It is said that when they shut down for the Sabbath those who lived nearby could not sleep in the eerie silence.

BEECHWORTH AND THE OVENS

On the day that Daniel Cameron [the diggers' friend and local storekeeper] was elected as parliamentary member for the seat of Ovens in September 1855, he led a procession of 80 supporters—some on foot, some on horseback, accompanied by William Brown's Circus Band—from the Woolshed diggings into Beechworth on a horse shod with golden shoes. The fact that the shoes were only put on the horse one mile out from Beechworth was not publicised—some say the shoes were at least 1oz. lighter on arrival.

Cameron had hired the horse from William 'Tinker' Brown, and both gentlemen 'saw a chance of making an *honest* penny out of the election'. Cameron's election committee widely publicised his proposed ride to the polling booth 'on a horse with golden shoes'.

William Craig was among the thousands who lined the streets to witness the procession. He was also a little bit cynical about storekeeper Cameron's extravagant display:

> The stream of population . . . was moving in the direction of the Ovens, where it was reported that gold was being unearthed in large quantities. An interesting feature of this rush was the intense excitement that ensued upon the rumour that gold was so abundant that even the miners' horses were shod with it![5]

Although Craig recalls in his memoirs that the horse had been borrowed from Brown's circus; that the shoes were merely gilded iron and the 'horse trained to lie on its back in the circus ring and flourish his heels in the air', most onlookers believed that those shoes were genuinely gold.

> 'Shoes of gold at the Ovens!' announced the newspapers in large letters. 'Shoes of gold!' echoed business men in Melbourne as they hurriedly despatched large consignments of goods to meet the requirements of the new rush. 'Gold-shod horses!' murmured crowds . . . along the high road . . . exclaimed thousands of people in far-off lands.[6]

Craig suggested that it was the worldwide reporting of Cameron's folly that caused thousands to leave their homes and rush to the Ovens. He claimed that it was a 'storekeeper's and shanty keeper's rush', and that there were more profitable diggings elsewhere—maybe not for Daniel Cameron.

Postscript: A notice for Brown's circus in the *Argus* newspaper [21 Nov. 1855] announced:

> the greatest feature in equestrianism ever produced in Europe, or in this colony—Raymond [sic] will then appear on his Favourite HORSE Castor, shod with pure gold, and go through his surprising tricks which will really astonish all beholders.

Post Office, Beechworth
Hand-coloured lithograph by A. J. Stopps, from a daguerreotype by Acley & Rochletz, James J. Blundell & Co., Melbourne, c.1856
(Rex Nan Kivell Collection, U2303. By Permission, National Library of Australia)

Mining at Cock's El Dorado Claim, 1897
(Burke Museum Beechworth Collection)

Miners' celebration on the Beechworth Diggings, c. 1880
(Burke Museum Beechworth Collection)

In a posed photograph miners 'celebrate their luck in finding a rich strike' out on the Nine-Mile, just out of Beechworth.

Beer by the bucket, and quart-pot, are the order of the day for this relaxed and joyous occasion—even if they are only acting.

Bourke Street. The Start for Beechworth
From *News Letter of Australasia*, 'A narrative to send to friends', No. 59, July 1867
(Picture Collection, State Library of Victoria)

It is midday as a fully-laden Cobb & Co. Coach is illustrated leaving from outside the Coaching Office, and the Albion Hotel, in Bourke Street Melbourne, on the journey to the diggings at Beechworth.

Opposite: *Spring Creek goldfields, Beechworth, c. 1857*

Above: *Spring Creek goldfields, Beechworth, c. 1861*
(Burke Museum Beechworth Collection)

Miners are seen building a water race along the severely-degraded gully just to the west of the township. Sluice mining had stripped the sides of the gully and tons of soil were washed into the old creek-bed.

OUR FIRST VICTORIAN HERO!
—Robert O'Hara Burke—

Irish-born Robert O'Hara Burke was at first a soldier, next an Irish constable, then a member of the goldfields police-force before he set off on his little pony to write himself into the annals of Australian history and posthumous fame as Victoria's greatest local hero.

No matter that it was his petulant, domineering, egotistic, know-all personality which eventually brought him undone, brought to a miserable and untimely death on the edge of the Simpson desert, his failed expedition brought the Colony of Victoria, and the Royal Society of Victoria into the spotlight.

Burke had served in the Hungarian Hussars and with the Royal Irish Constabulary before joining the Victoria Police in April 1853. He was stationed on the Beechworth diggings between 1854 and 1858 where, as Senior Inspector of Police, he was instrumental in bringing order to the Buckland River diggings after the attack on the Chinese in July 1857. Burke was transferred to the Police Camp at Castlemaine in November 1858.

Portrait of Robert O'Hara Burke
Lithograph by Edward Gilks, 1861
(Rex nNan Kivell collection, NK1931, by permission National Library of Australia)

The Buckland near the camp
Watercolour by Henry Bower Lane, 1862
(Picture Collection, State Library of Victoria)

Robert O'Hara Burke was Senior Inspector of Police, stationed at Beechworth between 1854 and '58.

He used his commanding presence and military bearing to bring order to the Buckland River diggings after the awful attack on the Chinese by European diggers in July 1857.

He was an impressive man, described as:

> a gentleman in the prime of life . . . tall, well-made, with dark brown hair; his broad chest was decorated with a magnificent beard . . . fine intelligent eyes, and a splendidly formed head.[7]

He sported a sabre cut, gained in the Austrian Army, which made him most attractive to the ladies who seem enchanted by this handsome, bold adventurer.

Burke was 'born to lead' and enjoyed the admiration and loyalty of those who served beneath him, and of those he served.

It was prominent industrialist John van Agnew Bruce who repaid Burke for settling a workers' dispute in his Castlemaine foundry by sponsoring his name to lead the expedition to the Gulf and attempt the first longitudinal [south to north] crossing of the continent.

Although he was almost incapable of maintaining any sort of normal order in his own affairs, had little knowledge of navigation, no experience at exploration, no bushcraft skills worth mentioning, his attractive and eccentric personality, and his Anglo-Irish pedigree, that ensured his name was put forward to lead the great Victorian expedition.

While the exploration party succeeded in reaching the Gulf of Carpentaria the whole enterprise failed to deliver any tangible benefit to the Colony of Victoria. All they found were miles and miles of almost impenetrable mosquito-infested mangrove swamp. Beset by interpersonal feuding, disease, malnutrition and the constipative effects of a diet consisting mainly of Nardoo leaves [which, unlike the natives they did not know how to treat] Burke and Wills perished at Cooper's Creek.

The deaths of Burke and his travelling companion William Wills at Cooper's Creek in June 1861, captured the imagination of the Colony and all those who had supported and sponsored Burke in his quest lined up to bask in his glory.

After news of their deaths reached Melbourne the Colony went into mourning. When their remains were brought back for interment in the Melbourne Cemetery, it was Councillor Gingell from Castlemaine, followed by the Castlemaine Light Dragoons, the Castlemaine Volunteer Band and the Castlemaine Rifle Corps who led the funeral procession through the streets of the city.

Right across the Colony citizens vied to be the first to erect fitting memorials to the greatest 'Victorian Heroes'—Burke and Wills.

On 1 July 1864 a slender, monolithic monument to Burke and Wills, overlooking Castlemaine from its vantage point in Wills Street was publicly unveiled before a crowd of more than 2,000 citizens, such was the place held in their hearts for Burke. Local draper William Froomes paid Burke this tribute: 'A man of rare chivalry . . . whom one could not but love'.

THE CENTRAL HIGHLANDS

Clunes and Creswick

Creswick became the scene of pioneering workplace reform in the mines, yet it was also the scene of the worst mining disaster on the goldfields when water burst through the face of the south-west drive of No. 2 shaft in the New Australasian Mine, on Tuesday, 12 December 1882. The deep mines sought ancient river beds far below the surface, and the miners had been shovelling out the loose gravel sandwiched between layers of basalt and shale when the tunnel burst.

Thousands of litres of water poured over the two men who were at work at the face, they were able to escape from the torrent and warn the plateman, who, showing great courage, ran a further 500 metres back down another drive to warn his cobbers.

Another twenty-nine men struggled through the rapidly rising waters, but only two of these managed to swim to safety in the total darkness, guided by ventilation pipes. The others climbed to the highest point in the tunnel, but as the air slowly ran out they collapsed and fell unconscious into the water. It took all the pumps on the surface two days to lower the level

The Port Phillip Gold Mining Company's Claim and the Town of Clunes
Wood engraving by Samuel Calvert, Ebenezer and David Syme, from *The Australian Illustrated News*, 19 June 1869
(Picture collection, State Library of Victoria)

There was limited alluvial gold on the Clunes diggings, and it was not until 1856, when the English company, Port Phillip & Colonial, began to follow the quartz reefs, that any real wealth was taken from Clunes.

By the end of the century the gold had all but played out, and the town, which had once been the fifth largest in Victoria, saw investments disappear, along with much of its population.

The Creswick Mining Disaster, 1882
Wood engraving from a sketch by our special artist, David Syme & Co., from *The Australian Illustrated News*, 23 December 1882
(Picture Collection, State Library of Victoria)

Twenty-two men drowned when water burst through the face of a drive in the No.2 shaft of the New Australasian Mine on 12 December 1882. Investigation into the causes of this, the worst mining disaster on the Victorian goldfields brought much-needed reform to work practices in the mining industry.

sufficiently for rescuers to enter the dark and watery tomb; twenty-two of the twenty-seven left below ground were found dead.

Fifteen thousand attended the funerals the following day. A relief fund raised £75 per family for the seventeen widows, and the 75 children left fatherless.

A Disaster Inquiry agreed that inaccurate surveys had led the mine manager to mistakenly allow tunnelling too close to older, water-filled workings. It was recommended that all mines be required to have better mine signalling and escape routes.

Creswick became the cradle of the trade union movement in Australia. Just as the miners at Clunes had banded together in December 1873, and defended their jobs against the Chinese, the miners at Creswick fought the bosses for their fair day's pay. In the 1880s miners worked an eight-hour shift for four shillings and six pence. An extra shilling, a hardship allowance, was paid to the men who worked at the mine face; these 'face men' often worked all day lying in the wet mud, shovelling gravel over their heads to their mates behind. They rarely lived beyond the age of 40. When mine owners sought

Mining scene, Creswick
Oil painting by Walter Withers, 1893
(Ballarat Fine Art Gallery)

This painting by Walter Withers, shows a whip on the Creswick diggings.

A whip was a horse-drawn pulley system that was used to raise and lower men, and ore, up and down the shaft. A horse would walk away from the shaft when pulling the bucket to the surface, and would walk backwards when lowering. Diggers would rely upon a steady horse to ensure safety in this operation.

This scene was painted 40 years after the first rush, at a time when company mining was at its peak. Here Withers has shown the old and the new. An old-timer with his pan just at the water's edge; the company crusher further up the hillside, and deep-shaft miners lounging in the shade at the pit-head while the whip-horse has a feed.

to employ contractors on 4 shillings per foot, rather than on an hourly rate, the miners once again joined in mass protest.

The spirit that led to the wearing of the red ribbon at Bendigo and Ballarat was reborn in protest at the avaricious mine-owners and their shareholders. The combination of water rising in the mines and continued organised labour resistance resulted in the eventual demise of the big mines.

Left: *Union leader, W. G. Spence*
(From 'Early Creswick' by John A. Graham, 1942)

Spence was brought up on the diggings at Jackass Flat, near Creswick. Although he had little education he was an inquiring and hard-working lad. He loved to read, with a fondness for history, philosophy and politics. He was particularly influenced by the utilitarian ideas espoused by John Stuart Mill.

In 1874 Spence was actively involved with the trade union movement helping to create the Creswick Miner's Union. His union activities took him far and wide. He became in turn General Secretary of the Amalgamated Miners Association and the President of the Amalgamated Shearers Union of Australasia. A member of the Australian Labour Party, Spence was elected to the first Federal Parliament in 1901.

Right: *Captain John Hepburn*
(Picture Collection, State Library of Victoria)

—Notable Nuggets—

Lady Loch [617 oz]
Sulky Gully, Creswick 23 August1887.
Midas Gold Mining Co.

Creswick Gold [1,697,500 oz]—
The combined output of the major mines at Creswick was 1,697,500 oz.

The Jim Crow Diggings

Daylesford, Blackwood and the Central Highlands

Some diggings took their names for obvious reasons: the name of the discoverer of the rush or the squatter's run, or simply from the topography or some remarkable feature of the landscape. Others, like the Jim Crow diggings, were a little more cryptic in the origin of their name.

The district, first opened in 1838 by seaman-turned-squatter Captain John Hepburn, was often difficult to negotiate. The hills and gullies were abrupt, then deep, twisting and turning, and falling away again into creeks rushing with the mineral-rich waters that were later to bring a different kind of prosperity to the region. Some said that the diggers had to adopt a kind of crow-like hopping gait to navigate the hillsides, and this name stuck; other reports were that it was named after the chief of the natives nearby, but who or what gave him this uncharacteristic name?

Hepburn had celebrated the discovery of the excellent natural spring water, but the discovery of gold overshadowed the benefits of the springs for a further thirty years, when a small bath-house was constructed at 'Hepburn Springs'. It became fashionable for travellers from Melbourne to take the railway to the European-styled mineral baths set in the middle of the Australian bush.

The Jim Crow diggings, c. 1859
Photograph by Richard Daintree
(Picture Collection, State Library of Victoria)

Richard Daintree, who had been a public servant in Queensland before he took his camera out into the field, was one of the many contemporary photographers whose work covered almost all of the Australian diggings, from Victoria to Queensland.

Simmons Reef, Mount Blackwood, 57 miles from Melbourne, Victoria
Oil on board by Elizabeth Shepherd, 1858
(Rex Nan Kivell Collection, T320. By Permission, National Library of Australia)
An inscription on the back of this painting states that Shepherd was on the goldfields between September 1855 and February 1884.

As the field had only opened in February 1855 and was not at its peak until September when it saw an influx of 15,000 diggers, Shepherd must have been among this rush.

The rushing waters fed by these springs were often far beneath the old creek-beds that were the source of wealth on other fields, and the diggers here often tunnelled straight into the hillsides following these beds, rather than driving shafts from above.

Carrier John Chandler had been offered a good price to get a load up to Daylesford, although it proved to be a difficult journey:

> When we got to the ranges, we had some very bad hills to go up and down, and one siding. We had the greatest difficulty to keep from capsizing. We got safe in with our loads and came back another way. We stopped at a spring for dinner. The water bubbled up like a fountain. It made the tea so strong we could hardly drink it. This is now the famous Daylesford mineral waters. We did not think much of it. At the foot of Mount Franklin we passed a tribe of natives. There was a lot of lubras and piccaninnies. We generally found it best to give them a wide berth, for they are such bold beggars that they will clean you out of all your tobacco, rum, tea, sugar, etc., and if you are alone and any way timid of them, then look out for yourself.[8]

William Howitt also writes of the Aboriginals encountered on his journeys through this region:

—*Notable Nuggets*—

John Bull [720 oz]

The John Bull nugget was found by three poor sailors in White Horse Gully on the Jim Crow diggings, between Castlemaine and Daylesford. The lucky fellow who actually discovered the John Bull, only inches below the surface, had only been on the diggings for a fortnight. The nugget weighed 45 lbs, and was sold by the sailors for £5,000 and taken to London, where it was put on public exhibition.

Unnamed. [600oz]

Yandoit. February 1860. A German and two Poles

Unnamed. [600oz]

Yandoit. April 1860. Four Irishmen

> ... we were surprised to see a number of natives haunting about [a] grog-shop in European costume; but learnt that they were from the aborigines station ahead of us, called Parker's Station, from the Protector [Edward Stone Parker]. The place in which they were found did not argue much for their progress in civilisation ...[9]

and writes also, this time with disgust, of the digger lounging at the same tent:

> a tall, dirty, unshaven, gallows-looking fellow who appeared at the door with a basin of broth, or liquid of the sort ... and answered our inquiries in the same favourite style of surliness.[10]

Howitt passed Hepburn's homestead, which he described as one of the largest he had ever seen, and mused on the good fortune that this master of a merchant-vessel had encountered when he traded 'ploughing the seas [for] grazing the Crown lands of Victoria'. He wondered when a digger would ever find a nugget so large that he, too, would be able to buy large tracts of land for one shilling an acre.

The area saw a great influx of southern Europeans; Italians established themselves in factories and farms; middle-European Jews came in their hundreds, drawn by the similarity of the 'mountain' region to that left far behind. The hardy little Cornishmen, whose expertise in deep underground mining was never equalled, followed the introduction of deep quartz mining.

What a mixture these diggings became! All the world was there—sober, hard-working Protestants working side by side with exuberant Italian Catholics,calculating Jews and the rowdy Tipperary mob—larrikins and ladies—all of them hopped about these diggings, up and down the steep gullies, with a 'Jimcra' gait*.

---

* The name Jimcra was derived from a popular song of the time which described the agitated dance movements of the black crow [a pejorative term for African slaves]:

> *Wheel about, an' turn about, an' do jus' so,*
> *Every time I wheel about, I jump Jim Crow.*

MOUNT ALEXANDER (CASTLEMAINE)

Mount Alexander was at the heart of Dr Barker's Ravenswood Run, a vast sheep-grazing station, typical of the holdings taken up by scores of squatters following the opening of the district by Major Mitchell's expedition of 1836.

Although there had been a number of reports of gold-finds in various parts of the fledgling colony none captured the public imagination until the discovery at Specimen Gully on the gently rolling terrain on the western edge of Barker's Run, at what is now known as Barker's Creek.

Maybe it was the names given to the region that attracted thousands of new chums to these diggings: Mount Alexander, Forest Creek, Ravenswood, Sutton Grange, Barker's Creek and Guildford—all conjure an image of 'old English' charm, but the reality that awaited the diggers in the summer months of 1851 would have been anything but reminiscent of home and hearth.

The alluvial diggings in the shadow of the mount lasted for several years. but after new rushes opened up to the north and north-west, and the larger centres developed deep-lead mines, the district of Castlemaine settled into a new era of prosperity.

The first regional railway steamed through the valley in 1861 bringing commerce and enterprise of a different kind to the goldfields, as Castlemaine developed its expertise in engineering and metal founding that had been learned on the diggings.

Above: *View of the Castlemaine Diggings*
From a drawing by George Rowe, 1857
(Author's Collection)

This engraving shows miners working in the old watercourse of Forest Creek. The bend in the creek beyond the bridge was eventually taken out as Castlemaine went to an inordinate amount of trouble to realign its landscape.

Hills were cut down, gullies filled, and undulating street levels cut away as the townsfolk sought to impose an ordered town-grid over the terrain.

'The Levels' occupied the minds of the citizens for many years. Where once buildings stood at street level, many in the oldest part of town had to re-align their front doors to meet the new levels, at times more than six feet lower than at the time of construction.

Opposite: *Forest Creek*
Watercolour by S. T. Gill, 1852
(Picture Collection, State Library of Victoria)

This view of the Mount Alexander–Forest Creek diggings was drawn within the first twelve months after the discovery by shepherds Worley and Peters, who found the first gold in the region in September 1851.

It was not long before the landscape was dotted with tents, and the thousands who had flocked to make their fortunes hurried about like restless ants.

On the left of Gill's watercolour can be seen the office of the *Argus* newspaper and Bryce Ross's Agency Office on the Red Hill at nearby Chewton. The mounted trooper is following the track heading towards the Government Camp, nestled between the hills at Castlemaine in the distance.

Castlemaine from Ten Foot Hill
Oil on canvas by Edwin Stocquelier, 1858
(Castlemaine Pioneers and Old Residents Association Collection)

Only five years after the first land sales Castlemaine already exhibits a well-settled air. While some diggers tents remain on the south side of Forest Creek, on the north substantial houses, churches, shops, warehouses and the first market buildings spread across the undulating landscape.

—Notable Nuggets—

Heron [1008 oz]
Fryers Creek—29/3/1855
Davis and Harriss

Unnamed [648 oz]
Taradale—27/5/1856
J. Williams, Geo. Stapleton and Jno. Matthews

Unnamed [600 oz]
Fryers Creek—1854
Finder Unknown

Store at Chewton, c. 1860
(Chewton Historical Museum Collection)

Chewton grew up on the site of the first Forest Creek diggings. It was also the site of the first Commissioners' Camp on Adelaide Hill.

The Camp moved into Castlemaine in October 1851, but Chewton remained an important junction as the diggings fanned out in all directions from this point: to Golden Point, Fryer's Creek, Forest Creek, Moonlight and Pennyweight Flats.

Bryce Ross established his 'Newspaper' office in Chewton.

The Garfield Wheel, c. 1898
(Castlemaine Art Gallery and Historical Museum Collection)

The waterwheel that drove the crushing mill at Quartz Hill near Chewton was the largest in the Southern Hemisphere: diameter, 72 feet; one revolution every 45 to 50 seconds.

MOBILE DAGUERREAN PHOTOGRAPHERS CAPTURE THE DIGGINGS

Benjamin Pierce Batchelder

Born in Beverley, Massachusetts in 1826, Benjamin Pierce Batchelder and his three brothers: Perez, Nathanial and Freeman, were partners in a far-flung photographic empire that at one time operated portrait galleries in Massachusetts, California and Australia.

They had embraced the new technology soon after it was first introduced, and by 1852 their unique and highly-mobile daguerrean carts [see also page 34] were soon a common feature across the American goldfields operating out of Stockton in San Joaquin County, California. One Californian gold miner, wrote in his journal in 1855 that he had his portrait taken by Benjamin Pierce Batchelder for five dollars 'a sort of Daguerreotype saloon on wheels at Fort Grizzly, El Dorado County'. The same miner visited Batchelder's cart again in Volcano [another diggings 80 km east of Sacramento] a month later. Batchelder's daguerrean darkroom was certainly mobile.

In 1856, Benjamin and his younger brother Freeman set sail for Melbourne to join Perez at the gallery he had established in Collins Street East. Benjamin and Nathaniel opened another in Sydney, but after Nathaniel's sudden death

Bendigo Hotel, Bridge Street, Sandhurst
Photograph by Benjamin Pierce Batchelder, c.1861
(Picture Collection, State Library of Victoria)

The Batchelder mobile-cart is well positioned for clear brand identification in the middle of this photograph. The same cart, and at times, the image of the photographer himself appear regularly in the series of photographs taken for the Sandhurst Council in 1861.

in 1860 Benjamin moved to Sandhurst where he opened a studio in Pall Mall just a few doors down from the Beehive building.

In 1861 the Sandhurst Borough Council commissioned him to create a series of views of the town's mining activities for display at the London International Exhibition the following year. He received an honourable mention for his photographs of the Volunteer Rifle Corps and Volunteer Fire Brigade.

Batchelder returned to America in 1868 accompanied by his wife Nancy who always worked with him in the gallery. In 1872 they opened the 'Photographic Art Palace' in El Dorado Street, Stockton and another, 'The Pioneer Gallery' on Main Street. Batchelder remained in Stockton until his death in 1891, Nancy kept the gallery open for several years after.

Nicholas Caire

Just like the Batchelders, Guernsey-born Nicholas Caire was fascinated by the new invention of the wet-plate photographic process. In 1860 he arrived in Adelaide, aged 23 years, in the company of his parents who had done little to dissuade him from pursuing a career in the photographic business.

While working as a hairdresser in Adelaide he was fortunate to be mentored by a professional photographer, the American Townsend Duryea, who was the first photographer to work outside of Adelaide, making trips into the

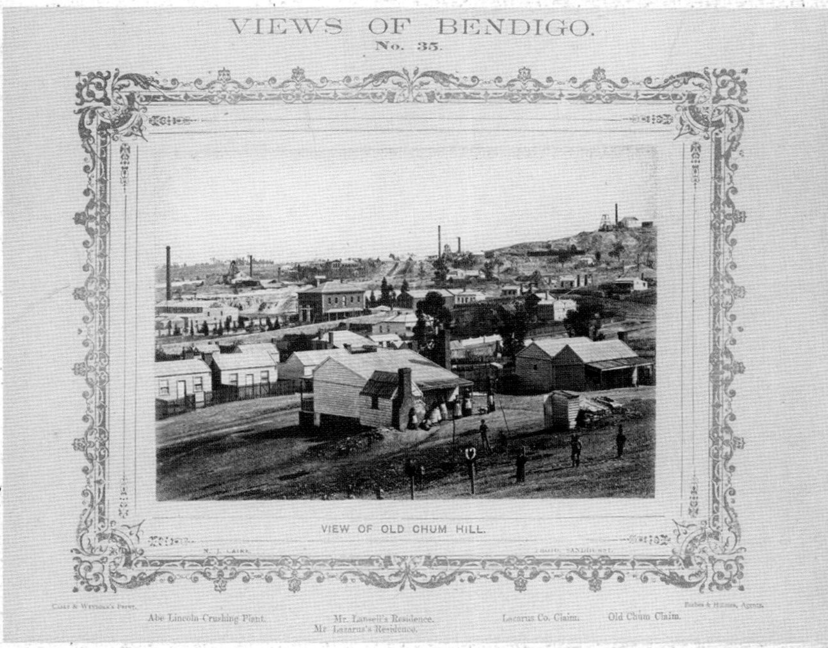

View of Old Chum Hill
Photograph mounted on card by Nicholas Caire, c.1875

Your photographer at work, c. 1886
(National Library of Australia Collection)

"This scene represents Mr. N. J. Caire, the celebrated '— Victorian Bush' photographer and author of this series of pictures, with his pack at work on the Gippsland mountains"

bush to places such as Burra, Clare, Goolwa and Kapunda. Duryea's experience must have encouraged Caire to also step outside. Although he had been producing quality studio portraits of his friends his next step was outdoors. In 1865 he travelled through Gippsland, carting his wet-plate box camera, recording images of the Strezlecki Ranges and photographs of Aboriginals at Lake Tyers.

In 1867 he opened his first studio in Adelaide. After his marriage to Louisa Master in 1870 he moved to Clunes on the Central Victorian goldfields where he supplemented his passion for photography with the proceeds of his hairdressing salon. Caire took the next step to becoming a professional when he opened a studio in Bendigo in 1871 and then, when he took over

T. F. Chuck's studio in the Royal Arcade in Collins Street, Melbourne in 1876 he was fully-established.

In 1885, the development of the dry plate process revolutionised the practice of outdoor, landscape photography. Although cameras were still cumbersome to cart about Caire dragged his all over the colony. He pioneered 'pictorial' photography; he photographed the high country previously known only to mountain cattlemen; his images of Bendigo are among the most comprehensive records of the mining district in its heyday; his human interest photographs of settlers doing it hard in the bush, and down on their luck, are a precursor to contemporary photojournalism.

Richard Daintree

Richard Daintree
(John Oxley library, State Library of Queensland)

Photographer Richard Daintree was born in Huntingdonshire on 13 December 1832. It was in his home village of Hemingford that he met Alfred Selwyn who was to become the first Government Geologist in the Colony of Victoria. Selwyn sailed for Victoria in August 1852, and it is presumed that Daintree came out on the same voyage, having been advised by his doctor to seek a better climate than Cambridge where he had studied theology and Slavonic languages.

On arrival in the colony at first Daintree went digging for gold. Like many others he thoroughly enjoyed the freedom of bush life but probably had little success at gold digging because when Selwyn's assistant

The Navarre Diggings
Photograph by Richard Daintree, c.1861
(Picture Collection, State Library of Victoria)

resigned his post in February 1854 Daintree did not hesitate in accepting the position. Ever the perfectionist he went back to England to study assaying. He returned to the colony in 1857 and had the position as Victorian Geologist until 1865 when he took up some land in northern Queensland. Four years later he was appointed Government Geologist for that region and recorded the first discoveries of gold-bearing country in north Queensland. Curiously, Daintree did not promote these goldfields for several years, others reaping the rewards that might well have been his to claim.

It is presumed that Daintree had previously met the prominent photographer Antoine Fauchery on the diggings, or in Melbourne, as he already showed an interest in the science of photography. While Daintree was back in England, Fauchery was in Paris. As both men arrived back in the colony at the same time it is also presumed that they travelled on the same ship as before long they were working together on a volume of photographic studies entitled Australia. While it is difficult to tell who took what picture in this study Fauchery was renowned for his portraits, and set *tableux*, while Daintree's primary interest was in the geology of the landscape and scientific exploration.

As government geologist he carried his camera everywhere he went and was the first to use a camera for scientific fieldwork anywhere in the world, translating his photographs to drawings and charts for reproduction when he returned to his office.

Daintree was made commissioner in charge of Queensland's contribution to the 1871 Exhibition of Art and Industry in London and was appointed as Queensland Agent-General in London the following year—a period not without controversy for Richard Daintree. His job was to encourage migration to Queensland, a task he undertook with great success, but his staff were lining their pockets without his knowledge and the political kerfuffle that followed stained his reputation at home in Queensland.

Daintree had maintained a close relationship with prominent clergyman and amateur geologist the Rev. W. B. Clarke all his professional life. Although Clarke was a man almost twice his age, their relationship became almost filial with Clarke sending Daintree geological samples for examination even while he was working in London. W. B. Clarke was one of the first men to report the existence of gold-bearing deposits in 1844, almost a decade before the first gold rush to New South Wales.

Daintree had always been troubled by indifferent health, the seeds of tuberculosis were with him since his days at Cambridge. Years of hard work, and bush living in the tropics had finally caught up with him, and the damp and foggy English winter of 1878 brought him undone. He died on 20 June after a short but unsuccessful period of convalescence in the south of France. By strange coincidence his mentor W.B. Clarke, ten thousand miles away, died the same week.

Antoine Fauchery

Self-portrait, Antoine Fauchery, c.1858

Antoine Fauchery travelled to the diggings from his native France in 1853. Unlike many photographers who restricted themselves to portraits of eminent figures or *carte-de-visites*, Fauchery also created tableaus of diggers working the creeks, groups of natives, and panoramic views of the townships and ravaged diggings that were often interpretative creations rather than simply captured observations. He pioneered the use of a lens, designed in Vienna, which gave sharp focus to the background making the subjects in the foreground appear almost in relief. His views of the towns and of the diggings are sharp all over. He called his prints taken in this way 'Stereomonoscopes'.

Landscape painter Eugène von Guérard, who was travelling with a large group of French artists and intellectuals, recorded that 'Fougery' was in Ballarat in 1853 after coming to Australia from California with his wife. Von Guérard had got it wrong: Fauchery had not been in California, and his travelling companion was not actually his wife at the time, but they were in Ballarat.

Like so many other diggers, Fauchery had both success and failure, and after going broke he used his few remaining pounds to set up a restaurant in Melbourne, catering for the large number of French diggers passing through. His takings from this helped fund his return to Paris, where he and his companion were finally married. They returned to Australia in 1857.

Washing out a good prospect
Photograph by Antoine Fauchery, c.1858
(Picture Collection, State Library of Victoria)

THE TARRANGOWER DIGGINGS. MALDON

Tarrangower (Maldon)

Once the easy pickings ran out, unlike most smaller communities, Maldon did not go into decline. There were incredibly rich veins running just below the surface, and mining companies were soon formed to tunnel into the earth.

The Nuggetty Reef, north of Mount Tarrangower, was discovered by young Alexander Pettit in November 1855. He and a couple of his mates quietly worked the reef until their secret got out in January 1856. Over the next five years £1,000,000 worth of gold was taken from these rich, yet mostly shallow, reefs. Little gold was found beyond 250 feet, making sustained deep mining quite a challenge.

In Maldon they worked around the clock, the sound of crushing batteries constantly pounded the air, and three times a day the streets were filled with hot and thirsty miners as they were hauled to the surface at the end of their shifts.

The town has remained virtually unchanged since the roaring days and it was honoured by the National Trust of Australia in 1966, when it earned the title of Australia's First Notable Town.

Miners on the Nuggety Reef
A group of Maldon miners pose along the rail-track of their small single-wheeled mine-head on the Nuggety Reef.

The Welsh Swagman

Joseph Jenkins, the Welsh Swagman

Joseph Jenkins (1818–98) was born in Cardiganshire, west Wales. His family had been farmers and men of letters, numbering some recognised Welsh poets among them.

He farmed at home until he married, when he moved to farm at Trecefel, Tregaron. The Jenkins had nine children, a prosperous farm, and Joseph held a position of respect in the community.

He held strong views on farming methods, favouring crop rotation, harrowing rather than deep ploughing, and was an advocate of the powerful properties of manure. He even badgered machinery makers for a combined dung-cart and distributor some sixty years before they were to become generally available.

At 51 years of age Jenkins packed his swag and set out for Australia, leaving his wife and seven surviving children behind. He arrived in Port Phillip in March 1869 and had travelled up to the Mount Alexander goldfields by the end of April.

After trying his hand at digging, he eventually settled in a hut in the bush near Lewis Road at Muckleford. He worked for many years around the district, helping farmers, clearing roads, digging the Maldon drains, and cutting great heaps of firewood.

All this time he recorded his adventures in his diaries. These records, which include many of his poems and songs, form the basis of the book *Diary of a Welsh Swagman*, in which he also extols the virtue of manure, unable to comprehend why the colonial farmer, complaining of the poor quality of the Australian soils, ignored the beneficial produce of their beasts.

He returned to Wales, aged 76, to spend the next, and last, four years of his life surrounded by his grandchildren.

Opposite top: *The Maldon Market Place*

Opposite bottom: *The Maldon Mines*
Watercolours by David Drape, c. 1855

Above left: *Carman's Tunnel Entrance, Parkins' Reef*
(Author's photograph)
Between November 1882 and December 1884 the impressively named Great International Quartz Mining Company drove a 570-metre tunnel into the south-western side of Mt Tarrangower.
The miners expected to cut across reefs that ran within the mountain, but for all their hard work chasing drives, opening crosscuts, galleries, following quartz veins, digging shafts, cutting, timbering and
laying tracks it was an unprofitable exercise and by 1888 the company stock was no longer listed.
A quartz crown was found on top of the mountain, but yielded only 2 oz per ton. It was declared 'not proving payable', and abandoned. Today, the long dry tunnel, 2.5 km from Maldon, is accessible to the public.

Above right: *Beer label, Maldon Brewery*
Several breweries were established in Maldon at the foot of Mt Tarrangower, where springs provided pure water, perfect for a good brew.

The Kangaroo Hotel, Maldon
(All Photographs,Courtesy of Maldon Historical Museum)

The Kangaroo at Maldon still stands today. Surprisingly, it is the only hotel so-named in Australia.

Most hoteliers seemed more intent on honouring their past than embracing their future, with pubs named—The Shamrock, Brian Boru, Old England, The Royal and Caledonian; there is even a Pig & Whistle in Central Victoria.

Warnock Bros., Beehive Stores, Main Street, Maldon, c. 1900

THE GOLDEN TRIANGLE

The district known as the Golden Triangle takes in the extraordinarily rich alluvial fields of Dunolly, Tarnagulla, Moliagul, Wedderburn, Rheola, Inglewood and Kingower. The number of significant nuggets taken from this region leaves all other goldfields well behind.

The Welcome Stranger nugget, the largest ever found in the world, was unearthed by John Deason and Richard Oates in 1869, at Moliagul, a small farming community in the heart of this coarse-gravelled, black-treed, harsh, dry country. All around this area great nuggets were discovered from the early days of the goldrush right up into the first decade of the twentieth century—the area justly earned its title as the 'Golden Triangle'.

—Notable Nuggets—

Welcome Stranger [2284 oz]
Moliagul—5 February 1869
John Deason & Richard Oates

Blanche Barkly [1743 oz]
Kingower—27 August 1857
R. & J. Ambrose, S. & C. Napier

Unnamed [1363 oz]
Old Lead, Dunolly—October 1857

Viscount Canterbury [1114 oz]
Berlin-Rheola—31 May 1853
S. Schlossman & J. Davis

Maryborough [1034 oz]
Blackman's Lead—22 January 1853
J. Dinon & Jas. Edinton

Poseidon [953 oz]
Tarnagulla—18 December 1906
Woodall, Condron, Brookes & Eva

Viscountess Canterbury [912 oz]
Berlin-Rheola—3 October 1870
Felstead & Party

Unnamed [893 oz]
Berlin Rush—12 March 1869
Pat & Jas. Hoare

Kum Tow [795 oz]
Berlin Rush—17 April 1871
Loo Ching & Party

Unnamed [782 oz]
Evans Gully, Kingower—February 1861

Leila [675 oz]
Poseidon—3 January 1907
C. Smith, J. Rodgers & G. Stephenson

Linger-And-Die Diggings, Tarnagulla, 1896
The Golden Triangle had some rich alluvial fields, several with unusual names such as Linger-And-Die, Strip-Me-Naked and Frying Pan Lead, so-named because the first gold was washed out in a frying pan.

Lucky diggers at their windlass, Tarnagulla
Diggers, Lockett and Scholes, pose at the head of their shaft after finding a 27 ounce nugget, 1902.

Main Street, Inglewood
Although some substantial buildings grace the streetscape, others are still roofed with canvas. In the centre a large gum-tree is posted with notices: 'The Diggers' Intelligencer' was a common feature across the diggings.
(Courtesy, Allan M. Nixon)

Martin's Timber Yard, Dunolly, c. 1865
Dunolly grew into a substantial town servicing the needs of diggers, farmers and settlers alike. At one stage, at the height of the rush there was a large Chinese community whose tent city lined the creek-bed for miles.
(Photographs courtesy Central Goldfields Shire, Historical Museum Collection)

WALHALLA AND WOOD'S POINT

Prospector William Gooley claimed to have been the discoverer of the Upper Goulburn goldfield in May 1861. However, at the same time there were countless numbers of diggers prospecting the icy streams of the Victorian Alps, as one by one the diggings opened up—Wood's Point, Gaffney's Creek, Jamieson, Matlock, Stringer's Creek and Walhalla.

In 1862 two experienced bushmen led a party of prospectors following the Goulburn River to its source, high in the Victorian ranges. At a fork in the river, one, a German named Dittmer Brehrens, took the left branch, and his companion, Corry, took the right. After considerable struggle, fighting his way through almost impenetrable scrub, Corry gave up. He cut across the mountain hoping to meet up with Brehrens. As he slipped down the other side he dropped into a secluded gully where he discovered the ground strewn with quartz, which showed a 'plentiful supply of gold'. He immediately staked out a claim and set to work.

His companion soon caught up with him, and before long others joined in the rush to what must have been the most difficult of all the goldfields to access.

At times bushmen and diggers would attempt to open a way through the dense bush by burning a path before them with a firebrand. When Duncan and Colin McDougall, who had been among Brehrens and Corry's exploring party, attempted to bring in machinery for quartz-crushing, the carriers they had engaged refused to push their horses any further. The McDougalls had to do it themselves. They named their mine 'The Morning Star', and although

Wood's Point, Mines on Morning Star Hill, c. 1864

they were only able to cart in a 'clumsy little machine, with wooden shanks to the old-fashioned water-engine, [it] turned out more gold than the large-stream driven batteries of Ballarat and Sandhurst'.[11] By the end of 1866 the claim had paid out over £164,000.

The mines in the often snow-covered mountain gullies of eastern Victoria were exceedingly rich. The Long Tunnel Mine, at Walhalla, at the time of its closure in 1913 was the single largest producer of gold in Victoria, yielding 13.5 tons of gold between 1865 and 1911. The shaft of the Long Tunnel was 1100 yards deep, and the tunnel extended over 5 miles underground.

Walhalla Gold Mining column, 1887
(Picture Collection, State Library of Victoria)
The photograph shows a group of miners in their best clothes, standing around a column on a marble plinth. Segments of the column record the amount of gold mined in Walhalla within two-year periods, commencing with 1870. The photograph probably records the placing of the top segment which records the amount of gold mined in 1884 and 1885.

Packhorses Bringing Supplies to the Diggings
(Rex Nan Kivell Collection. National Library of Australia)

The mountainous terrain of the Upper Goulburn diggings was so difficult to access that packhorses were at first the only way to carry in supplies.

The English novelist Anthony Trollope toured these goldfields on horseback, and found the track into Walhalla so steep that at times he could hardly remain in the saddle. Imagine his surprise when he discovered a piano and billiard table in the hotel on arrival.

An enterprising carrier, Louie the Frenchman, carried dancehall girl Kitty Cane up the hillside into Walhalla for 9d a pound, which wasn't such a bad deal for him, as Kitty weighed 22 stone!

The crushing machinery designed for McDougall & Company's Morning Star Mine was made to measure. No single piece of the eight-head stamping battery could weigh over 200 lbs, as each had to be carried on horseback, and had to be assembled on site.

Although the entire crusher weighed less than three tons, it took them over three months to carry it up to Wood's Point, and almost a year to bring the entire project to completion.

The gullies were so steep on this goldfield that little flat ground was available for building. The settlement at Walhalla followed the meandering watercourse, winding in and out of the valley, some buildings even straddling the creek.

When the miners wanted a place for recreation they simply removed the top of a hill, truncating it to provide a level playing field. The Walhalla Cricket Ground is still today only reached by a climb of over 600 feet. It was on this field in 1907 that Warwick Armstrong, captain of the Australian cricket team, bet that he could hit a six by landing it on the roof of the Star Hotel. (He didn't quite manage it, and was caught out on the boundary for twelve.)

In the cemetery some of the diggers are buried in graves cut vertically into the hillsides, so valuable was horizontal space.

Where once stood proud forests, barren hillsides remained. The Long Tunnel itself fired eight steam boilers, 24 hours a day. Where lack of water was the bane of some goldfields, at Walhalla there was often too much, with miners forced to work all day in mud and slush, miles underground.

'I allus has wan at eleven'

This famous poster for Carlton Beer was based on a photograph taken around the turn of the century by Melbourne-based photographer, G. M Sinclair.

Sinclair had gone into a bush pub at Walsh's Creek, an old gold diggings in the Upper Yarra/Warburton region, north-east of Melbourne, where he observed this old fossicker, Sam Griffin, approach the bar and raise a glass of beer to his lips with what appeared to be almost spiritual dedication.

When he had drained his glass he let out a long sigh of deep satisfaction. Sinclair commented, 'You seem to be enjoying your beer, my friend?' Sam replied, 'I do indeed sir, I allus has wan at eleven'. A photograph was taken, and later adapted by a commercial artist to the now-famous poster for Carlton.

There is an amusing rejoinder to Sam's reply. He may have said that 'He allus had wan at eleven', but the original advertisement continued, 'It's something wot's gotta be done, cos if I don't have wan at eleven I allus has eleven at wan!'

WARANGA, WHROO AND THE BALACLAVA MINE

The Waranga diggings had been troublesome around the time of the 'Red-ribbon' rebellion in Bendigo. Diggers on this scrubby, dusty, goldfield cared little for the requirements of the troopers and gladly added their names to the document that was to become known as 'the Bendigo Petition'. Unfortunately most of the signatures from these diggings were lost in the McIvor Escort robbery and were never placed before the governor in Melbourne.

To the east of the McIvor diggings, on the undulating plains near the Goulburn River, there was once a bustling township that was home to over 20,000 diggers and their families. Today nothing is left of Whroo but a huge hole in the ground and an abandoned cemetery, whose metal and wooden headstones bear testament to the hardships endured on these rough-and-ready diggings.

There were rich alluvial fields around Rushworth, but it is the story of the Whroo diggings that is the most intriguing.

The discovery of the Balaclava Reef just a few miles out of Rushworth saw mining methods that were most unusual. Shafts were cut down into the hillside following the rich veins of gold-bearing quartz. The miners removed entire veins leaving open fissures in the rock that were propped apart with timbers, leaving the hillside like a giant honeycomb.

An attempt was made to blast the hill apart with an enormous charge of explosive, but this was not successful. All that was left was a hill too dangerous for further shaft mining. A gaping hole, blasted into the side of the hill, allowed the miners to cut away material in what was to become one huge open-cut mine.

The ore to be crushed was taken away by tramway through a tunnel cut through 100 yards of solid rock.

The gold won from the Balaclava mine at Whroo financed the building of the majestic Menzies Hotel in Victorian Melbourne.

At various times attempts were made to reopen the pits, speculation on the possibilities of reworking the old shafts was always defeated by the element that had caused so many to close—water. Towards the end of the twentieth century mining took on a new form, huge drives were opened miles away from the reefs to be worked, trucks and excavators driven straight in, to reach the working face far underground. No more winding cables or poppet heads, no more clattering cages or sound of the steam whistle or ringing of bells—all were replaced by the growl of the diesel engine.

The Balaclava Syndicate, 1932
(Courtesy Q. C. Binks Collection)

There were few mines still working on the Victorian goldfields when this photograph was taken, yet there were plenty who still believed in the diggings.

A group of investors, friends and families pose on the hillside at the re-opening of the Balaclava Mine in 1932.

NEW SOUTH WALES

Beyond The Blue Mountains

Bathurst is Australia's oldest inland settlement, first settled after Governor Macquarie travelled to the 'newly discovered country' in 1815. Although the land was ripe for agricultural development, such development in the region was unusually slow, as several years of successive droughts and economic depression deterred squatters from expanding into a region so remote from the coastal ports.

Just as explorer Thomas Livingston Mitchell was to wax lyrical about the 'great south countrie' he had crossed on his expedition from Sydney into Victoria in 1836, when he titled the central region 'Australia Felix', Assistant Surveyor-General G.W. Evans had also described the rich plains of central New South Wales—as 'the handsomest country I ever saw'.

The Sort to Catch Gardiner—The Right Man on the Right Horse at the Right Place
No matter where the venturer dared to roam, the possibility of encountering one of the 'Kings of the Road', a bushranger, was real. Most did not consider the police to be much of a threat to their liberty, and although most traps were not too smart few bushrangers lived to a ripe old age.

Just as Evans had been the first to lay foot on the Bathurst plains and herald the influx of Scottish squatters and sheep-herders, so too did Mitchell herald the migration of the Sydney Scots to take up large squatting runs right across the best tracts of land in Victoria.

The discovery of gold at Ophir, only 35 km from Bathurst, brought thousands onto the squatters' runs in 1851, as did the discovery of gold in the central Victorian highlands see the end of the squatters' reign on those rich plains. The story repeated itself on almost every goldfield: shepherds walked away from their flocks; shopkeepers put up their shutters, packed their wares and headed for the diggings, where their next store was a simple plank set across two boxes and roofed in canvas. Sailors abandoned their ships, police resigned, gaolers threw in their keys, parsons, priests, prosecutors and prostitutes all headed for the diggings where each expected their fortune was to be made.

The diggings around the old centre of Bathurst—Young, Forbes, Mudgee, West Wyalong, Parkes and Eugowra are also names that feature prominently in the tales of derring-do on the diggings—a disproportionate number of notorious characters ended up on these New South Wales goldfields.

'Darkie' Gardiner, Ben Hall, Johnny Gilbert and John Bow were some of the more famous of the 'currency lads' who roamed these diggings. They were known to be at Lambing Flat at the time of the riots there. The Clarke Brothers (Thomas and John) and their extended family terrorised the area

Ophir diggings, Summer Hill Creeks, 1851
Hand-coloured lithograph from a drawing by G. F. Angus, published J. Hogarth [London], 1851
(Rex Nan Kivell Collection, NK703. By Permission, National Library of Australia)
This almost arcadian scene belies the reality of the rush to these parts. This lithograph was first published in June 1851, just one month after Hargraves had made his discovery, and obviously before the creek had been churned to mud by the thousands of diggers who crowded onto these green banks.

around Yass and Goulburn until they were captured at Jindera in April 1867. 'Mad Dan' Morgan, who started his career in Castlemaine and finished it on the Ovens near Beechworth, instilled fear into the hearts of the honest settlers around Wagga Wagga and Tumbarumba for many years.

The apparent isolation of these diggings drew the misfits, the outcasts, the errant ticket-of-leave men, the bold lads who defied the law and demanded that they too had a right to pursue their destiny as free men. Unfortunately these bushrangers saw the easy way out: if digging was hard, sitting astride a stolen horse and pushing a pistol under the nose of a coach-driver was easy, and there was always gold a-plenty ready for the taking. The law, however, did prevail—and there are numerous lonely bushrangers' graves dotted throughout the bush.

The Naming of Ophir

Edward Hammond Hargraves named the diggings where he found the first gold at Summer Hill Creek, 35 km from Bathurst, Ophir, after the biblical 'city of gold' (as had been Ophir County in California).

KIANDRA: THE COLD FIELDS

Gold was discovered in the Eucumbene River, high in the snow-covered mountains of southern New South Wales in January 1860.

The alluvial diggings were all but finished in Victoria, and around Bathurst, so diggers rushed to stand once again in freezing creek-beds, searching for a bit of colour.

By the middle of the year most of the miners were unable to work because of the heavy snow. George Preshaw, who had grown up on the Castlemaine diggings, where his father had a doctor's surgery at Campbell's Creek, entered service with the Castlemaine branch of the Bank of New South Wales in 1855, was transferred to the Kiandra agency at the beginning of the rush. He was shocked to find the conditions in his new bank (a tent) on arrival:

> On entering I saw a young man behind the counter . . . he was perched on a piece of bark which rested on two logs, a stream of water running under him . . . I was puzzled to account for this, but on examination found it was caused by the snow, which was a foot or two deep at the back of the tent, thawing.[12]

Kiandra in 1860
(By permission, National Library of Australia)
Even though the conditions on the Kiandra goldfield were generally inhospitable, the lust for gold proved irrisistable. More than £2,000,000 worth was won from the usually snow-covered hillsides.

By June the miners devised a scheme to engage all the Chinese in the region to bring up much-needed supplies, as it was impossible for pack-horses to get through.

A great feature of Kiandra was Kidd's Hotel, and its restaurant provided hot meals for the diggers where: 'Commissioners, bankers, squatters, swells, come to see the rush, burly diggers just as they had left their work, shanty-keepers, bullies, loafers pierced with cold and impelled by hunger . . .'[13] crowded into the single room in which two narrow tables ran the entire length of the building.

Nearby Carmichael's Empire Hotel opened a dance-room in September 1860; however, there were only three dance-girls. Diggers who missed out on a female partner had to take a 'hairy-faced gentleman or not dance at all'. The floor of the Empire Hotel was thick with mud, and Preshaw recorded:

> It struck me as a queer sight to see hairy-faced men in pea jackets, and long boots, with pipes in their mouths, dancing together.[14]

BATHURST AND LAMBING FLAT

The winter of 1860 had been so harsh that only the hardiest remained on this cold field.

Alongside dancing, drinking and brawling (which they did just to keep warm) the Kiandra diggers were the first in Australia to go skiing, swooshing down the slopes with palings strapped to their feet.

The Kiandra rush only lasted until after an extremely cold spell in the middle of 1861, when the rush to the warmer climes of Lambing Flat [near

---

Gold diggers arriving at Bathurst on their way to Ophir
Lithograph published by Woolcott & Clarke, Sydney; 1851,
from a drawing by G. F. Angas, 1851
(Rex Nan Kivell Collection, NK672. National Library of Australia collection)

Bathurst had been settled for almost half a century before gold was discovered. Unlike the Victorian goldfields there was a well-established township already standing when the diggers passed through on their way to the diggings.

The town had been officially gazetted in 1833, but development was slow. After the discovery of gold the entire region boomed as, typically, thousands of diggers flocked there in search of riches.

After railways were established in the southern colonies Cobb & Co., relocated its headquarters to Bathurst in 1862. The entry into the town of its 103 horses, eighty in harness, pulling ten red-painted coaches and two feed wagons was described as resembling 'the triumphant entry of a first-class equestrian troupe'. By 1870 the company was running 30,000 horses across the eastern colonies, all centred on Bathurst.

Walter Russell Hall and his brother Thomas, diggers from Ballarat at the time of the Eureka Stockade had taken over control of Cobb & Co. from the original owners. Thomas became manager of the Queensland National Bank where they invested in a syndicate to develop the Mount Morgan mine. When Walter Hall died in 1913 his estate was valued at £2,915,513.

Young] enticed the diggers, along with the bank-teller George Preshaw down off the mountain.

The roads of the Riverina were the favourite haunts of the most notorious of New South Wales bushrangers, and as he crossed the country to take up his new posting at Lambing Flat Preshaw had to be careful to avoid being asked to 'bail up' on the lonely roads. On the way a young man on horseback had informed him that:

> Lambing Flat was deserted; that there had been a great 'roll-up'; the bankers had fled for Yass with their treasure; the military had been telegraphed for ... the courthouse had been burned down ... and the town was in a complete state of uproar.[15]

Preshaw dismissed this news, but on arrival he found it all to be true. He had arrived at Lambing Flat in the middle of the riots against the Chinese.

He telegraphed Sydney for instructions, and was ordered to proceed to Yass where, with all of the other bankers, he waited until peace had been restored.

THE TAMBAROORA FIELD

The story of Bernard Otto Holtermann, posed proudly with 'his' famous nugget in his renowned photograph, is an interesting tale of opportunism at its best.

Holtermann migrated to Australia from Germany in 1858. After spending some years at various positions in Sydney and at times abroad, Holtermann eventually joined a fellow-countryman, Louis Beyers, at Hill End, just out of Bathurst.

Hill End, and the nearby goldfields community of Gulgong, were developing into a rich, deep-lead mining district. It was at Hill End that Holtermann and Beyers established their Star of Hope mine.

At one stage Holtermann was short of funds, and sold his share in the mine to another digger at Hill End, a ticket-of-leave man known as 'Northumberland Jimmie'. He hurriedly bought back his share after Beyers showed him the floor of the mine littered with small nuggets following a successful blast. Jimmie was less than pleased when he discovered the reason for Holtermann's undue haste.

German-born prospector, Bernard Otto Holtermann poses with the nugget that made him famous

(From an original advertising poster for Holtermann's Life Drops)

The mass of gold and quartz weighing 630 lbs, and valued at £12,000, was unearthed by miners working for Holtermann and his partner, Louis Beyers, in the Star of Hope mine in 1872.

Holtermann used this gold-encrusted quartz monolith as an emblem for the rest of his life.

Holtermann appointed himself as mine manager after the Star was floated, and a company was formed on 17 April 1872. Seven months later they unearthed the largest specimen of reef gold ever discovered. Holtermann demanded that the mass should be removed from the underground shaft in one piece. Of course, this was a difficult operation for the miners as the heavy lump had to be dug away from all sides, but Holtermann already had a great plan for this piece of gold.

The famous photographic portrait of Holtermann standing next to 'his' nugget was never actually taken. The image that he was to use over and over again for the rest of his days was a montage created by the A&A Co. photographic assistant, Charles Bayliss, from a shot of the nugget taken on the day and a

Whim and Shaft Houses, Hawkin's Hill
(Holtermann Collection, Mitchell Library, State Library of New South Wales)

The harshness of the weather high up on the central New South Wales plateaus made for some ingenious bush architecture. On observing these examples of bush carpentry one correspondent wrote:

> the horse which works the whim is in every case sheltered from snow and rain by a very picturesque octagon building roofed to a point in bark . . . the make of these whims displays no mean proficiency in bush carpentry and the liberality with which they are supported by struts and braces is marvellous.[16]

Henry Beaufoy Merlin, 1872
Merlin was the photographer who established his American & Australian Photographic Company's Studios at Hill End.

shot of Holtermann leaning against a studio prop. The two negatives were brought together years later, well after the nugget had been to the crusher.

Both Holtermann and Beyers became very wealthy men. Holtermann set about doing good works, became involved in public affairs, constructed buildings and churches, and built a large turreted mansion in Sydney, where he even had a stained-glass window created of this image.

He invested in all sorts of schemes, one of the most curious being the creation of Holtermann's Life-preserving Drops, which according to his advertising claimed to cure:

> asthma, biliousness, cramps in the stomach, colds, diarrhoea, dysentery, fevers, ailments of children [especially while teething] and for the COMPLAINTS of FEMALES, under any circumstances—*October 1876.*

The advertising material used to promote Holtermann's patent medicine featured his portrait standing beside the famous nugget.

With his new-found wealth Holtermann also invested in a long-term project which funded the photographic documentation of the goldfields. Starting with Hill End and Gulgong the A&A Photographic Company recorded the buildings, and mines, in those towns. Other settlements in New South Wales and the great centres in Victoria were also recorded and form the most comprehensive archive of historic photographs of the later goldrush period. Known as the Holtermann collection hundreds of these photographs are kept in the State Library of New South Wales.

Northumberland Jimmie eventually struck it rich in the mine he worked at Hawkins Hill with Black Nat, an escaped African-American slave. Black Nat had travelled to Australia on the same boat as Edward Hargraves.

Northumberland Jimmie had his moment of goldfields glory. He trotted into the history books one day when he shod his pony with golden shoes and trotted through the streets of Hill End. This act, however remarkable it may have seemed to the diggers at Hill End, was repeated on several other diggings—such was the exuberant extravagance of the fortunate digger, no matter where Lady Luck had found him.

A&A Photographic Studio in Tambaroora Street, Hill End, in 1872

The Holtermann Collection

Holtermann owned the land that the A&A studio occupied. He had an interest in the company, and in the *Hill End Observer* that occupied the building next door.

Here photographer Charles Bayliss, who took over after the death of Henry Merlin, in 1876, stands in the doorway, with the studio and darkroom assistant just behind. Their caravan driver stands to the left of the doorway, and the young boy in white is thought to be the driver's son, as he is often seen in photographs taken by A&A.

(All Photographs Holtermann Collection, Mitchell Library, State Library of New South Wales)

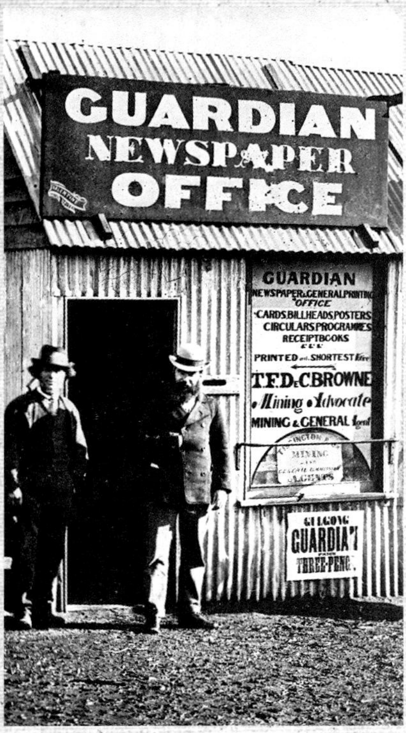

Above left: *The editor of the* Gulgong Guardian, *T. F. De Courcy Browne, with his runner, Henry Beal, outside the Gulgong office*
Browne was a fierce advocate for miners' rights, and suffered many writs for libel in the course of his public duty.

Above right: *Smith's Cheap Jack Tobacco & Fancy Goods Warehouse (Wholesale & Retail)*
This, the smallest shop on Clarke Street, Hill End, probably has the most impressive title.

All of that in a building that measured only eight feet [2.4m] across.

Opposite top: *Henry Hilton's Golden Age Hotel*
This rough weatherboard hotel building was constructed for successful miner Joseph Dietz in 1870, who been one of the party who found the first gold on Red Hill at Gulgong.

Dietz sold the hotel the following year and built another, The United States Hotel, on the Canadian Lead. Henry Hilton became the third licensee in June 1872 and changed the name soon after this photograph was taken to the Hotel de France. Such descriptive and varied European names indicate the multi-national population that inhabited these diggings at that time.

By 1873, only three years after it had opened, and three owners later, it was closed, and became the home and shop front for a series of chemists, including Dr Zimmler.

Opposite bottom: *Dr Charles Zimmler's Dispensary*
Mr White, who had been the manager of Barnes's Mudgee Drug Store, poses for the camera in his doorway opening onto Queen Street, Gulgong.

GOLDEN AGE HOTEL
DINING ROOMS

GULGONG
CHEMIST
DRUGGIST
DISPENSARY
DR ZIMMLER

The photographs shown here, taken from the Holtermann collection, were used by Australian designer Gordon Andrews as part of a collage of images behind the portrait of Lawson on the first Australian $10 note [1966].

Lawson's stories often reflected the hardship and determined pioneering spirit he observed as a boy on the goldfields of the New South Wales highlands.

Left: *Donald's Circulating Library*

Right: *Times Bakery, Gulgong*

Left: *American Warehouse & Fancy Goods Emporium*
The four men shown here standing in front of the American Tobacco Warehouse & Fancy Goods Emporium appear on the first Australian $10 note.

Right: *Scurrah's Shampooing & Hairdressing Saloon*
Barber T. B. Scurrah, leans against the doorpost of his Shampooing and Hairdressing Saloon in Gulgong.

Apart from his tonsorial skills, Scurrah was also known to belt out a good song: 'Does Yer Want to Buy a Dorg' and 'My Farder Kept a Brewery' being among his particular favourites.
(All Photographs Holtermann Collection, Mitchell Library, State Library of New South Wales)

Henry Stuart's Great Western Store
This building on Tambaroora Street, Hill End, is one of the few still standing today. Stuart sold a huge range of goods from these substantial wide-fronted premises.

LAWSON AND GULGONG GOLD

Henry Lawson, also known as 'the bard of the bush', was born in a tent at Grenfell on the New South Wales goldfields in 1867.

His parents split up when he was only fourteen years of age, and Lawson moved to Sydney, where he took jobs working in factories by day, attending school at night, hoping in vain to gain entry to university. He eventually abandoned this goal, and began to submit his poems to the *Bulletin* magazine. He was a regular contributor to the *Bulletin* by the time he was twenty. By 28 he had become a compulsive drinker. His love of the bottle would eventually ruin a marriage and ruin him as well.

Often embittered by his alcoholism and envious of the growing reputation, and apparent financial success, of his lifelong 'nemesis', the lawyer-son of a country grazier, 'Banjo' Paterson. Lawson jousted against Paterson in print.

Where Lawson expressed a left-wing egalitarianism that revered the working poor, while debunking the affectations of the 'nobs', Paterson gloried in the beauty of the land and the works of man. Lawson wrote of the hardship of settler life in the Australian bush—the shearers strikes, the lust for gold, the faceless workers in nameless streets; his pen conjured an image of the iconic battler—he was the worker's mate and championed the working class against all odds.

His collected work, *While the Billy Boils* [pub., A&R 1913], is full of the wry humour and rough mateship that typifies the Australian bush.

He was found dead in a rented cottage on 2 September 1922. This son of a Norwegian migrant, who was born poor and died destitute, had so enriched the nation that he was honoured with a state funeral.

Portrait of Henry Lawson, 1867-1922
Photograph by Sir Lionel Lindsay, c. 1900
(By Permission, National Library of Australia)

Opposite: *Holtermann [second from left], Beyers and mates with gold-bearing reef taken from their Star of Hope Mine at Hill End*
(Holtermann Collection, Mitchell Library, State Library of New South Wales)

Next page: *Mine head and group of miners, Gulgong*
This group of diggers posing atop their shaft and at the windlass obviously could not afford the luxury of a whip horse, which would have cost them about £50. Here everything is winched up and down by hand. Although this was the norm on the shallow alluvial fields, the deep shafts at Gulgong would have made this a back-breaking and laborious exercise.

—The Roaring Days—

by Henry Lawson [selected verses]

The night too quickly passes
And we are growing old,
So let us fill our glasses
And toast the Days of Gold;
When finds of wondrous treasure
Set all the South ablaze,
And you and I were faithful mates
All through the roaring days!

Their shining Eldorado,
Beneath the southern skies,
Was day and night for ever
Before their eager eyes.
The brooding bush, awakened,
Was stirred in wild unrest,
And all the year a human stream
Went pouring to the West.

Oh, who would paint a goldfield,
And limn the picture right,
As we have often seen it
In early morning's light;
The yellow mounds of mullock
With spots of red and white,
The scattered quartz that
glistened
Like diamonds in light.
The azure line of ridges,
The bush of darkest green,
The little homes of calico
That dotted all the scene.

I hear the fall of timber
From distant flats and fells,
The pealing of the anvils
As clear as little bells,
The rattle of the cradle,
The clack of windlass-boles,
The flutter of the crimson flags
Above the golden holes.

Oh, they were lion-hearted
Who gave our country birth!
Oh, they were of the stoutest sons
From all the lands on earth!

—Notable Nuggets—

Kerr's Hundredweight [700 oz]
Louisa Creek, [later named Hargraves]—July 1851.

An Aboriginal shepherd-boy named Daniel discovered this nugget in a tributary of the Meroo Creek on Dr Kerr's 'Hargraves' Station. The nugget-encrusted quartz—three gold specimens side-by-side—weighed 75 pounds [48 kg] and contained 700 ounces of gold. It had to be broken up to remove it from the earth and transferred to Bathurst.

The area around Hargraves was rich indeed offering up scores of nuggets, both big and small.

The most notable were:

Unnamed [840 oz] Meroo Creek—1851

Unnamed [720 oz] Meroo Creek—1851

Unnamed [366 oz] Meroo Creek—1851

The Brennan Nugget [364 oz] Meroo Creek—1851

The King of Waterworn Nuggets [2680 oz] Meroo Creek—1852

Unnamed [157 oz] Meroo Creek—1852

Unnamed [82 oz] Louisa Creek—1852

Unnamed [71 oz] Meroo Creek—1852

Darby's Nugget [312 oz] Louisa Creek—1852

5 Hundredweight Nugget [2800 oz] Louisa Creek—1856

Turner's Nugget [197 oz] Louisa Creek—1856

John the Dutchman's Nugget [103 oz] Louisa Creek—1856

Bryant's Nugget [89 oz] Louisa Creek—1856

Reids Nugget [77 oz] Louisa Creek—1856

Winnan's Nugget [77 oz] Louisa Creek—1856

Turner – 2 pieces [73 oz] Louisa Creek—1856

Cork Jack Nugget I [72 oz] Louisa Creek—1856

Cork Jack Nugget II [36 oz] Louisa Creek—1856

Maitland Bar Nugget [344.78 oz] Meroo Creek—1887

Unnamed [357 oz] Hargraves—1887

Unnamed [200 oz] Hargraves—1887

Unnamed [47 oz] Hargraves—1887

TILBA TILBA AND MT DROMEDARY

In 1877 the Cowdroy brothers found the reef they had all been searching for, about 500 yards from the summit of the granite mountain, at the foot of the last steep rise. Although the terrain was almost impossible to work, there was a small mining boom that worked the mountain reefs until 1906. The Mount Dromedary Proprietary Gold Mining Co. Ltd pegged its first claim in 1878, and the lease situated close to Cowdroy's yielded 42,522 grains of gold by the end of the nineteenth century.

Numerous settlers had taken an interest in the region around the Wallago Lake on the New South Wales Coast, 185 miles south of Sydney, since the first Europeans explored the area in the early years of the nineteenth century.

The Curlewis Brothers, who farmed at Ballalaba, staked a claim near Cobargo in 1833, and Dr Thomas Braidwood Wilson sent a party from Braidwood to establish his claim in the same region.

Crown Land Commissioner Lambie was on one of his periodic inspections to the region from his base at Cooma in 1839, when he came across the station called 'Tolbedilbo', which consisted of one slab hut, two acres of wheat, 301 cattle, and two horses, spread out over eight square miles.

The first resident to settle in Tilba Tilba was Henry Jefferson Bate, who arrived in 1869, setting up his farm on a block he called 'Mountain View', near the site of the present settlement of Tilba.

The Photographs of William Henry Corkhill

The photographs reproduced here are from the collection of William Henry Corkhill, whose family had long been acquainted with the Bate family in England.

Corkhill, who was born in Cumberland, came to Australia with his family in 1854. He visited the Bates at Tilba in 1882, and stayed. He took a position as cheese-maker at Henry Bate's farm, and in 1883 married his daughter, Frances.

Bate had began to construct shops and dwellings for lease near his homestead, and these buildings ranged across the hillside that formed the town of Tilba Tilba. The buildings remained in the Bate family until the first buildings were sold in the early 1970s.

Pioneer photographer William Henry Corkhill settled in Tilba Tilba in 1882. *(TT83)*

He photographed Tilba, and the surrounding district, over many years leaving a record that shows a goldfields town little changed in more than a century.

Central Tilba, c. 1897
(TT835)
Bate's original twin-roofed, verandahed store can be seen to the left of the photograph facing the road.

Corkhill also developed a passion for photography, and for the next twenty years he recorded almost every aspect of the district he had grown to love. Corkhill died in 1936, but his photographic record shows a community that changed little in his lifetime, the town owned for so long by the one family remained almost intact into the present age.

Opposite:
(TT374)
Striking miners picnic at Half Way Rock on Mt Dromedary Road, 1898.
(All Photographs, National Library of Australia. William Henry Corkhill Tilba Tilba Collection)

Next page:
(TT836)
A system of flumes and waterwheels drove the battery of the Enterprise Mine, Mt Dromedary.

Mt Dromedary

(TT186)

The Cole family pose under the verandah of their neat little slab-and-shingle hut.

The men worked in the Mt Dromedary mine, which by 1899 employed around fifty people.

RUSH TO THE OUTBACK

By the end of the nineteenth century the spirit of the diggings had changed. Where once men simply wandered from rush to rush and gold found almost strewn upon the ground, now it was to be sought deep within the earth and took a collective enterprise to win it.

The romance of the diggings was soon replaced by the frenzy of the stock exchange as investors jostled each other to buy into almost any mining venture. The Great Boom could not last forever. Where once there had been surety, the period of rapid expansion underwritten by gold was followed by a decade of economic depression, starting in 1890, that created a generation no longer prepared to leave good fortune just to good luck. The workforce unionised.

Towards the end of the century exploration for new goldfields moved away from the south-eastern colonies and new mining centres were opened in some most inhospitable territory. Gold was found in the South Australian

The Diggings in the Barossa, c. 1885
(Photograph Courtesy of the State Library of South Australia)

Gold was first discovered in the Barossa in October 1868. Some of the claims there were very rich, yielding at times as much as £1000 per man.

To gain such a reward required a lot of hard digging, but by this time the pressure of the licence fee no longer applied. There were, however, few diggers who could be bothered with such sustained digging to depths of over 20 feet through the hard conglomerate and sandstone of these diggings.

The lure of gold did persist, and in 1886 there was another great rush. This time the polite society of Adelaide stayed at home while the Teetulpa diggings in the inhospitable desert country, closer to the New South Wales border, drew thousands, once again, to scratch about in the dust seeking their fortune.

desert, the great Queensland mines opened, and the Golden Mile in the West drew thousands more across the blistering desert sands. These new mining camps became the latest frontier towns, they attracted a new breed of desperate men: the gamblers, boozers, the shady characters; and the scores of freshly painted ladies from Europe and the Orient, ready and willing to keep them company—and share their success.

The age of the new-chum digger may have been long gone, but the spirit of the 'wild colonial boy' was still evident out on the ragged edges of civilisation in the decade prior to the Federation of Australian colonies.

South Australia

If it was the similarity between the landscape around Bathurst and the hills of Sacramento that encouraged Edward Hargraves to prospect at Summerhill Creek in 1851, it is hard to imagine why Thomas Brady was scratching around in the shale on the desert sands near Waukaringa, in north-eastern South Australia, in 1886.

The landscape there must be one of the most uninviting of all the Australian goldfields. Where Assistant Surveyor-General Evans had extolled the beauty of the Turon, and Major Mitchell championed the 'great south countrie', what poet ever sang of the charms of the Teetulpa field?

Gold Diggers Camp, c. 1895
(Photograph courtesy of the State Library of South Australia)
A digger and his wife pose proudly beside their makeshift canvas home on the goldfields. Although these diggings were some of the roughest, hottest and driest, there was no need for a woman to stay away from all the excitement.

Baker's Cart Arrives at the Diggings
From *Cassell's Picturesque Australasia*, 1889
(La Trobe University, Bendigo, Library Collection)
There was little enough water but no fuel sufficient for the diggers to make even their own damper on the Teetulpa goldfield.
As on most of the later diggings in the desert or the outback, the simple necessities of life proved to be the most difficult to obtain, expensive for some, and most profitable for others.

> The coach journey was slow and wearisome, owing to rough roads and fagged horses. At sundown, on rising to the crest of a low hill, the passengers beheld at their feet Brady's Gully, then in its infancy. There was nothing attractive in the view. Few goldfields, perhaps, have been so devoid of picturesque features as that of Teetulpa . . . hardly any trees were to be seen, and no water ever ran in the watercourse, except during heavy rain. In all directions could be seen reefs of white quartz standing out in clear relief amid the prevailing colours of blue and salt-bush.[17]

Just to the north lay a great sandy plain, the only vegetation some acacias that stood where water sometimes flowed after heavy rain. The rush began in one such watercourse. The upper soil had been washed away in a strong flood, exposing the auriferous gravel and loose sand. Brady took shelter in that gully in a rare downpour and, after the rain had cleared, a shaft of sunlight lit up a piece of gold exposed by the rain.

The rush that followed saw 5000 diggers make the hot and dusty journey from Adelaide [200 miles to the south], and pitch their tents under the blazing desert sun.

Teetulpa City
(Photograph courtesy of the State Library of South Australia)
The desert country offered almost nothing for the comfort of the diggers. All provisions had to be carted in, all food, grog, goods and gear carried across the desert to the tent city.

Lack of water was the bane of this goldfield, the closest being at Tonkin's Well about two miles from the diggings, and all the wash-dirt was carried to the well for washing. Eventually water was pumped up to holding tanks at the southern end of Brady's Gully.

Provisions were also scarce. However, one enterprising butcher drove a small mob of 60 sheep to the diggings each day, and a baker's cart carried 400 loaves a day 16 miles to the hungry diggers. All were sold within minutes of their arrival. The baker could get as much as 2 shillings for each 2 lb loaf, and the fresh loaves were almost 'worth their weight in gold' to the baker, who didn't even have to lift a shovel to make his fortune.

There were some fortunes to made on this field. One hot day a digger was lying stretched out on his claim in the creek-bed scraping at the gravel with his butcher's knife. Sweeping aside the gravel, he uncovered 'The Joker', a nugget the size and shape of a man's hand; it weighed 30 oz and was worth £120.

Afraid that others would see what he had found, and swarm across his patch, he sat bolt upright and placed his hand over the nugget.

Another digger, working in the claim next to him, looked up, 'Found anything?' he asked. 'No! Seen the colour, that's all', he replied. He asked the digger to throw him his coat, which was lying close to the next claim. He said he wanted to have a smoke.

Diggers Crowd the Water Course at Tonkin's Well, 1886
Diggers had to carry dirt from their claims on Brady's Gully to wash at Tonkin's Well, two miles from Teetulpa.
(State Library of South Australia)

'Here you are, mate. But what's the matter? You look pale. Don't you feel right?' enquired the digger as he handed him his jacket.

'I'm all right; only the sun is a bit hot', he replied. Unable to contain himself any longer, he placed his coat over the nugget, laughing uncontrollably, until he became almost hysterical. Those around him thought he had a touch of the sun, and when he had calmed down he picked up his coat—and nugget—and went to his tent.

It was another ten days before the news of the discovery of 'The Joker' was broadcast, but few knew where his claim was to be found. A few days later nuggets were also found at Goslin's, an abandoned 'duffer' of a claim, where in one day a lucky digger unable to find a spot at Brady's scratched £100 worth from a nest of nuggets found in a hole in the rock.

The spirit of the first rushes in the eastern colonies was rekindled at Teetulpa. This goldfield was not dominated by managers and shareholders watching their investments grow from the comfort of a gentlemen's club in the city, this was a goldfield of muscle and men, of sweat and toil, of dirt and dust—and more dust—and mateship.

The diggings once again offered the spirit of adventure that men could not get standing behind a shop-counter in the city, or chasing behind some fat squatter's sheep. No matter how hard the work was, the pioneering life provided adventure for the lucky, and disappointing memories for those who failed.

Teetulpa diggings, South Australia
Wood engraving published in *Australasian Sketcher*, 2 December 1866
(Picture Collection, State Library of Victoria)

1. The road to the diggings from Manna-Hill;
2. Smith, the discoverer of the field;
3. The prospector's claim;
4. Brady's Gully;
5. A half-way halt at Salt Creek;
6. Tonkin's Dam;
7. The claim in which the 30 oz. nugget was found;
8. A dust storm on the diggings.

GOLDFIELDS OF THE DESERT

Gold had been found in the Kimberley in the mid-1880s, and rich deposits discovered beneath the shifting sands of Southern Cross (Coolgardie) in 1892, but it was not until an Irishman, Patrick ('Paddy') Hannan, found the first nuggets at Kalgoorlie in 1893 that the great rush to the western goldfields began.

Australia was in the grip of economic depression, the boom that had followed the first goldrush forty years earlier had burst. Where once labour had been impossible to find, there were now masses of unemployed and disappointed diggers desperate for work.

The great mines of Bendigo and Ballarat were closing down one by one. Mine owners were eventually defeated by water flooding into the deep

—*Discoveries in Western Australia*—

1885—The Kimberley
Mr E. T. Hardmann, W.A. Government Geologist found gold in the Kimberley

1888—The Pilbara

17 September 1892—Coolgardie
Arthur Bayley & William Ford

14 June 1893—Kalgoorlie
Patrick 'Paddy' Hannan

Paddy Hannan Statue, Kalgoorlie
Photograph by Aaron Bunch, 1995
(Rex Nan Kivell Collection. By Permission, National Library of Australia)

underground tunnels. When the miners joined together to demand a fair day's pay for a hard day's work, and to demand to work only eight hours a day, deep mining became a precarious investment. The freewheeling great adventure had soured.

The finds in the west caused a rebirth of the digger spirit. Thousands of eager diggers once again rushed to the fields coming overland by bicycle, by dray, on horseback, wagon and camel caravan. The diggings on the western edge of the great Nullarbor Plain were not all like the verdant granite hills in the east, but beneath the desert sands lay the 'richest square mile on earth'. In time, more than £100,000,000 worth of gold was won from these dusty fields.

The Golden Mile

A story typical of the hardships and the excitement encountered by miners on the Golden Mile is that of one miner's trip from the Bendigo goldfield to the West, recalled in the following excerpts from the diary kept by William Hocking [the author's paternal grandfather]. The Hockings had migrated to Australia from Penzance in Cornwall, with William aged one, and he had grown up steeped in mining culture and the fellowship of the tight Protestant mining community that worked the Bendigo shafts.

In 1902 William Hocking set out to make his pile in the west:

> Bendigo, 29 January 1902—Having made up my mind that God willing I would go and try my luck in the West like a lot more I left working at the Great Southern Bendigo on January 29.[18]

After a train journey to Melbourne, William boarded a steamship bound for Fremantle, with one stop at Adelaide on the way. He was surprised to meet quite a large contingent of other miners from Bendigo on board, and, although he was too seasick to join them in the second

William Hocking [the author's grandfather], kept a diary of his journey to the west and his time on the East Murchison goldfields. Born in Cornwall, he left England aged one year, was taken first to California then to Queensland, with the family finally settling on the Bendigo diggings.

Excerpts from the diary of his expedition to the goldfields in the west, which were entered between January 1902 and August 1903, are reproduced in this chapter. *(Hocking Family Collection)*

saloon for Sunday service, he recorded in his diary that 'I was up on deck and heard it all, felt it done me good, the singing was nice'.[19]

A large number of the Bendigo deep-lead miners were Cornish Methodists, whose life revolved around work, church and family; and for the Methodists, singing ability was of utmost importance. William takes particular note to record in his diary the varying ability of the different congregations he joined up with on his journey to the west.

Miners from all over Australia were making their way west, but not all were of the same persuasion, which seemed at times to shock young William. After arriving in Fremantle, and a few days 'knocking about' in Perth he took an overnight train for Kalgoorlie:

> . . . travelling all night. Grand country to travel through up till the time I could see . . . at east Northam 2 chaps got in, one I used to work with back Little 180 Bendigo—Paddy Sullivan and his brother—all went well until we got to Southern Cross and there 6 navvies got in with their swags—off the Pipe track going to Coolgardie—the language they were using being terrible and the beer flowing freely. Got out and changed carriage at Boorabbin—found it more pleasant than such disgusting company . . . one told me that I would not be on the fields long before I drank also, Lord forbid that such be the case.
>
> Got on coach at 1-25 pm arrived Leonora 3 pm . . . left again 4-25 pm full load on, on the way to first stopping place saw Geo. Roberts who used to drive Lansell's Big Battery Engine about 2 miles out—reached Diorite King 8-30 pm.[20]

The train journey continued for several days, stopping at Doyle's Well and Poison Creek, and then on to Lawler, where he:

> . . . had to stop at a Hotel—no other places in these parts and was put in Bar parlour—did not smell too sweet—had three Austrians for companions and hear the Billiard Balls and the drink going on till about 12 o'clock.[21]

He was on the goldfields for some time before he found employment, but eventually was taken on to work the nightshift at the Leinster Mine about 20 miles from Lawler:

> . . . of all the mines I worked in the Leinster is the worst—Hot as fire and everything so slushy and greasy—have to keep washing your hands and tools. Put in timber. Drinking water and the heat turned me up but put the shift, cannot help drink in here. How the mine is so Hot and only 160 feet deep surprises me . . . all hands go up to surface for crib when they fire. Have to leave it for 1/2 an hour or more for the smoke to clear and when you go down the smoke is very thick.[22]

He goes on to wonder why he left the grand old mines of Bendigo for the west, and complains of the incessant nuisance of the little black flies that

Miner's Camp, West Australian diggings, c. 1902
(Hocking Family Collection)
A group of Cornish miners from Bendigo pose outside their scrub and canvas camp on the East Murchison goldfields; William Hocking is on the right. The difficulties faced in the construction of this shanty and other forms of abode are recorded in his diary:

> I went out into the bush for a stroll looking for poles for a tent but never found any long enough . . . after breakfast went out looking for poles—went 2 or 3 miles got 5 after a terrible amount of trouble and left 3 behind thinking to go back for them—near got bushed this mulga scrub being very difficult to distinguish it

and after a terrible thunderstorm at 4 o'clock one afternoon:

> the rain simply pours. My bed and blankets, boots and my portmanteau got all wet, over your boot tops in the tents—had to dig a drain all round to let water away—a typical West Australian experience . . . the tent being new let the water through.[23]

robbed him of his daytime sleep, and the poor quality of the drinking water that constantly turned his stomach:

> . . . there is a sly-grog shop here and some of the men get hold of this poison which quickly upsets them . . . a little excitement—Coach arrival from Lake Way with Gold Escort. Mounted Constable riding behind Rifle and Revolver foot Constable on Coach with Rifle also. This goes through every four to five weeks. Went down and seen it off—Leinster gold went with it. Two nice ingots about 900 oz—Blacks around Lawlers very poor specimens—Mixing with Australians has not done them any good. Women smoke as well as men—terrible cadgers—the disease among them is very bad—The Leinster is a great place [for] stacks of flies, ants, insects get in amongst the bread, weevils in the flour—Menzies, Boulder or Coolgardie far before this place—would never bring a woman here, not a fit place but the Lord's way is

Bayley Street, Coolgardie, 1894
Photograph by Roy Millar
(Roy Millar, Kalgoorlie, W.A., Album 283. Rex Nan Kivell Collection, NK10699, By Permission, National Library of Australia)

When Arthur Bayley and William Ford made their first discovery they found 6 lbs gold in the first three hours of digging.

By the time they rode into the little settlement of Southern Cross on 17 September 1892, Bayley was carrying more than 30 lbs of the precious metal in his saddlebags.

Within six months 1000 men had rushed to peg their claims in the desert sands. By the end of 1893 Coolgardie was declared a town, and the first two-storeyed building was under construction.

Coolgardie grew rapidly, like so many other gold towns, but it was a hard place to live for the almost entirely male population.

Its isolation from the main coastal settlements and the absence of women led to the usual alcoholism and aggressive criminal behaviour that also typified the earlier eastern goldfields.

not ours—What a grand lesson to learn like the Apostle Paul 'In whatsoever state to be content' (but it's a hard one)
March 28—They have put poppet legs up at the claim—up about a week or more (Iron) looks more like a mine now and they are skidding the shaft and going to put cage on as soon as it is ready . . .
June 23—Heard 2 men suffocated at Mt Sir Samuel (dynamite fumes) were working in a winze firing out, one went down away a good while so his mate went down and he never came up so a third man went down after them—but by this time there were a few men there who got him up but he was pretty bad.[24]

Coolgardie, Bayley Street, Northside, 1894
(Ms Collection, Ms3747, By Permission, National Library of Australia)

William moved up to the mines at Moyans after underground workers were put off at Leinster, and for a number of weeks continued to present himself at the mines several times a day until he was lucky enough to be picked to start on the night-shift:

> Nov 9th—Went to Church Sunday evening, good congregation.
> Nov 10th—up twice to the mine looking for work at 8-half past, no show—over 30 there at night concert in aid of Wesley Church we stood outside and heard it all.
> Nov 11th—up again twice no chance.
> Nov 12th—up again twice no show. Bob Matthews got a start night-shift on machine.
> Nov 13th—up again twice no show—really thought we would have been on—its disheartening. There's such a crowd there every time over 20 men every day . . .
> Nov 16th—to my great surprise was told to come on Sunday night night-shift on the machines . . . got on allright up a rise at the 500 foot level . . .[25]

In the early months of 1903 the diaries show that shifts were becoming irregular, one day short here, a half day lost there until the heat, dust and flies drove William back to Bendigo. He boarded the train for Perth on Easter Monday, 13 April 1903:

Hannan's Warden's Court, Kalgoorlie, 1895
Photograph by Roy Millar
(Roy Millar, Kalgoorlie, W.A., Album 283, Rex Nan Kivell Collection, NK10699, By Permission, National Library of Australia)
At the beginning of the rush most buildings were crude shacks created from scrub or whatever materials were at hand, while corrugated iron was the easiest material to carry across the desert plains. The hessian-covered shacks and iron buildings were gradually replaced with timber, brick and stone, the towns losing their frontier appearance and taking on the appearance of a prosperous mining town. Most goods were carried to these diggings by camel train.

> May 6th—[came up] by the Express and arrived at Golden Square a little after 8pm after 15 months absence none the worse for my trip. Thankful to God for all his mercy toward me in sparing me to get back home amongst all my loved ones again.[26]

The next entry in his diary records:

> Arrived Rufton New Zealand on Monday night Aug 10th 1903, stopped at Railway Hotel two nights . . . started work Tuesday, afternoon 18th August . . .[27]

William married Emily Jane Nankervis, and together they started married life on the New Zealand diggings. He worked at the Otago mines for several years before they returned to Bendigo with the first three of their seven children. After a trip to America in 1916 where he met with relatives, spending

William and Emily Jane Hocking, with the first of their seven children, in the snow outside their miner's cottage in Otago, New Zealand
(Hocking Family Collection)

A far cry from the brush and canvas humpy he had lived in on the East Murchison goldfields, this charming little timber-framed house is typical of miner's cottages found anywhere on the goldfields by the end of the century

his days inspecting winding gear, and visiting various churches, William died of miners' phthisis (a common lung complaint caused by inhalation of dust and grit) in 1932.

His story is typical of the thousands of young men on the goldfields who had little more to trade than their muscle in what seemed like an almost spiritual need for hard work, a strong dose of the Protestant work ethic and a burning desire to prove themselves fit and worthy of their hire.

TROPICAL FEVER

Queensland and The North

Although there were some early rushes to Queensland in the 1850s it was not until the alluvial gold in the southern colonies had played out and companies were searching for new deposits that the Queensland mines came into being.

Men with experience on other fields were seeking for opportunities to apply that knowledge and to make their mark in Australia's goldfields' history. Some of the early rushes to Queensland were disastrous. The worst came early in 1858 when some gold was found at Canoona, on the Fitzroy River (north of where Rockhampton now stands). There was some speculation that this rush was completely fabricated to inject an instant population into the newly separated colony of Queensland.

More than 15,000 diggers came from the south, but, when the rush proved to be a shicer [no good], they were left stranded more than 1000 miles from Sydney. There were no provisions, no stores, and very little gold for trading, even if there had been any supplies. The diggers were eventually brought out of the isolated diggings by sea in a rescue operation financed by the Victorian government and through public subscription. Victoria felt an obligation to the large number of diggers from that colony who had been seduced by the promise of riches in Queensland; they also felt some responsibility for the deeds of unscrupulous shipowners and agents who had largely concocted glowing reports of the Fitzroy River goldfield with the express purpose of bringing hearty, working men into the new Colony of Queensland.

The remoteness of the tropical region, and the almost total lack of facilities and difficulties in obtaining supplies, left many diggers stranded, starving, and sorry they had ever stepped aboard a ship bound for the tropics.

Thorvald Weitemeyer was a digger from Denmark who recorded in his diaries his experience of these goldfields:

> When I landed there [Cooktown] looked wild enough. There were some thousands of people camped out in tents . . . all the loafers, pickpockets and card-sharpers seemed to have trooped up from Brisbane, Sydney and Melbourne . . . and the robbing of tents was an everyday occurrence . . . although it had been known far and wide that any one who wanted to go to the Palmer must either starve or carry six months rations with him, still many destitute and good-for-nothing people could be seen wherever one looked. Men would walk about among the tents and . . . beg. There was a great deal of sickness . . . it was a common sight to see men lying helpless, writhing with pain on the ground, some of them bellowing out for pity or mercy . . . men would pass such a poor object with the greatest apathy.[28]

Mount Morgan Gold Mine, near Rockhampton, Queensland
Watercolour by Ethel M. Turner, c. 1890
(Rex Nan Kivell Collection, T2255. By Permission, National Library of Australia)
Thomas Hall, who had been in the Eureka Stockade during the troubles in 1854, was part of the syndicate who formed the Mount Morgan Gold Mining Co. in 1886. He was joined in this very successful enterprise by his brother Walter, who had been operating as Cobb & Co's. Sydney Agent since taking it over in 1861.
The old Ironstone Mountain behind the two largest chimney stacks has since completely disappeared; it is now a huge hole in the ground.

The colony was prone to torrential rain, and rivers would flood almost without warning, leaving diggers cut off once again from supplies. One such flood on the Normanby River left a large group of miners stranded on one side of the raging river, while those on the other side had rations to spare: 'There we were, looking across at one another—they shaking their gold-purses at us, and we showing them the flour-bags'.[29]

Two men attempted to cross, and were swept away and drowned. No further attempts were made. Weitemeyer tells of a shipmate of his who had become separated from his main camp by rising waters, and was not found until after the wet season had passed:

> His dead body was found in his tent . . . he had died of hunger, yet under his head was a bag with eighteen pounds' weight of gold in it . . .
>
> The country around is very poorly off for game; besides they had no powder, and so they had been eating their horses, their dogs, and at last their boots! It is a fact that they used to boil their blucher boots for twenty-four hours and eat them with weeds! It takes something to make a Queensland miner lie down and die . . .[30]

Queensland Blacks Attacking Chinese Diggers on the Gilbert River
Wood engraving from *The Illustrated Australian News*, Ebenezer and David Syme, 30 January 1873
(Picture Collection, State Library of Victoria)

The Queensland Aboriginals were hostile to both Europeans and Chinese alike.
At the time there many rumours of cannibals eating Chinese killed in the Palmer River area, near Cooktown.

Charters Towers to Croydon

Jupiter Mosman, a young Aboriginal stockman out looking for a stray pack-horse, first found some nuggets on the Burdekin River flats on Christmas Day 1871. Prospectors Hugh Mosman (Jupiter's boss), George Clarke and James Fraser rushed back to Ravenswood to lodge a claim reward.

The district was named after the mining warden of Ravenswood, William Eurbank Melbourne Charters, who first registered the claim. Reminiscent of the hilly outcrops in Devon and Cornwall known as tors, the area was duly named Charters Tors; it was not long before the name suffered from Australianisation, and was thereafter known as Charters Towers.

Sometime around 1880 another stockman, William McKinley, made a find on Ironstone Mountain [as Mt Morgan was then known], but, because

RAVENSWOOD—CHARTERS TOWERS GOLDFIELD, QUEENSLAND.

Ravenswood, Charters Towers goldfield, Queensland
Wood engraving by Samuel Calvert, Ebenezer and David Syme,
from *Illustrated Australian News*, 9 August 1875
(Picture Collection, State Library of Victoria)

he had been swindled out of a claim before, he decided to prospect over the whole mountain until he found the best claim of all. However, when Fred Morgan, the owner of the Criterion Hotel in Rockhampton, got an inkling of McKinley's activities, he himself pegged out a claim. He soon found some good stuff, formed a partnership with his brothers, Ned and Tom, and three other mates [Thomas Hall, William Pattison and Knox D'Arcy], and they began to mine the mountain.

After four years the Morgan brothers sold out to Hall, Pattison and D'Arcy, who were then joined by Walter Hall; and the Mount Morgan Gold Mining Co. Ltd was formed. It was floated on the stock exchange in 1886, and soon became the talk of the colonies, as at the time only eight men held one million £1 shares each, which in any one's language was a phenomenal amount of money.

Within the first few years the company grew twenty-fold, and more than 80 tons of gold taken from old Ironstone Mountain, gold that was described

Flooded Street in Gympie, c. 1873
(John Oxley Library, State Library of Queensland Collection)
Gympie was always troubled by rising waters. the town sits high along the banks of the river, yet in every generation the waters of the Mary River rise to wet the floorboards of the town.

as the purest ever poured in Queensland. Ironstone is no more, so much dirt was cut away that a huge crater lies where once a mountain loomed, and the area is now known as the 'big hole'.

The east-coast ports of Rockhampton, Cairns and Cooktown and Normanton on the Gulf of Carpentaria to the west were established to provide communication and supplies in and out of the goldfields as the population of the separated Colony of Queensland grew from 30,000 to 100,000 in the first seven years of the gold rush. Normanton became a busy port for a few years after gold was discovered in 1885 at Croydon, 150 miles inland. At the height of this rush 7000 diggers were camped on this scrubby, white-ant-ridden, waterless plain. There were 36 hotels in Croydon during the rush, but today almost nothing remains. More than twenty-one tons of gold were taken from this goldfield by the end of the century.

Gympie [Nashville]

A field had also opened at Gympie in September 1867, following the discovery there by a wandering prospector, James Nash. Nash had dumped his swag on the banks of the Mary River, lit his fire, got his billy going, and panned a while as he waited for it to boil. He struck it lucky. The *Maryborough Chronicle* described the find as a 'reef loaded with gold like

Gold digger's sale, Queensland, c. 1864–70
Photograph by Richard Daintree
(Rex Nan Kivell Collection, T3218. By Permission, National Library of Australia)
Most diggers came to the goldfields for only a short time, to get rich quick and return home, set up for life. Most joined into working parties, pooled their resources, and kitted themselves out for the journey.

When they had tired of the adventure, fallen on hard times, or won a prize in this glittering lottery, they sold all their goods before quitting the goldfields—and there were always eager new chums ready to purchase the scarce goods and equipment on offer at a digger's auction.

This hand-coloured photograph is presumed to be from the eighty or so photographs Daintree had tinted in oil and watercolour for the London Exhibition in 1871.

plums in a Christmas pudding'. Within days nearby Maryborough became a virtual ghost town. Gympie grew just like every other gold town—like topsy. Tents were thrown up all over the place; shanty stores, shambles and rough-and-tumble pubs lined the crooked streets, filled with brawling, drunken diggers who caroused from dusk until dawn.

There was an influx of more than 600 Chinese into Nashville [as Gympie was known at the time]. It was their custom to take up claims abandoned by European diggers. The *Maryborough Chronicle* reported on 16 May 1868:

> The Mongolians have lately been arriving in gangs. Their favourite place seems to be the flat at the end of Nash's Gully. They are orderly and harmless and we presume there can be no objection to them.

It was not long though, before the European diggers protested over the success the Chinese had from the abandoned field. The Chinese took

James Nash, who found the gold that started the Gympie goldfields
(John Oxley Collection, State Library of Queensland)

By the time that James Nash was wandering around in the hills of Queensland there had been many attempts to discover a viable goldfield in that new colony.

Wherever men roamed, whether squatter, settler, shepherd or wanderer, they all cast an eye over the terrain hoping to recognise a gold-bearing landscape.

After taking up land in Northern Queensland Richard Daintree, on his geological explorations of the region, discovered several potential goldfields but did not publish them as such. He guided others to the sites but did not profit from these discoveries himself. It appears that he may have had enough of digging in Victoria and found the life of the squatter and itinerant scientist much more rewarding.

In the early days few of Daintree's fields were sustainable, but the rush that followed Nash lasted for almost half a century.

Cape River miners take it easy in front of their old bark hut
Photograph by Richard Daintree, c.1870
This was one of Daintree's favourites and it was used to convince English migrants that life in the colonies would agree with them.
(John Oxley Library, State Library of Queensland)

Mullock heaps surround the shafts on the early Gympie field, c. 1868
Photograph by Richard Daintree
(John Oxley Collection, State Library of Queensland)

—Notable Nuggets—

Curtis Nugget [957 oz. 906 oz of pure gold]
Gympie Creek—5 February 1868
George Curtis

Unnamed [804 oz]
Sailor's Gully, Deep Creek, Gympie—1868

Unnamed [336 oz]
Top Camp, Cloncurry—1868

Unnamed [258 oz]
Mount Wheeler, Rockhampton—1868
A prospector named Cadden

The Nashville Diggings, Queensland, 1868
Wood engraving, published by Ebenezer and David Syme, 18 July 1868
(Picture Collection, State Library of Victoria)

thousands of pounds worth of gold from the field, leaving only rubble to welcome the diggers as they fell back on Nashville after the other rushes proved unsuccessful.

By mid-1868 a 'roll-up' was called, and, just as their fellow-countrymen had suffered before them in California, on the Buckland River and at Lambing Flat, the 'Celestials were [sent] flying helter-skelter, taking flying leaps over claims, sometimes into them, when they would be dragged out by their pig-tails and cuffed on again'.[31]

The Chinese were driven from these diggings, but came back in greater numbers when the next wet season forced most Europeans out of their old, damp holes.

A great flood rushed through Gympie in 1893 when the Mary River rose to 90 feet above its normal level. All the mines were flooded, and over 120 houses were seen floating downstream.The floods were largely the result of clearing the forests for timbers, and the runoff was incredible. The last of the mines, the North Phoenix, closed in 1925.

THE TERRITORY AND LASSETER'S LOST REEF

The Darwin Rush

Gold had been discovered in the Northern Territory as early as 1865, when some 'specs' were taken back to South Australia by a failed government exploration party that had been attempting to establish a settlement at Escape Cliffs. In 1869 the survey party that marked the site of Darwin found gold in the Blackmore and Charlotte Rivers, and some at Tumbling Waters. The discovery that started the rush to Palmerston (as Darwin was then known) came later in 1871, when the construction gangs that were building the overland telegraph found gold at Pine Creek.

Diggers from all over Australia rushed to the north: once again shiploads of diggers sailed from Port Phillip, from Sydney Harbour and Adelaide eager to get at this, the latest rush. No matter how remote the goldfield, an almost insatiable appetite for gold lured the diggers onward. Many also travelled overland, following the newly-built telegraph line into Darwin.

Thousands of Chinese workers, who had been brought into the territory from Singapore as cheap labour, also rushed to the diggings. By 1896 most of the mines were controlled by English companies. Syndicates had been formed at the start of the rush as investors bought up the diggings, using information that was passed down the wire. Most of these were worthless, and most failed.

Port Darwin Rush—The SS Omeo *Leaving the Sandridge Railway Pier*
Wood engraving from *Illustrated Australian News*, 10 October 1872
(Picture Collection, State Library of Victoria)

DEPARTURE OF THE STEAMSHIP GOTHENBURG FROM ADELAIDE FOR PORT DARWIN.—SEE PAGE 98.

Departure of the Steamship Gothenburg from Adelaide for Port Darwin
Wood engraving from *Illustrated Australian News*, 17 June 1873
(Picture Collection, State Library of Victoria)

The Loss of Harold Lasseter

In 1897 an Afghan camel-driver found the exhausted body of Harold Bell Lasseter sprawled in the dust near the central Western Australian border to the west of Ayer's Rock.

Recovering in a surveyor's camp, Lasseter claimed that he had discovered a glittering gold-bearing reef almost six miles long near the border in the Petermann Ranges. Although the rock samples that Lasseter had in his pockets when he was found proved to be encouraging to the surveyor, when questioned on the precise whereabouts of his reef Lasseter himself proved to be somewhat taciturn.

For the next thirty years he kept the location of the reef to himself, until in 1930 he was able to raise the funds and mount an expedition, with himself as guide, back to his mythical reef.

Before long, however, there was dissension within the expedition party, and Lasseter struck out on his own, taking a few camels with him. As he departed he cried out, 'If I don't find the reef, I'm never coming back'.

His departing remark proved prophetic: he was never seen alive again. Bob Buck, an experienced bushman, led a search party and claimed to have discovered Lasseter's body in a cave at Winter's Glen. Buck returned with Lasseter's papers, which like those other ill-fated adventurers half a century earlier, Burke & Wills, had been buried beneath a tree marked 'DIG'.

The final note written by Lasseter to his wife suggests the hopelessness that can surround those seduced by the dream of gold:

> I am paying the penalty with my life, may this be a lesson to others . . . Good Bye Rene darling wife mine and don't grieve . . . but it does seem cruel to die alone out here—my last prayer is 'God be merciful to me as a sinner and be good to those I leave behind' . . . xxx Harry x

Lasseter had spent his last days tagging along with a party of desert indigenes, who were at turns suspicious of the lone white man, yet appreciative of his ability to shoot down fresh game. It is believed that Lasseter was 'boned' by a jealous 'Kaditcha', or medicine man, and from then on believed his fate was sealed.

Bob Buck retrieved a torn, burnt note from the ashes of a fire beside Lasseter's remains, where his revolver and false teeth lay by his side. In this last note Lasseter expressed disappointment at his treatment by the natives:

> They have made no [attempt] to build me a [shelter or] anything for shade . . . 78th day no . . . food I realise my end is [near] . . .

Bob Buck buried Lasseter's remains and carved his name on an old gum-tree a short distance from the roughly-fenced grave.

Another note, written in invisible ink, and lodged with a Sydney bank years earlier was marked to be opened in the event of Lasseter's untimely demise. It reads:

> This envelope, with contents under seal, is only to be delivered to persons presenting an authority from me and signed as shown on margin hereof. It contains a record which is as near as possible correct, having regard to the unreliable nature of the scientific instruments used, of a rich gold bearing reef known to exist in the interior of Australia prominent landmarks are described, and cross-bearings given on same. Compass bearings were taken by a compass which varied 2 1/4° at Carnarvon in 1897—L.H.B. Lasseter.

However, the compass bearings indicated by Lasseter—even taking into account the noted variability of the unreliable equipment have never located that glittering prize.

Today, Lasseter's Reef remains an enigma. No-one knows whether it ever existed at all.

HASSARAC'S OATH OF REVENGE.

SCENE LAST.—*BANQUETING APARTMENT*—grand entertainment—the merchant robber.

Pantomimical Tambourine Dance *By Morgiana.*

DEATH OF THE ROBBER.

SPLENDID APPEARANCE OF THE

FAIRY OF THE LAKE IN THE STAR OF ELYSIUM,

Surrounded with BRILLIANT FIRES.

To be followed with an entirely new Ballet Divertissement, arranged for this occasion, to be called

Squatters

AND

GOLD DIGGERS,

Or, Which is my Choice.

Fairy of the magic wand—Miss Veilburne. Susan, the fair maid of Victoria——Madame Veilburne.
Annet, her sister—Mrs Davis. Dame Grompy—Mrs Webster. Jooferry—Mr Charles
Mr Barlamb sheepface, a squatter———Mr Meadows. Nuggity Spar, a gold digger——Mis Stubbs.
Oliver Bounce, a policeman—Mr Turner. Jack Tar—Mr Holloway. Bill Roe— Mr Shearcroft.
Bill———Mr Coppin. Tom Tittle———Mr Opie.

The most striking incidents in this Local Production consist in a

Sylphide Pas Seul - - - - - - - - Miss Veilburne.

NOTES

Author's Note

1 The *First Gold Rush at Melbourne* from *The Earl's Choice and Other Poems* by Sir William à Beckett, former Chief Justice of Victoria, Smith, Elder and Co, London, 1863
"*Declinat cursus, aurumque volubile tollit*" —trans. 'She changes her course and picks up the rolling gold'.
This quote is taken from Ovid *Metamorphoses* [Book 10, line 667] and is the story of Hippomanes who, in a race with Atlanta, which he had win to gain her hand or forfeit his life, dropped golden apples in her path which she could not resist. In stooping to pick them up she lost the contest.

I.
How it moves us—how it proves us—
This bewildering tale of gold!
How they glisten—how they listen—
Eyes and ears when it is told!
How it sets us all a-raving,
How it sets us all a-craving,
Thinking of what might be got,
If we were but on the spot!
Gone are many, some still linger.
Waiting with unquiet heart,
And few feel not itching finger,
As they see the rest depart,
II.
In the bush, and in the city,
"*Gold's*" the universal ditty,
Not alone the pauper—miser—
Slaves of avarice and want,
But the wealthier and the wiser
Seek for baptism at its font.
Men who'd think it a base libel,
If 'twas hinted they were poor;
Men who talk about their Bible,
And plates hold at the church door—
Labour-hirer, working man,
Clerk, mechanic, artisan,
Washed and unwashed—high and low,
Mingle in the current's flow
That doth to the "diggins" go.
III.
What is this strange scene we near,
New to eye and new to ear?
See them delving there below,
Ev'ry dig a gamester's throw;
What is this they pause to view—
Turning o'er and looking through?
Ha!—the glittering ore appears,
Gone are all their long-felt fears;
Dig, my boys—behold, behold—
Dig away—for this *is* gold!
IV.
Look around on all the scene,
Much that's mournful doth it mean.
See how they eye one another,
Should thus brother look on brother?
Yonder scowling visage mark,
Well it is not lone or dark,
For if murder could be done,
There, to do it, standeth one.
V.
Night is come, and here and there
Sleepers close their their eyes in prayer;
There is drinking, gaming, brawling—
Ending oft in challenged fight
To be fought by Sabbath light,
If, perchance, the coming morn
Of a week-day should be born—
For e'en hatred can keep cold
Sooner than stop work for gold,
Digging for it, as if God
Had hid salvation 'neath the sod!
VI.
Gold! supreme is thy dominion,
God of church upon whose creed
Every nation is agreed;
Where's another one on which
Holds mankind the same opinion—
'Tis expedient to be rich?
Missionary in Christ's name,
By the side of him who came
Thy evangel to proclaim.
With a faith that never falters,
With a trust that heeds no shock
Millions kneel before thy altars,
Millions to thy temple flock.
Never yet was homage found
Unto King of earth or heaven
As to thee so freely given—
Thee the *monarch underground!*

[Sir William à Beckett was Chief Justice of the Colony of Victoria from 1852–1857. His tenure co-incided with the onset of the goldrush—through all the troubles on the diggings and the Eureka trials. He left the bench in 1857, returning to England six years later. He died in 1869 and is buried in West Norwood Cemetery.]

CHAPTER 1
Gold! Gold! Gold!

1 From *Hutchings California Magazine*, November 1857.
2 ibid.

3 Secretary of State Earl Grey to Governor La Trobe, 12 January 1852.
4 From the diaries of William Swain; recalled in J. S. Holliday, *The World Rushed In*, Simon & Schuster, USA,1983, pp. 312–29.
5 ibid.
6 From the memoir of Eugene Ring. A New Yorker, Ring began his adventures in California in 1848 after a long illness. He travelled across the Panama isthmus and up the coast to San Francisco, returning to New York in 1851.
7 ibid.
8 ibid.
9 Swain, op. cit.
10 JoAnn Levy, *They Saw the Elephant: Women in the California Gold Rush*, University of Oklahoma Press, 1992.
11 ibid.
12 ibid.
13 ibid.
14 The Burlingame Treaty was signed between the United States and China, which regulated commerce and emigration. The treaty allowed for a free flow of emigration and travel between the two nations.
The treaty was named after Anson Burlingame, a former American ambassador to China who was largely responsible for the negotiations.

CHAPTER 2

First Gold in Australia?

1 George Sutherland, *Tales of the Gold-fields*, George Robertson, Melbourne, 1880, p.14.
2 James Flett, *The History of Gold Discovery in Victoria*, Hawthorn Press, Melbourne, 1970, p. 421.
3 John A. Graham, *Early Creswick: The First Century* [Facsimile Edition], Creswick Historical Museum, 1987, Creswick, Vic., pp. 174–5.
4 Flett, op. cit., p. 419
5 William Howitt, *Land, Labour & Gold*, Lowden, Kilmore, Vic., 1972, Letter X, 25 December 1852, p. 93.
6 Flett, op. cit., p. 350.
7 Antoine Fauchery, *Letters From a Miner in Australia*, Georgian House, Melbourne, Vic.,1965, p. 51.
8 William B. Withers, *The History of Ballarat* [Facsimile Edition], Queensberry Hill Press, Carlton,Vic., 1980, p. 9.
9 C.W. Langtree, Secretary of Mines [1888], in Flett, op.cit., p. 351.
10 Flett, op. cit., p. 61.
11 ibid., p. 62.
12 Clacy, Mrs Charles. *A Lady's Visit to The Gold Diggings of Australia in 1852–55*, Lansdowne Press, Melb., Vic., 1963, p.124.
13 From *Cassell's Picturesque Australasia*, first published 1889 [Facsimile Edition], Child & Henry, Fine Arts Press, Gordon, NSW, 1978, p. 790.
14 ibid.
15 Clacy, op.cit., p. 124.

CHAPTER 3

A World Turned Topsy-Turvey

1 John Dunmore Lang, *The Australian Emigrant's Manual or, A Guide to the Gold Colonies of New South Wales and Port Phillip*, Partridge & Oakley, London, 1852. p. xvi.
2 John Capper, *Phillip's Emigrant's Guide to Australia*, 1852, p. 18.
3 Lang, op.cit.
4 Lang, op. cit., p. 5.
5 ibid., p. 3.
6 Capper, op. cit., p. 21.
7 Quoted in Serle, p. 68, from the diary of W. Rayment. Geoffrey Serle, *The Golden Age*, Melbourne University Press, Carlton, Vic., 1963.

CHAPTER 4

The Last of England

1 Henry Kingsley, *My Adventures on the Australian Gold-fields*, ch. 1.
2 J. B. Barnes, quoted in Serle, op. cit., p. 49.
3 Kingsley, op. cit.
4 Dante Gabriel Rossetti, *A Victorian Romantic*, London, 1849, p. 114.
5 Advertisement, Truro, Cornwall, England, 19 August 1839.
6 Clacy, op. cit., p. 136.
7 Severyn Korzelinski, *Memoirs of Gold-Digging in Australia*, first published in Cracow, 1858, trs. Robe, University of Queensland Press, St Lucia, Qld, 1979, p. 132. Korzelinski was in Australia between the years 1852 and 1856, and the diaries recalling his adventures on the Victorian goldfields were published in his native Poland following his return home.
8 ibid., p. 135.
9 Howitt, op. cit., Letter X, 25 December 1852, p. 94.
10 ibid., pp. 94–5.
11 ibid., Letter III, 29 September 1852, p. 22.
12–13 ibid.
14 Clacy, op. cit., p. 63.
15 ibid., p. 102.
16 Howitt, op.cit., p. 94.
17 ibid.

CHAPTER 5

The Road to the Diggings

1 Thomas Arnot diaries, 7 August 1852, MS 8464, Australian Manuscripts Collection, State Library of Victoria.
2 Howitt, op. cit., Letter XV, 29 March 1853, p. 145.
3 Clacy, op.cit.
4 From Donald Friend, *Hillendiana*, Ure

Smith, Sydney, 1956. Friend was a noted Australian artist who rented a cottage in Hill End for many years. He travelled there at various times with fellow-artists Russell Drysdale and Brett Whiteley, whose earlier works celebrated the torn landscapes of this historic gold-mining region.

5 Rev. D. Mckenzie, *The Gold Digger, a Visit to the Gold Fields of Australia in Feb. 1852, with Information for Intending Emigrants.* London, 1852.

6 *Records of the Castlemaine Pioneers*, Rigby, Melbourne, 1972, James Robertson, 31 March 1882, p. 47.

CHAPTER 6

Under Southern Skies

1 Fauchery, op. cit., p. 40.
2 Frank McKillop, *Early Castlemaine*, New Chum Press, Castlemaine, Vic., 1999, Essay 28, p. 81.
3 ibid., Essay 6, p. 25.
4 Howitt, op. cit., Letter XVII, 28 May 1853, p. 171.
5 ibid., p. 175.
6 John Chandler, *Forty Years in the Wilderness*, Loch Haven Books, Main Ridge, Vic., 1990, p. 67. John Chandler came to Australia from England at the age of 11. When gold was discovered, he and his father joined the rush and had some good luck. He operated as a carter of goods to and from the diggings, and it was this trade that brought him the most success.
7 ibid., p. 83.
8 James Bonwick, *Notes of a Gold Digger and Gold Diggers Guide*, E. Conebee, Melbourne, 1855.
9 Marjorie Tipping, *An Artist on the Goldfields: The Diary of Eugène von Guérard*, Melbourne University Press, Carlton, Vic., 1992, p. 61.
10 Clacy, op. cit., p. 57.

CHAPTER 7

A Glittering Lottery

1 John Sherer, *The Gold Finder in Australia*, Penguin, Ringwood, Vic., 1973, p. 183.
2 ibid.
3 David Tulloch, *Five Views of the Gold Fields of Mount Alexander and Ballarat, in the Colony of Victoria*, Thomas Ham, Melbourne, Vic., 1852.
4 Fauchery, op. cit., pp. 76–7.
5 ibid.
6 ibid.
7 ibid.
8 Sutherland, op. cit., p. 84.
9 John Arthur Phillips, *Gold-mining and Assaying: A Scientific Guide for Emigrants*, John J. Griffin & Co., London, 1852, pp. 38–40.

CHAPTER 8

No Place For a Lady

1 Capper, op. cit., p. 172.
2 ibid.
3 ibid.
4 ibid., p. 173.
5 Clacy, op. cit., p. 137.
6 ibid., pp. 62–3.
7 ibid., pp. 55–6.
8 ibid.
9 Chandler, op. cit., p. 123.
10 ibid., p. 124.
11 William Kelly, *Life in Victoria: or Victoria in 1853 and Victoria in 1858*, Chapman & Hall, London, 1860, pp. 132–135
12 Sherer, op. cit., p. 196.
13 Capper, op. cit., p. 49.
14 Clacy, op. cit., p. 137.
15 ibid., p. 136.
16 Gronn, op. cit., pp. 80–2.
17 *Mount Alexander Mail*, 11 December 1854
18 ibid.
19 ibid.
20 ibid.
21 William Craig, *My Adventures on the Australian Gold-fields*, Cassell & Co. Ltd, London, 1853, pp. 222–3.
22. ibid.
23 *Mount Alexander Mail*, 11 December 1854.
24 Craig, op. cit., p. 224.
25 ibid., p. 225.
26 ibid., p. 229.

CHAPTER 9

'Show Us Yer License'

1 Howitt, op. cit., Letter XXII, 15 August 1853, p. 216.
2 ibid., Letter XIV, 1 March 1853, p. 131.
3 Chandler, op. cit., p. 50.
4 Edwin Canton Booth, *Australia in the 1870s*, Virtue, London, 1873–76, p. 24.
5 Howitt, op. cit., p. 219

CHAPTER 10

The 'Red-ribbon' Rebellion

1 Earl Grey, Secretary of State, 12 January 1852.
2 William Howitt, op. cit., Letter XIV, 1 March 1853, p. 135.
3 David Tulloch, op. cit.
4 Howitt, op. cit., Letter II, 28 September 1852, p. 11.
5 Howitt, op. cit., Letter XXII, p. 224.
6 The Bendigo Petition, State Library of Victoria.
7 Howitt, loc. cit., p. 225.
8 ibid., Letter XXIII, 27 September 1853, p. 229.
9 ibid.

CHAPTER 11

The Battle at Ballarat

1 G.W. Rusden, *History of Australia*, 3 vols, Chapman & Hall, London, 1883, p. 680.

2 Raffaello Carboni, *The Eureka Stockade.* Melbourne University Press, Carlton, Vic., 1963; first published 1855.
3 *Argus*, 10 April 1855.
4 Carboni, op. cit., p. 99.
5 From Hotham's despatch to Sir George Grey, Secretary of State, 20 December 1854, quoted in Serle, op. cit., p. 173.

CHAPTER 12

A Law Unto Themselves

1 Korzelinski, op. cit., p. 36.
2 Captain John Hepburn, *Letters from Victorian Pioneers*, 10 August 1853, Public Library, Museums and National Gallery of Victoria, Government Printer, Melbourne, p. 55.
3 Recorded in *Chronicle of Australia*, ed. John Ross, Penguin, Ringwood, Vic., 1993, p. 291.
4 Chandler, op. cit., p. 102.
5 *Records of the Castlemaine Pioneers*, Walter Wilson [essay], 24 September 1886, p. 97.
6 ibid., J. F. Hughes [essay], 30 September 1887, p. 2.
7 ibid.,William Ottey [essay], 25 March 1887, pp. 56–7.
8 ibid., W. H. Wilson [essay], 26 September 1890, p. 157.
9 Clacy, op. cit., p. 97.

CHAPTER 13

The Celestials

1 G. Mackay, *Annals of Bendigo 1851–1867*, Mackay & Co., Bendigo, Vic., 1867, p. 61.
2 Fauchery, op. cit, pp. 102–3. Quong-Chew was a fifth cousin of the Mandarin Ta-Quang-Tsung-Loo, who also owned several gardens near Macao. His social standing, combined with his eloquence, entitled him to assume the role of spokesman for the Chinese community.
3 Denovan, in a letter to the *Bendigo Advertiser*, 22 May 1859.
4 Mackay, op. cit., p. 61.
5 Quoted in David Horsfall, *March to Big Gold Mountain*, Red Rooster Press, Vic., 1985, p. 143.
6 *Australasian Sketcher*, 27 December 1873, p. 167.
7 Arthur C. Bicknell, *Travel and Adventure in Northern Queensland*, 1895. Bicknell was an English writer who was in Queensland at the height of the Chinese troubles.
8 ibid.

CHAPTER 14

The End of the Roaring Days

1 Anthony Trollope, *Australia and New Zealand*, Geo. Robertson, Melbourne, 1873, p. 268.
2 J. C. Patterson, *The Gold-fields of Victoria*, 1862., quoted in A. W. Strange, *Ballarat*: A Brief History, Lowden, Kilmore, Vic., 1971, p. 24.
3 ibid.
4 Mackay, op. cit., p. 15.
5 Craig, op. cit., p.195.
6 ibid., p.196.
7 Quoted in Tim Bonyhady, *Burke & Wills: From Melbourne to Myth*, David Ell Press, Balmain, NSW, 1991, p. 40.
8 Chandler, op. cit., p. 111.
9 Howitt, op. cit., Letter XXXVI, 16 May 1854, p. 374.
10 ibid.
11 George Sutherland, op. cit., pp. 73–9.
12 George Preshaw, *Banking Under Difficulties: or Life on the Gold-fields ofVictoria, New South Wales and New Zealand.* Edwards Dunlop & Co., Melbourne, 1888, p. 56.
13 ibid. p. 57.
14 ibid. p. 67.
15 ibid. p. 56.
16 Quoted in Keast Burke, *Gold & Silver: Photographs of Australian Gold-fields from the Holtermann Collection*, Penguin Books, Ringwood, Vic, 1973, p. 254.
17 *Cassell's Picturesque Australasian*, op. cit., p. 721.
18 From the diary of William Hocking, unpublished manuscript, 1902.
19 ibid.
20 ibid.
21 ibid.
22 ibid.
23 ibid.
24 ibid.
25 ibid.
26 ibid.
27 ibid.
28 Thorvald Weitemeyer, *Missing Friends and Adventures in Northern Queensland*, T. Fisher Unwin, London, 1892; quoted from Gympie Gold, Angus and Robertson, Sydney, NSW., 1973.
29 ibid.
30 ibid.
31 E. B. Kennedy, quoted from *Gympie Gold*, op. cit., p. 107.

BIBLIOGRAPHY

à Beckett, Sir William. *The Earl's Choice and Other Poems.* Smith, Elder and Co., London, 1863

Anderson, Hugh [ed.]. *Charles Thatcher's The Gold-Diggers' Songbook.* Red Rooster Press, Ascot Vale, Vic., 1980.

Bate, Weston. *Victorian Gold Rushes.* McPhee Gribble/Penguin, Ringwood, Vic.,1988.

Blackman, Grant & Larkin, John. *Maldon: Australia's First Notable Town.* Hodder & Stoughton, Melbourne, 1978.

Bolton, G. C. Richard Daintree. *A Photographic Memoir.* The Jacaranda Press, Brisbane, Queensland, 1965.

Bonyhady, Tim. *Burke & Wills: From Melbourne to Myth.* David Ell Press Pty Ltd, Balmain, NSW, 1991.

Booth, Edwin Canton. *Australia in the 1870s.* Virtue & Co., London, 1873–76.

Bowman, John S. *The American West Year By Year.* Crescent Books, New York, 1995.

Bride, Thomas Francis. *Letters from Victorian Pioneers.* Published for the Trustees of the Public Library, Public Library, Museums and National Gallery of Victoria, Melbourne, 1898.

Burke, Keast. *Gold & Silver: Photographs of Australian Goldfields from the Holtermann Collection.* Penguin, Ringwood, Vic., 1973.

Carboni, Raffaello. *The Eureka Stockade.* Melbourne University Press, Carlton, Vic., 1963; first published 1855.

Cecil, Lord Robert. *Gold Fields Diary, 1852.* Melbourne University Press, Carlton, Vic., 1935.

Chandler, John. *Forty Years in the Wilderness*, ed. Michael Cannon. Loch Haven Books, 1990; first published by the author, 1893.

Chronicle of Australia, ed. John Ross. Penguin, Ringwood, Vic., 1993.

Clacy, Mrs Charles. *A Lady's Visit to the Gold Diggings of Australia in 1852–55: Written on the spot by Mrs. Charles Clacy.* Lansdowne Press, Melbourne, 1963; first published 1853.

Craig, William. *My Adventures on the Australian Gold-fields.* Cassell & Co., London, 1853.

Crux Australis [Journal of the Flag Society of Australia], vol. 12/4, no. 52, 1999.

Currey, C. H. *The Irish at Eureka.* Angus & Robertson, Sydney, 1954.

Cusack, Frank. *Bendigo: A History.* Heinemann, Melbourne, 1973.

Duyker, Edward [ed.]. *A Woman on the Gold-fields: Recollections of Emily Skinner 1854–1878.* Melbourne University Press, Carlton, Vic., 1995.

Evans, William [ed.]. *Diary of a Welsh Swagman, 1869–1894.* Sun Books, Melbourne, 1975.

Family History and Genealogical Record of Thomas Hiscock, Pioneer and Discoverer of

Gold in Victoria, 1849. Hiscock & Sons Pty Ltd, Standard Office, Benalla, Vic., 1936.
Fauchery, Antoine. *Letters from a Miner in Australia*. Georgian House, Melbourne, 1965; first published in French 1857.
Flett, James. *The History of Gold Discovery in Victoria*. Hawthorn Press, Melbourne, 1970.
Friend, Donald. *Hillendiana*. Ure Smith, Sydney, 1956.
Gibney, H. J. & Hoyer, N.C. *Taken at Tilba: Photographs from the William Henry Corkhill Tilba Tilba Collection*. National Library of Australia, Canberra, 1983.
Golding, D. J. [ed.]. *The Emigrant's Guide to Australia in the Eighteen Fifties*. Hawthorn Press, Melbourne, 1973, first published 1853.
Goodman, David. *Gold Seeking: Victoria and California in the 1850s*. Allen & Unwin, St Leonards, NSW, 1994.
Haigh, Christopher [ed.]. *The Cambridge Historical Encyclopedia of Great Britain and Ireland*. Cambridge University Press, New York, 1985.
Hocking, Geoff. *Castlemaine: From Camp to City*. Five Mile Press, Melbourne, 1994, 2nd edition 2007.
Holliday, J. S. *The World Rushed In: The California Gold Rush Experience*. Simon & Schuster, New York, 1983.
Horsfall, David. *March to Big Gold Mountain*. Red Rooster Press, Ascot Vale, Vic., 1985.
Howitt, William. *Land, Labour & Gold, or Two Years in Victoria with Visits to Sydney and Van Diemen's Land*. Lowden, Kilmore, Vic., 1972; first published 1855.
Kaplan, Fred. *Dickens: A Biography*. Hodder & Stoughton, London, 1998.
Kelly, William. *Life in Victoria: or Victoria in 1853 and Victoria in 1858*, Chapman & Hall, London, 1860,
Kerr, Colin and Margaret. *The Gold Seekers*. Rigby, Australia, 1975.
Korzelinski, Severyn. *Memoirs of Gold-digging in Australia*, trs. by Stanley Robe. University of Queensland Press, St Lucia, Qld, 1979; first published Cracow, 1858.
Lang, John Dunmore. *The Australian Emigrant's Manual, or A Guide to the Gold Colonies of New South Wales and Port Phillip*. Partridge & Oakey, London, 1852.
Lerk, James A. *Bendigo's Mining History 1851–1954*. Bendigo Trust, Bendigo, Vic.,1991.
Levy, JoAnn. *They Saw the Elephant: Women in the California Gold Rush*. Archon, Hamden, Ct, 1990
McDougall, Cora [ed.]. *Gold! Gold! Diary of Claus Gronn: A Dane on the Diggings*. Hill of Content, Melbourne, 1981.
MacFarlane, Ian. *Eureka: From the Official Records*. Public Record Office of Victoria, Melbourne, 1995.
Mackay, G. *The Annals of Bendigo*. Mackay & Co., Bendigo, Vic.,1867.
McKillop, Frank. *Early Castlemaine: The Municipal Council, ed. G. Hocking*. New Chum Press, Castlemaine, Vic., 1999; first published Mount Alexander Mail, 1908.
Newnham, W. H. *Victoria Illustrated, 1857 & 1862: Engravings from the Original Editions by S. T. Gill & N. Chevalier*. Lansdowne Press, Melbourne, 1971.

Pearsall, Ronald. *The Worm in the Bud: The World of Victorian Sexuality.* Penguin, London, 1971.
Preshaw, George Ogilvie. *Banking Under Difficulties; or Life on the Goldfields of Victoria, New South Wales and New Zealand.* Edwards Dunlop & Co., Melbourne, 1888.
Prospectors' Guide [Victoria]. Issued by Geo. Brown, Secretary for Mines, Govt Printer, Melbourne, 1936.
Records of the Castlemaine Pioneers. Rigby, Melbourne, 1972.
Rolls, Eric. *Sojourners: Flowers and the Wide Sea.* University of Queensland Press, St Lucia, Qld,1992.
Rosa, Joseph G. *The Taming of the West: The Age of the Gunfighter.* Salamander Books, London, 1993.
Rusden, G. W. *History of Australia.* Chapman & Hall, London; S. Mullen, Melbourne, 1883.
Serle, Geoffrey. *The Golden Age: A History of the Colony of Victoria.* Melbourne University Press, Carlton, Vic.,1963.
Sherer, John. *The Gold-Finder in Australia.* Penguin, Ringwood, Vic., 1973; first published 1853.
Stacpoole, H. J. *Gold at Ballarat.* Lowden, Kilmore, Vic., 1971.
Strange, A. W. *Ballarat: A Brief History.* Lowden, Kilmore, Vic., 1971.
Sutherland, Alexander. *Victoria and its metropolis, past and present.* McCarron, Bird & Co., Melbourne, Vic., 1888.
Sutherland, George. *Tales of the Goldfields.* George Robertson, Melbourne, Vic., 1880.
Thomas, David. *Artists of the Bendigo Goldfields: 1852–1864.* Bendigo Art Gallery, Bendigo, Vic., 1989.
Thomas, David. *S. T. Gill's Bendigo.* Bendigo Art Gallery, Bendigo, Vic., 1993.
Tipping, Marjorie. *An Artist on the Goldfields: The Diary of Eugène von Guérard.* Melbourne University Press, Carlton, Vic., 1992.
Victoria the Golden: Scenes, Sketches and Jottings from Nature by William Strutt. Melbourne, Victoria 1850–1862. Library Committee, Parliament of Victoria, Melbourne, 1980.
Walhalla Chronicle – Facsimile Edition. Harrington & King, Waverley Offset Publishing Group, 1978.
Weitemeyer, Thorvald Peter Ludwig. *Missing Friends and Adventures in Northern Queensland,* T. Fisher Unwin, London, 1892.

Websites

Online Archive of California. www.oac.cdlib.org
Trails to the Goldrush. www.over-land.com/trgold.html

ACKNOWLEDGMENTS

The intention in preparing this book was to bring together as wide a range as possible of pictorial images [paintings, engravings, photographs and ephemera] that would tell the story of the mass migration to the Australian goldfields of the 1850s.

I wanted to express the hopes and desires, the fantastic finds and devastating failures that were the stuff of legend on the goldfields. I wanted to understand why this period still holds our fascination today, to search for the meaning of this event, the impact it had on the world and the reasons why so many of our forefathers pulled up their roots and sailed halfway around the globe into uncertain future, but exhilarating adventure.

This story had to start with the rush to the California diggings. In the writing of this work I learned that my great-grandfather went first to California, then Montana, and then onto Australia. This sent me on a fascinating journey of exploration into the electronic world of the worldwide web. Where once my great-grandfather walked, I was now surfing; the Californian sesquicentennial celebrations of the discovery of gold in 1848 left a valuable legacy of information and images that helped me to draw out the link between the Californian diggings and the discoveries in Australia three years later.

I thank all those across the Pacific with whom I have enjoyed fruitful electronic discussions: Tracy Melings of the University of Berkeley, California; Courtney De Angelis of the Amon Carter Museum of Fort Worth, Texas; Jeff Kram of the Oakland Museum of California.

All have been most generous with their time and efforts in ensuring that works requested from their collections found their way to the Antipodes.

I also acknowledge the assistance given from the other side of the world, in particular by Iain Harrison of the Birmingham Art Gallery and Museum, Birmingham, the counter staff of the Nottingham Library, and the National Portrait Gallery, London.

I wish to thank all those who have given me such generous assistance over the time of the preparation of this book. Without the efforts of the many librarians, picture researchers, gallery curators and private collectors who have given their time and lent the works under their care, books such as this would not be at all possible.

In particular I acknowledge the generous assistance of Scott Jessop of the Burke Museum, Beechworth; Sally Routledge formerly of Bendigo Regional Library; Karen Quinlan and Anonda Bell of the Bendigo Art Gallery; Peter Perry of Castlemaine Art Gallery & Historical Museum; Maldon Historical Museum; Gael Ramsay of the Ballarat Fine Art Gallery; Jenny Molony of the National Gallery of Victoria; Alice Livingstone of the Art Gallery of New South Wales; Oxley Library, State Library of Queensland; Jennifer Broomhead of the State Library of South Australia; Art Gallery of Western Australia; Anne Armstrong and Diane Reilly of the State Library of Victoria; State Parliamentary Library of Victoria; Marika Tolghesi of the National Library of Australia; Young Historical Museum; John Zulic, Director Creative and Design—Sovereign Hill, Ballarat, Victoria; the special collection of the library at La Trobe University, Bendigo; and Colin Bourke of Stock Photos, Melbourne.

Thanks also go to John Menzies and Marion Colman of Sovereign Hill, Ballarat.

There are numerous individuals who have also lent works from their private collections. I thank Graeme and Lyn Bennett, late of the Diggers' Store in Campbell's Creek, Victoria, who have joined in the new rush to the Northern Territory; my father-in-law, Q. Clifford Binks, whose private collections still remain a mystery to us all, but things do appear when most needed; the late Frank Cusack of Bendigo, a greatly respected historian, who generously allowed the use of some images from his own works; author Allan M. Nixon for permission to use his photograph of Inglewood; Doug Mills and Felix Cappy of Castlemaine, who lent me their prized Colt revolvers and to Margaret Freeeman, also of Castlemaine, whose letters from her great-grandmother Margaret Kennedy are shown on page fifty of this book.

There are also numerous groups and individuals who have over the years given me pictures and ephemera, often for use in other projects. I have attempted to acknowledge all such images to their source; if I have failed to do this accurately I apologise. Every attempt has been made to trace the source of material and to give proper acknowledgement.

I also acknowledge the work of others who have researched this topic before me. Geoffrey Serle's *The Golden Age*, James Flett's *The History of Gold*

Discovery in Victoria and Frank Cusack's *Bendigo: A History* are invaluable texts. James Lerk, another historian from Bendigo, has always been a constant and reliable source of information, and I thank him for sharing his wide knowledge whenever asked. There is also an army of authors working at the local history level who, through their brochures and smaller texts, provide a wealth of excellent resource material. I thank them all, and urge them to continue with the task of keeping our history alive.

Lastly, I thank my wife, Christine, for once again leaving me alone to follow my obsession, for holding the camera bag, wandering through endless museums with me, sitting in the car for hours as we drove through pouring rain—just to see the Lambing Flat flag, and then to turn around and drive all the way back home again.

It takes determination to bring such a book to fruition, but it also takes the support and the tolerance of family, friends and colleagues; for that support I thank you all.

Geoff Hocking, Castlemaine

Postscript: Thanks to David Cunningham, of Castlemaine, who cast his expert eye over the book before it went to print, and once again shared his boundless knowledge.

INDEX